CURRENT PERSPECTIVES ON INTERNATIONAL TERRORISM

Current Perspectives on International Terrorism

Edited by

Robert O. Slater

Director of Research
Defense Intelligence College
Washington, D.C.

and

Michael Stohl

Professor and Director of Graduate Studies
Department of Political Science
Purdue University

St. Martin's Press   New York

First published in the United States of America in 1988

Printed in Hong Kong

ISBN 0-312-01379-5

Library of Congress Cataloging-in-Publication Data
Current perspectives on international terrorism/edited by Robert O.
Slater and Michael Stohl.
p.   cm.
Revised papers from a conference held in December 1985 and
sponsored by the Defense Academic Research Support Program (DARSP).
Includes bibliographies and index.
ISBN 0-312-01379-5 : $30.00 (est.)
1. Terrorism—Congresses. I. Slater, Robert O. (Robert Owen),
1950- . II. Stohl, Michael, 1947- . III. Defense Academic
Research Support Program (U.S.)
HV6431.C87 1988
303.6'25—dc19   87-23582
                                                               CIP

For the joys of my life –
Valerie, Evan, Lindsay

For the women of my life –
Cynthia, Rachel, Ilene

Contents

Contents

Preface

This book is the result of a conference on International Terrorism held in December 1985 and sponsored by the Defense Academic Research Support Program (DARSP). The objective of DARSP, managed by the Defense Intelligence College in the United States Department of Defense, is to facilitate open and constructive dialogue between US government analysts and the academic community on issues such as terrorism.

The papers presented at this conference have been substantially revised for publication in this book. They represent the current thinking of leading international scholars on key aspects of terrorism, including a number of issues not adequately addressed in the literature.

We owe a debt to the authors for their willingness to undertake major and timely revisions of their papers based both on the comments of the editors and the extensive discussion which took place at the conference. We also owe a special debt of thanks to the panelists and audience at the conference whose extensive comments on the papers contributed immeasurably to the overall quality of this book. Each of the authors has cited those whose specific comments contributed to the revisions of their chapters. Finally, we would like to acknowledge the endless energies of the staff at the Defense Intelligence College, particularly Steve Dorr and Patricia Lanzara; without their contributions there would not have been a conference.

ROBERT O. SLATER
MICHAEL STOHL

Notes on the Contributors

Dr Martha Crenshaw is an Associate Professor of Government at Wesleyan University in Middletown, Connecticut. Before joining the Wesleyan faculty in 1981, she was an international relations analyst in the Foreign Affairs Division, Congressional Research Service, Library of Congress. Dr Crenshaw is the author of *Revolutionary Terrorism: The FLN in Algeria* and editor of *Terrorism, Legitimacy and Power: The Consequences of Political Violence*. A contributor to various American and British books on terrorism, she has published articles on the nuclear and other aspects of that subject in American and foreign journals.

Dr Ted Robert Gurr is Professor of Political Science and Director of the Center for Comparative Politics at the University of Colorado in Boulder. Dr Gurr has written, coauthored, edited and published scores of books, papers, monographs and studies focusing on contemporary and historical politics, violence, crime and terrorism. His *Why Men Rebel* won the American Political Science Association's Woodrow Wilson Foundation prize for the best book in political science in 1970. Dr Gurr has served as a consultant to numerous American and foreign government agencies and was codirector of the Task Force on Historical and Comparative Perspectives on Violence in American for the National Commission on the Causes and Prevention of Violence.

Mr Brian Jenkins is Director of the Rand Corporation's Security and Subnational Conflict Program, a position he has held since the establishment of the programme in 1979. Mr Jenkins, an internationally recognised expert on terrorism, has been influential in creating an international community of scholars, government officials and military officers concerned with understanding and responding to terrorism and other forms of subnational conflict. He is the author of *International Terrorism: A New Mode of Conflict* and coauthor of *Terrorism and Personal Protection*, as well as numerous other books and articles on terrorism. Mr Jenkins has taken part in major international conferences and intergovernment discussions on terrorism and frequently testifies before the US Congress on this issue.

Dr Alex Schmid is Associate Professor of International Relations at the Department of Political Science of Leiden University, the Netherlands. He is also Senior Research Fellow at the Center for the Study of Conflicts (COMT) at the same university. Dr Schmid is currently a visiting Scholar at the Program on Non-violent Sanctions in Conflict and Defense in the Center for International Affairs, Harvard University. Dr Schmid has authored numerous books on military intervention and political terrorism including *Soviet Military Interventions Since 1945* and *Political Terrorism: A Research Guide to Concepts, Theories, Data Bases and Literature.*

Dr Robert O. Slater is Director of Research at the Defense Intelligence College, located in Washington, DC. Dr Slater also directs the Foreign Language and Area Studies Program for the Department of Defense. Before joining the College in 1985, Dr Slater worked for major research and consulting firms in the Washington, DC area directing research projects focusing on US Government clients. Dr Slater holds a Ph.D. in International Relations from The American University and has authored articles on political risk analysis and coauthored articles on military *coups d'état* in the *American Political Science Review.*

Dr Michael Stohl is Professor and Director of Graduate Studies in the Department of Political Science at Purdue University in West Lafayette, Indiana, where he has been since 1972. His teaching and research interests centre on international relations, with special reference to violence and politics, political terrorism, US foreign policy, and international political economy. Dr Stohl has edited, coedited and contributed to numerous books on terror and political violence, including *The Politics of Terrorism, The State as Terrorist* and *Government Violence and Repression.* His articles on terrorism have been published widely in journals.

Dr Grant Wardlaw is Senior Criminologist at the Australian Institute of Criminology in Canberra. Before joining the institute in 1976 he was a psychologist with the New Zealand government's Department of Justice in Auckland and a member of the faculty in the Department of Psychology at the University of Auckland. A graduate in International Law from Australia's National University, and also a political scientist, Dr Wardlaw is a specialist on terrorism, criminals, drug abuse, the drug trade, and international relations. Dr Wardlaw is the author of *Political Terrorism: Theory, Tactics and Counter-measures* and the forthcoming *Public Order Policing.*

Professor Paul Wilkinson is Professor of International Relations at the University of Aberdeen. His books include: *Political Terrorism, The New Fascists,* and *Terrorism and the Liberal State.* He jointly edited *Terrorism: Theory and Practice* and edited *British Perspectives on Terrorism.* Since 1980, Professor Wilkinson has been General Editor of *Key Concepts in International Relations,* academic editor of Kraus reports on the history of political violence, and Editorial Adviser to the *Contemporary Review.* In 1986 he was appointed Special Consultant to CBS, America and Chairman of the Trustees of the Research Foundation for the Study of Terrorism.

1 Introduction: Towards a Better Understanding of International Terrorism

Robert O. Slater and Michael Stohl

INTRODUCTION

United States Secretary of Defense Caspar W. Weinberger in remarks made recently to an American Bar Association National Conference on terrorism stated that:

> The face of international terrorism is constantly changing as it increases in scale... The number of terrorist groups has multiplied. We have also seen the advent, or at least resurgence, of suicidal terrorists and of fanatical, pseudo-religious doctrines that extol terrorism. Terrorists have developed collaborative networks. They have gained better access to international arms markets and have acquired more sophisticated weapons and explosives ... Terrorists have refined their planning, intelligence and targeting methods, often surveilling their victims for months ... Terrorists have discovered new sources of funding through crime. In addition to their traditional bank robberies, they have entered the lucrative narcotics trade. Terrorists have become skilled managers of their financial assets using secretive banking channels and investing large sums in legitimate businesses in the United States and elsewhere. Finally, we are confronted with the spread of state-sponsored terrorism
>
> (Weinberger, 1986, p. 1).

These comments do reflect an evolution in the understanding of international terrorism, suggesting a deeper understanding of terrorists which goes beyond the traditional and outdated perspective of terrorism as an act performed only by madmen.[1] In another sense though, the Secretary of Defense's remarks seem indicative of

1

a continuing lack of commitment to a deeper understanding of the motives and actions which underlie terrorism and of a continuing sense of ignorance concerning the mechanisms through which terrorists groups operate. While we increasingly recognise that knowledge of belief systems and ideologies is a necessary ingredient of a better understanding of terrorists, we have not actually seen a significant increase in this knowledge.[2] On an optimistic note, we have begun to see evidence that we have moved further along the learning curve concerning our desire to know more about the factors which form the foundations for international terrorism as a form of behaviour which is likely to continue for decades to come.

THE LITERATURE ON TERRORISM

Along with the realisation that international terrorism is likely to prevail as a factor of international politics has been the development of a rather voluminous literature on the subject.[3] However, the extant literature on terrorism has contributed only marginally to an overall systematic understanding of the major factors involved in international terrorism. This is due to a number of factors. First, terrorism is a popular area in which to publish and has attracted countless scholars who have seized upon the subject as a good 'one-time' opportunity. This has led to a somewhat disjointed literature lacking the continuity usually found in sub-fields of research. Secondly, while the literature abounds with case-studies of individuals, groups, and terrorist movements little systematic comparison or application of frameworks is found. Third, another subset of the literature is rich with theories of international and Soviet conspiracy as the major explanation for the existence of international terrorism in the world today. Finally, frequent attempts have been made to apply our knowledge of civil violence and insurgency to the phenomenon of terrorism. Unfortunately, this very rich empirical literature has thus far shown to be only marginally relevant to the study of terrorism – and continued attempts at simplistic application has led to a fundamental misunderstanding of the basic issues of international terrorism.

The study of terrorism requires the same rigorous analysis as any other field.[4] Yet, it is plagued with a number of handicaps somewhat peculiar to this field. There is clearly an abundance of definitions of terrorism without a consensus on how it ought to be defined. Indeed a recent Symposium on International Terrorism held by the US Department of Defense revealed almost as many definitions as there were speakers. While considerable uneasiness is frequently expressed concerning our apparent inability to come to definitional terms with terrorism, the importance of discussing the *concept* is also frequently emphasized. It is precisely the problem of definition, and its associated conceptual issues, which handicaps us in our attempts to grasp the critical issues.[5]

Furthermore, the data available to us in our analysis of terrorism remain rather unsystematic and unreliable. At best, the unclassified data on terrorists and terrorist incidents are seen through the prism of the media, often itself an instrument of terrorism. Finally, the rhetoric surrounding terrorism compounds the problem of understanding the phenomenon. It is argued that the major problem of terrorism today is state-sponsorship, both direct and indirect – yet the publicly available evidence which supports this contention, is often intuitively palatable yet not particularly substantive.

DEFINING TERRORISM

As we have already discussed, agreeing on the definition of terrorism remains as difficult a task as any in increasing our understanding of this form of behaviour. In fact, one could argue that it is often more convenient *not* to define the concept. As shown at the Symposium already mentioned as well as countless others, many experts express frustration at the extensive debate over the meaning of the term and it is not unusual to hear the comment somewhat akin to the recent debate on pornography in America, 'when I see it, I know it'. We are told that definitions of terrorism seem to 'box us in' and might tend to exclude certain actions that states might prefer to include as terrorism, for obvious policy reasons.[6]

In the chapters which follow, each author describes terrorism somewhat differently reflecting the overall nature of the concept. It is arguable that we are dealing with a form of behaviour which is not susceptible to a single definition; that it is a type of behaviour, policy, tool or instrument used by individuals, groups and nations, attests to the fact that its definition depends on the perspective from which it is viewed. In this vein, Wardlaw, in his essay, argues persuasively *against* the use of the word terrorist since it conjures up so many disparate meanings. Short of this unlikely occurrence, however,

Wardlaw suggests a more rational and even-handed use of the concept: 'an act committed by a friendly nation which fits the definition of terrorism should be condemned'. The important point of this definition should not be lost: that in order to understand terrorism better we must avoid the heavy-handed political and cultural biases which so frequently influence our research.

In spite of this lack of definitional clarity which appears endemic to the study of terrorism, a number of critical insights can be made about how it is viewed, particularly in the context of the systematic approach taken in this collection of analyses. First and foremost, terrorism is a phenomenon of international relations and should be analysed as such. As Wardlaw points out in his essay, terrorism can influence the foreign policy of nations, can disrupt and perhaps destroy political processes which are of importance to the international community and does present a real threat to international order and stability. Furthermore, as Gurr points out, terrorism should be regarded as *tactics* used in political conflicts within countries and among them. Clearly, we must begin to understand terrorism in the same vein that we have attempted to understand civil violence, insurgency, revolution and, more recently, low-intensity conflict. It must be subject to the same systematic scrutiny as any other type of behaviour studied in the course of international politics. Furthermore, terrorism must not be conveniently defined to suit an individual's political beliefs. As Wardlaw, Schmid and Stohl each state, acts of terrorism must be defined as such regardless of the perpetrator.

Terrorism is purposeful. A consensus appears to be emerging that abandons the more traditional view of terrorism as predominantly irrational behaviour.[7] As Crenshaw points out in her essay on psychological factors, the concepts of rationality and irrationality are culture-bound, and terrorists rationally hold convictions that the majority of society sees as deluded. Even if it may not necessarily be the case, as Wilkinson argues, that every international terrorist movement or group requires an extremist ideology or belief system for motivation, the fact remains that there is a set of beliefs or justification system which in some sense guides the actions. Thus, in our definition of terrorism, we assume that terrorism is a purposeful act which is intended to affect an audience either directly or indirectly (as Schmid discusses at length in his analysis of terrorist goals and objectives).

SEVEN CRITICAL PERSPECTIVES ON INTERNATIONAL TERRORISM

As we have already suggested, the study of international terrorism is replete with case-studies and ideological arguments on the causes of terrorist behaviour. All too little systematic analysis of terrorism as an international behavioural phenomenon exists in the current literature. In the next few pages we will outline what we believe to be the seven most critical issues or perspectives on international terrorism. These seven areas represent perspectives which are pre-requisites to a rational policy for dealing with and responding to international terrorism.

Perspective 1   Psychological and Ideological Factors

The progression of thinking about terrorists as more than irrational actors inevitably leads to a more systematic examination of how the terrorist individual perceives the political/social/cultural milieu and the influences on that individual which play a role in the choice of terrorism. While a rich literature exists on belief systems – both how they are formed and how they influence behaviour – only recently has this research been applied to the study of terrorists. One explanation for this is the relative lack of data on terrorists; certainly when compared with data available on major political actors, the amount of information available on terrorists is meagre at best.

It is not enough to understand the individual in isolation. Crenshaw's contribution is to portray clearly the importance of *group* explanations of terrorism. For many, the initial attraction is to the group. What attracts individuals to such groups and what provides the impetus to remain totally obedient to group norms is a critical piece in the puzzle of understanding terrorists.

An equally important issue is what an understanding of the psychology and ideology of the terrorist means. Does an increased awareness of these factors lead to a more knowledgeable and effective means of dealing with terrorism?

Perspective 2   Goals and Objectives

Traditionally defined, the goal of terrorism is generally seen as an attempt to produce a feeling of anxiety in an individual, group, nation, etc. In our attempt to understand terrorism, we generally view it as a unidimensional type of behaviour without paying sufficient attention to its different manifestations. Terrorism is multifaceted – it represents a set or type of behaviour which is used to achieve a varied agenda of goals. Much of this depends on the origin of terrorism and its intended affects. Much of our failure to grasp the multiple goals of terrorism extends from a fascination, particularly on the part of the media, with the direct targets of terrorist activity. While clearly a target of terrorism, the victim is often a surrogate for those who are truly the targets of influence. In order to begin to understand what goals and objectives are related to terrorist activity, a systematic analysis and identification of the *real* targets of terrorism is critical. Schmid's contribution to our thinking about goals and objectives is significant in that he defines targets as not only those who are the victims but also those who are placed in fear, immobilised, influenced or manipulated. It is this argument – that terrorism can not only move or remove a target but also effectively manipulate a diverse target population – that we must pursue if we are to comprehend better the *modus operandi* of terrorists.

Perspective 3 Analysing Terrorism

No area has advanced more slowly than the application of research methods to the study of terrorism. Like many fields of inquiry in their infancy, the study of terrorism has been dominated by a great deal of impressionistic research and little attention has been paid to establishing a mode of inquiry based on systematic, well-grounded approaches. Although not lacking an impressive array of scholars, the field of terrorism analysis is a high visibility area for those who wish to publish. Consequently, research on terrorism has suffered from a general lack of accumulation of systematic evidence.

Certainly, a significant problem is a lack of systematic and reliable data. Continued reliance on superficial reports of terrorist events relegates much of the analysis of terrorism to second-rate status. Furthermore, the fact that much of the data are oriented to *specific* interests of government agencies, and are not made available for unclassified analyses, creates a tremendous accessibility problem for analysts of terrorism. The recent debate in the USA and Western Europe over evidence which may or may not prove that Libyan involvement is state-sponsored terrorism, highlights the problem of data made available only to prove certain policy contentions and not made available for analysis.

Even more significant than the lack of data may be the types of questions which are asked, and clearly the types of analysis to which these questions lead. As Gurr points out in his essay, his concern is more that we are asking the wrong questions by not looking more intensively at the *causes* of terrorism as opposed to its trends, effects and potential responses. Only when research begins to examine terrorism as a phenomenon which results from structural/societal factors has it made significant strides in improving our overall understanding.

Perspective 4   Support Mechanisms

A factor often neglected in research is the question of where and how terrorist groups derive their support, not simply financial but ideological and motivational. Clearly left over from the less-informed and more-traditional perspectives is the view of the terrorist as a societal outcast living in isolation and forced to rob banks to support activities. Such myths of the terrorist are disappearing rapidly, particularly with the significant contributions of such students of terrorism as James Adams, whose recent study of financial aspects of terrorism represents a ground-breaking effort (see Adams, 1986). Even with this major contribution by Adams, we have only begun to scratch the surface in understanding the vast and complex nature of the financing of terrorism. The study of terrorism has become so complex that a sub-field and sub-specialty in narcotics and terrorism has emerged (see Steinitz, 1985).

While our increased understanding of the financing of terrorism is critical, other support mechanisms exist which are also crucial to the survival of terrorist groups. As Wilkinson points out in his essay, there are numerous prerequisites for mounting terrorism, including a degree of training and organisation, leadership and access to targets. The prerequisites vary depending on the indigenous versus multinational/international operations of terrorists. Most significant is the ideological and motivational support from the populace and often from various segments of the international community. While the evidence in support of an international terrorism conspiracy is less than over-whelming, certainly there are cooperation and coordination among terrorist groups – indeed, coordination which crosses international boundaries.

Perspective 5   State-sponsored Terrorism

Probably most controversial is the study of state-sponsorship of international terrorism. Most disturbing to analysts of terrorism is the fact that the state-sponsored variety poses a more obvious threat and can and has been successful in influencing and disrupting political policies. It is significant that the concept of state-sponsorship permeates virtually every aspect of the analysis of terrorism as is evidenced by its appearance in virtually every chapter of this volume.

While there is evidence of state involvement in international terrorism, the issues of defining what constitutes terrorism and identifying specific instances of direct or indirect state involvement make the issue highly ambiguous and ideological. To many, state-sponsored terrorism has become a catchword for Soviet-sponsored terrorism (see Schmid, 1983). To others, state-sponsorship is synonymous with Libyan activities. Yet, as Stohl points out in his essay on state-sponsorship, there is considerable debate concerning the meaning of state involvement and the cost associated with such involvement. Even more problematic seems to be an unevenness in the application of definitions of state-sponsorship. As Stohl wrote in a recent essay:

> The Reagan administration indicated its confusion on the Israeli policy . . . in the wake of the Israeli raid on the PLO headquarters in Tunis. The White House initially had characterized the bombing as a 'legitimate response' to 'terrorist attacks'. The following day, the White House described the action as 'understandable as an expression of self-defense' but added that it 'cannot be condoned'. Following this, the United States abstained on, rather than veto, a Tunisian requested condemnation of the bombing by the United Nations Security Council . . . Finally three weeks later John Whitehead, Deputy Secretary of State, who had been sent to Tunisia to mend some fences stated in reference to the Israeli action that 'We deplore it, as we deplore all acts of terrorism wherever they may occur' (Stohl, 1986, p. 13).

Stohl, in his essay, argues that there are three types of state terrorist behaviour: (i) coercive diplomacy; (ii) covert behaviour, including clandestine state-terrorism and state-sponsored terrorism; and (iii) surrogate terrorism. The significance of these definitions is that they go beyond the traditionally unidimensional characterisation of state-sponsored terrorism and require an analysis of the form of behaviour, its intent and the 'costs' of employing one type versus another (see Bernstein, 1986).

Perspective 6   Avenues for State Response

In his address to the American Bar Association quoted at the beginning of this chapter, Weinberger (1986) argued that there was a need for new approaches to terrorism that combine pragmatism and moral vision. 'The phenomenon of terrorism does not fit neatly into our present system of laws ... We will fail to address the reality of terrorism and to deal with it effectively if ... we confine our thinking to familiar concepts of criminal process or customary international law.'

Pragmatism is clearly the operative word in considering an appropriate and effective policy for responding to international terrorism. An examination of responses must be embedded in an overall systematic and coherent understanding of the concept of terrorism without exaggerating its threat, while maintaining an overall sense of legitimacy in structuring our response.

Wardlaw, in his essay, persuasively argues in favour of a balanced approach in dealing with and responding to international terrorism. This balance should reflect the nature and level of threat posed by international terrorism to the vital interests of democratic states. Most critical is the ability to distinguish between different types of terrorist threat and that past exaggeration of the *real* threat posed by terrorists has in many ways restricted the options of politicians. In considering response options, it is imperative that due consideration be given to the less 'glamorous' alternatives including increased intelligence activity, regional and bilateral agreements designed to discourage terrorism, and other more imaginative diplomatic and political options designed to place pressure on sponsor states.

Perspective 7   Future Trends

While it is easiest to assume that the trend in international terrorism is toward greater and more widespread violence it is critical that a systematic examination of the most likely future of this phenomenon be included in our overall analysis. Most important is to place international terrorism in the appropriate perspective – just how prevalent is it today and what are its likely manifestations in the future? An inherent assumption in much research on analysis is that it has indeed *grown* as a phenomenon. Is this the case or have different types of terrorism appeared with differing modes of operation which make it appear that it is indeed increasing?

Additional concerns are the future tactics of terrorists; will they change and how? Jenkins, in his essay, argues that there is little to suggest major innovations in tactics. The tactics of terrorists appear to be evolutionary but not highly innovative – those that work will tend to be pursued and imitated and innovations will occur when needed.

Notes

1. For an analysis of the problem of viewing the terrorist as only a madman see Hacker (1976), Miller (1980) and Stohl (1983).
2. See Schmid's (1983) trenchant criticism of this problem.
3. Schmid's 1983 bibliography runs to 4091 entries and identifies 78 other bibliographies. See also Mickolus (1980) for an annotated bibliography on the terrorism literature.
4. See Nicholson (1986) and McCamant (1984).
5. See Vought and Fraser (1986), Farrell (1982), and Jenkins (1980).
6. For a witty and vitriolic attack on the use and non-use of definitions see Hitchens (1986).
7. For early analysis see Schelling (1966) and Dror (1971).

References

Adams, James (1986). *The Financing of Terror* (New York: Simon & Schuster).

Bernstein, A H. (1986) 'Iran's Low Intensity War Against the United States', *Orbis*, vol. 30, no. 1, Spring, pp. 149–67.

Dror, Y. (1971) *Crazy States* (Lexington, Massachusetts: D C Heath).

Farrell, W. R (1982) *The US Government Response to Terrorism: In Search of an Effective Strategy* (Boulder, Colorado: Westview Press).

Greenberg, M. (1979) *International Terrorism: An Annotated Bibliography as Research Guide*. (Boulder, Colorado: Westview).

Hacker, F. (1976) *Crusaders, Criminals, Crazies: Terror And Terrorism in Our Time* (New York: W W. Norton).

Hitchens, C. (1986) 'Wanton Acts of Usage, Terrorism: A Cliché in Search of a Meaning', *Harpers*, September, pp. 66–70.

Jenkins, B, (1980) 'The Study of Terrorism. Definitional Problems', in Y. Alexander and J. Gleason (eds) *Terrorism: Behavioral Perspectives* (New York: Pergamon).

McCamant, J. (1984) 'Governance Without Blood: Social Science's Antiseptic View of Rule or the Neglect of Political Repression', in M. Stohl and G. Lopez (eds) *The State as Terrorist* (Westport, Connecticut: Greenwood Press).

Mickolus, E. (1980) *The Literature of Terrorism* (Westport, Connecticut: Greenwood Press).

Miller, A. H. (1980) *Terrorism and Hostage Negotiations* (Boulder, Colorado: Westview Press).

Nicholson, M. (1986) 'Conceptual Problems of Studying State Terrorism', in M. Stohl and G. Lopez (eds) *Government Violence and Repression* (Westport, Connecticut: Greenwood Press).

Schelling, T. (1966) *Arms and Influence* (New Haven, Connecticut Yale University Press).

Schmid, A. (1983) *Political Terrorism: A Research Guide to Concepts, Theories, Data Bases and Literature* (New Brunswick: Transaction Books).

Steinitz, M. (1985) 'Insurgents, Terrorists and the Drug Trade', *Washington Quarterly*, vol. 8, no. 4, Fall, pp. 141–56.

Stohl, M. (1983) 'Myths and Realities of Political Terrorism', in M. Stohl (ed.) *The Politics of Terrorism* (New York: Marcel Dekker).

Stohl, M. (1986) 'Terrorism, States and State Terrorism: The Reagan Administration in the Middle East'.(Unpublished paper).

Vought, D. B. and Fraser J. H. (1986) 'Terrorism: The Search for Working Definitions', *Military Review*, July, pp. 71–6.

Weinberger, C. W. (1986) 'Framing an Appropriate Response to Terrorism', *Defense Issues*, vol. 1, no. 36. Reprint of remarks prepared for delivery at the American Bar Association National Conference on Law in Relationship to Terrorism, Washington, DC, 5 June.

2 The Subjective Reality of the Terrorist: Ideological and Psychological Factors in Terrorism

Martha Crenshaw

The actions of terrorist organisations are based on a subjective interpretation of the world rather than objective reality.[1] Perceptions of the political and social environment are filtered through beliefs and attitudes that reflect experiences and memories. The psychological and ideological factors that constitute the terrorist's world-view are only part of a complex web of determinants of terrorist behaviour, one of which is surely a strategic conception of means and ends. It is clearly mistaken, however, to assume that terrorists act in terms of a consistent rationality based on accurate representations of reality. In fact one of the aims of terrorist organisations is to convince sceptical audiences to see the world in their terms. An important aspect of the struggle between governments and terrorists concerns the definition of the conflict. Each side wishes to interpret the issues in terms of its own values.

Given this premise, that the way in which members of the terrorist organisation see the world influences their behaviour, it becomes essential to analyse the content and structure of the political beliefs of members of terrorist organisations. Commonly-held systems of beliefs may be derived from numerous environmental sources. The political and social context in which the terrorist organisation operates and from which it developed constitutes one set of origins. General cultural influences (history, tradition, religion, literature) imparted to individual members of society through socialisation patterns as well as formally constructed ideologies or political philosophies, are additional sources of terrorist beliefs.

12

Many people are exposed to the impact culture or political ideas; however, only a few select terrorism. Explaining the receptivity of the small minority who turns to terrorism requires analysis of the psychological functions of beliefs. Psychological traits do not stand in isolation from social learning, but individual variations in susceptibility to social and political setting must be emphasised. Furthermore, the situation in which terrorists exist is stressful and uncertain, which contributes to extreme and unrealistic beliefs that are psychologically functional, durable, and resistant to change. Both cognitive processes and motivational factors encourage reliance on a set of unchanging beliefs that inhibit flexibility and openness. This combination of factors explains the tenaciousness of terrorist beliefs despite their growing deviation from reality. It may also explain the bitterness and violence that control dissent within terrorist organisations. The dynamics of the group encourage cohesiveness and solidarity that stifle challenges to the dominant beliefs in the terrorist organisation.

Any psychological analysis must proceed with caution. The data are scarce and imprecise, as terrorists do not readily submit to acting as experimental subjects. The 'mindset' of the terrorist has yet to be systematically analysed. As Jenkins (1979) claims, the perspective of the terrorist and the effect of context and circumstances on behaviour remain areas of uncertainty. It is also important to be sensitive to cultural differences and to avoid assuming that what is unusual by Western standards is also abnormal. The concepts of rationality and irrationality commonly employed in social-scientific analysis are culture-bound. Terrorists rationally hold convictions which the majority of society see as deluded. As Joseph Conrad (1963, p. 9) explained, 'perverse reason has its own logical processes'.

The policy implications of this preliminary analysis should be carefully drawn. In general, governments should avoid reinforcing the subjective reality of the terrorist. The aim of policy should also be to loosen the hold of the group over its members and to make the individuals who have become committed to terrorism more responsive to reality. In hostage situations in particular, government decision-makers must use their knowledge of terrorist perceptions and beliefs to induce flexibility and compromise. Terrorists must be persuaded to look at a longer-run future and to develop a less abstract world-view.

THE CONTENT AND STRUCTURE OF BELIEFS

Members of terrorist organisations act in terms of organised belief systems that structure their interpretations of the world and filter the information they receive. As Holsti (1967, p. 18) contends, the belief system 'may be thought of as the set of lenses through which information concerning the physical and social environment is received. It orients the individual to his environment, defining it for him and identifying for him its salient characteristics.' What terrorists believe affects perception and action. The questions to be asked here concern whether or not sets of common beliefs can be identified. If not similar in terms of specific political positions, shared beliefs may be comparable in terms of general orientations or attitudes toward the world. Collective beliefs may also be like in structure if not content. That is, terrorists may not believe the same things, but their beliefs may resemble each other in degree of complexity, abstractness, or flexibility.

It is possible to view the beliefs of individual terrorists as extensions of the extremist mentality. Traditional 'extremism' theory holds that radicals of both left and right will display less sophisticated reasoning than moderates because they are attempting to simplify an overly complex reality. Sidanius (1985), however, argues the contrary. Extremists, including political terrorists, exhibit greater cognitive complexity and flexibility (Sidanius, 1985, p. 641).

The proposition that the terrorist belief system may be cognitively complex is supported by the research of Hopple and Steiner (1984). Through content analysis of documents from the German Red Army Faction (RAF), the Italian Red Brigades, and the Basque Euzkadi ta Askatasuna (ETA) they found that terrorists view the world causally. That is, terrorists employ a variety of categories used to identify the causes of events: individual terrorists, the group, competitors or rivals, political parties, the public, the media, corporations, the situation, government policy and institutions, ideology, and foreign states (Hopple and Steiner, 1984, pp. 18–19 and 80–2). In no case did terrorists consider a single cause as sufficient explanation. The beliefs held by members of these three groups fluctuated as the organisation developed, although it is not clear whether these changes resulted from shifting attitudes or from shifting composition of the group. Given the high rate of attrition in terrorist organisations, membership is unlikely to remain stable. Although these three groups may not constitute a representative sample of all terrorist organisations, they include both revolutionaries and national-separatists. The differences between types appeared minimal.

Another question raised by the consideration of terrorism as a form of extremism is whether or not there are significant differences between left and right extremists, Sidanius (1985, p. 657) found that links between the organisation of the belief system and left-versus-right ideology were difficult to demonstrate. Horowitz argued that it does not make sense to distinguish between left and right terrorism. He asserted that 'terrorism is a unitary phenomenon in practice and in theory' (Horowitz, 1983, p. 48). Terrorist beliefs represent a fusion of jumbled symbols. Abstractions provide a blanket ideology for terrorists on the left and the right and permit multiple meanings and interpretations. Sheehan (1981) found right terrorists in Italy to have sophisticated metaphysical justifications for their actions. Their beliefs seemed as complex as those of the revolutionaries and nationalists that Hopple and Steiner studied.

However, Hoffman (1982 and 1986) distinguishes sharply between right and left terrorists. The beliefs of right-wing extremists in Europe and the USA are nationalistic and racist. Adherents to these views oppose Communism and all forms of socialism, whereas to the left the opponent is the capitalist state. Furthermore, the beliefs of the right are more emotional, confused, and facile than those of the left. They tend toward hero-worship and obsession with power and strength. In Italy, rightist groups often derive their beliefs from fantastical conceptions in history and literature.

There are other differences among groups that should not be obscured. Not all terrorist belief structures are as complex as those of the RAF and the Red Brigades. The Weathermen, for example, exhibited a much greater naiveté. Jane Alpert (1981, p. 155) demonstrates a combination of over-simplification and grandiosity when she explains why she never discussed the violent activities of two members of the Front de Libération de Québec whom she had sheltered: 'The rationale behind the bombings was too obvious to require explanation. They wanted to topple the power structure as quickly and effectively as possible and ultimately install a revolutionary regime'. To Bernadine Dohrn, the social basis for revolution in the USA was equally simple and self-evident: 'Freaks are revolutionaries and revolutionaries are freaks' (Jacobs, 1970, p. 510).

The beliefs of terrorists of both left and right are characterised by the high level of abstraction Horowitz mentioned. For example, one of the most significant components of the belief system of an adversary in a conflict situation is the image of enemy (Holsti, 1967). To terrorists, the concept of the enemy is a depersonalised and monolithic entity. The Red Brigades defined the enemy as the 'Multinational Imperialist State', abbreviated to 'SIM' (Salvioni and Stephanson, 1985, pp. 494–5). Both the Red Brigades and the RAF regarded the state as merely the agent of distant external forces, not as an autonomous actor within the domestic context or as in any sense issuing from the people. The RAF considered German social democracy merely an arm of the oppressive system of American capitalism and militarism. They saw Germany as an occupied territory under the grip of 'exterminators' *(Textes des prisonniers*, 1977, especially pp. 63–7 and 75–82). Palestinian organisations base their strategy of terrorism on the belief that Israel is an artificial state; not a reality but an outpost of Western imperialism that can be driven out of Arab territory. In the light of the general acceptance of the proposition that the relationship between the media and terrorists is symbiotic, each benefitting from the other (Schmid and de Graaf, 1982), it is interesting to note that the RAF viewed the mass media with great suspicion as a tool of the capitalist enemy (Hopple and Steiner, 1984, pp. 49–50, and *Textes des prisonniers*, 1977).

The Weathermen presented colourful if somewhat infantile images of the enemy. In the series of communiqués released from the underground in 1970 (announced as a declaration of war) the enemy is described variously as 'American imperialism', 'institutions of American injustice', the 'killer–pig', or the 'monster-state' Jacobs, 1970, pp. 509–16). The threat posed by this enemy was nothing less than genocide.

To the Italian neo-fascists, the enemy is anyone who poses obstacles to their aspirations for an organic state. According to Ferracuti and Bruno (1981, p. 208) 'the enemy is non-human, not good enough. He is the enemy because he is not a hero and is not friendly to the hero'. Fascist terrorists often blame vague and faceless conspiracies of élites and despised classes, such as bankers and Jews, capitalists and Marxists (Hoffman, 1982, and Wilkinson, 1983). To American rightists such as 'The Order', the enemy is defined as the government, all non-whites , and Jews. Anti-semitism is a predominant element in all these sets of rather disconnected conspiracy theories.

Most political belief systems are affective as well as cognitive. That is, they not only order information so as to make it meaningful but establish values by which behaviour is judged. The beliefs of terrorists, in addition to being excessively abstract, also seem to be highly moralistic. The world is seen in black-and-white terms and there is a strong concern with justification for terrorist actions. Two well-known traits of terrorist propaganda exhibit these tendencies. Terrorists usually employ elaborately legalistic terminology and practice. From the viewpoint of the Red Brigades, Aldo Moro was captured, held in prison, tried, convicted, and executed. They also view the conflict with the government as a war in which the terrorists are soldiers. Terrorist organisations are self-styled armies or brigades. To Ferracuti and Bruno (1983, pp. 308–10), the 'fantasy war' aspect of terrorism is extremely important to its practitioners. The desire to appear as soldiers appears to be common to all types of terrorists. In their turn, terrorists of the right are concerned with cleansing communities of alien and immoral influences.

Both legalistic and military self-conceptions may be regarded as essential justificatory beliefs. As Menachem Begin explained, 'in order to maintain an open underground you need more than the technique of pseudonyms. What is most necessary is the inner consciousness that makes what is 'legal' illegal and the 'illegal' legal and justified' (Begin, 1977, p. 108).

The strength of the military self-image is shown in the Irish Republican Army's insistence on a military organisational structure long past its practical usefulness in Northern Ireland. Its power may also explain why the Provisional IRA has not resorted to the hijackings and kidnappings that have become popular techniques of contemporary terrorism.[2]

For revolutionary terrorists, the concern with justifying violence is often accompanied by a strong emphasis on perceived injustice done by the state to a weak and helpless populace and the related necessity for revenge. Emma Goldman protested against the popular image of the nineteenth-century anarchist–terrorist as a lunatic or 'wild beast', when 'those who have studied the character and personality of these men, or who have come in close contact with them, are agreed that it is their super sensitiveness to the wrong and injustice surrounding them which compels them to pay the toll of our social crimes' (quoted in Laqueur (ed.) 1978, p. 194). The Red Brigades 'participated at the outset in social questions like the

Milanese campaign for free mass transportation, but, slipping further into the underground, they soon moved on to ''justificational'' violence: that is, retribution for what they considered injustices against the working class' (Salvioni and Stephanson, 1985, p. 493). A high level of abstraction was consistent with justification. Hopple and Steiner (1984, pp. 56 and 62) found that abstract or vague references to ideology tended to dominate the Red Brigades' thinking. Over time, their rhetoric became 'strident, dense, and lacking in intellectual content. The targets are general and symbolic and the victims are not linked to specific wrongdoings'. Their goals became more ambitious and less feasible.

The beliefs of left terrorists generally appear to be interrelated and interdependent. That is, the components of their belief systems are not autonomous. They specify relationships among the enemy, the people, and the terrorists. The missing ingredient of the terrorist belief system, however, is the victim. How to sustain the conception of acting in the interest of the people in the light of the isolation of the small underground from the masses and the absence of popular support poses difficult theoretical problems. One way of explaining the distance between terrorist organisation and domestic public opinion was, for the RAF, to conceive of its role as representative of the people of the Third World, not just the German proletariat. The ostensible goal of the RAF was not to overthrow the German state but to liberate the Third World from American imperialism. The destruction of the German regime was merely a means to that end. Ulrike Meinhof also insisted that the people could not recognise the RAF's representational role until the actions of the 'urban geurrilla' had shown the way. According to the RAF, the objective fact of the alienation of the masses necessitated a war of liberation whether or not the people consciously sought it (*Textes des prisonniers*, 1977, pp. 36–9).

As for national separatist organisations, ETA also encountered problems in defining its role. In particular, nationalist and working-class interests in the revolutionary process appeared to diverge. The dominant 'military' branch of ETA could only resolve this dilemma by advocating that the Basque people organise themselves independently from the terrorist underground and severing its ties with the popular masses (Bereciartu, 1985). Although Basque grievances against the Spanish regime run deep, the situation is not colonial and the working classes might not benefit by national autonomy.

Terrorists of both right and left seem to see themselves as a morally superior élite to whom conventional standards of behaviour do not apply. They perceive their role as an obligation, not a choice. In this aspect of terrorist belief-systems, there may be a sharp divergence between revolutionaries and nationalists on the one hand and neo-fascists on the other. Terrorists of the left see themselves as avenging the victims of injustice and oppression, often extending the scope of their responsibility to the global level. Terrorists of the right do not share this concern with the people. Their justification seems to lie in their identification with transcendental forces of history rather than with the masses whom terrorism is intended to mobilise. To right terrorists, the struggle between themselves and historical forces is two-sided. To revolutionaries and nationalists, the struggle is three-sided: state, people, and *avant-garde* resistance.

The distribution of beliefs among members of a terrorist organisation is likely to be uneven. Given the extent of role differentiation within terrorist organisations, it is reasonable to expect that the leadership may possess more complex and differentiated belief structures than do followers. The basis for the authority of leaders may lie precisely in the ability to articulate beliefs held implicitly by followers. Or authority may derive from the relevance of the leader's background to the general belief system. Andreas Baader, for example, may have gained his position in the RAF not so much because of his theoretical ideas as his credentials as a member of the proletariat (*Textes des prisonniers*, 1977, p. 188). It also seems to be the case that the original founders of terrorist organisations are more ideologically inclined than are the successor-generations. Their beliefs continue to dominate the organisation even after they are removed from active positions. The emprisoned 'historical nucleus' of the Red Brigades possessed strong influence over the subsequent development of violence. Appeals to their authority became a legitimating device within the outside organisation. No subsequent leaders possessed their degree of control, and the organisation was divided by rivalries between managerial and ideological leadership styles. Moretti, an important 'second-generation' leader, based his authority on organisational expertise rather than doctrinal inventiveness. He was challenged by Senzani, a professor of criminology 'who had risen quickly in the ranks because he was one of the few capable of writing theoretical documents' (Salvioni and Stephanson, 1985, p. 501; also Moran (ed.) 1986).

In conclusion, this overview suggests the following observations.

The beliefs of terrorists are characterised by abstraction, impersonality, and impracticality. They may be complex to the point of abstruseness or naively simple. The provision of moral justifications for violence is an integral component. The world is divided between good, represented by the terrorist organisation, and a much stronger and pervasive evil, usually embodied in governmental authority and the social classes identified as supporting the state. The terrorists see themselves as élites of superior consciousness and perceptiveness, acting alone through necessary and appropriate violence, with eventual victory guaranteed by the forces of history. Moral objectives are, for the left the freedom of the people, and for the right, the restoration of traditional or mythical values of order and hierarchy. Their moral duty is to destroy a corrupt state and society, whether they see that corruption as materialism and inequality or as a racial impurity and social permissiveness. The categories in which terrorists think are rigid and undifferentiated. The enemy's hostility to the terrorists is implacable and unchangeable. Victims are by definition agents of the system – 'genocidal robots', according to the Weathermen (Jacobs, 1970, p. 518).

ENVIRONMENTAL SOURCES OF TERRORIST BELIEF SYSTEMS

Inquiry into terrorist belief systems is concerned not only with the content or nature of beliefs about world and self but also with how these conceptions are formed or determined. On the one hand, beliefs are the product of social learning and thus reflect their context. On the other hand, beliefs are a product of the psychological characteristics of the individual. These two modes of understanding are not incompatible, but the first problem is to ascertain how the members of terrorist organisations – a minority of a given social group – are influenced by widely diffused environmental factors.

A possible method of selecting decisive influences from the universe of social surroundings is to search for those that provide the individual with a place in a historical process, that suggest a model for action appropriate to acquiring this status, and that furnish a vocabulary and a framework for articulating beliefs and justifying them to an audience. Both cultural and political environments can establish scripts or macronarratives that place present events in a historical continuity, linking the past to the future (see Himmelweit *et al.*, 1981, p. 191; Gergen and Gergen, 1983; Tololyan, 1985). In addition to providing a universal explanation, these macronarratives must be directive, in the sense of answering the individual's problem of how to act in specific political situations and thus providing a role, or micronarrative. The macronarrative is an autonomous, comprehensive interpretation of reality, independent of current events, reaching far back into history and forward into the future to explain how events are related to each other. Within this essentially dramatic script is a role for the individual, a model for appropriate and justifiable action. (Gergen and Gergen, 1983, argue that in psychological terms every individual self-conception exists in terms of a narrative, but that not all narratives need be directive.) These narratives are activated only under the types of political circumstances that make them salient and relevant. At non-crisis times they lie dormant. These propitious situations may involve threats to strongly-held values, newly-opened opportunities, or puzzles – events significant to the individual and his or her community which are otherwise inexplicable.

The sources of these narratives or scripts may be cultural or political. The social, religious, literary, and linguistic traditions and myths ingrained in centuries of historical consciousness yield a pattern of socialisation. Not only values but models of action are internalised and assimilated. In ethnic cultures (or subcultures), especially those in national communities struggling to preserve an autonomous existence in the face of majority pressure, such narratives are especially influential.

The second important source of narratives is political ideology. Ideas or philosophies are usually learned from adolescence on. They are explicitly elaborated and articulated as guides for political interpretation and action, which often specify the circumstances under which they are appropriate. It seems logical to assume that ideologies would be stronger in homogeneous, non-divided, modernised, secular societies. Yet examination of cases reveals that reality is more complex than this dichotomy might suggest.

That such myths, derived from centuries of experiences and embedded in oral and written sources, should motivate separatist terrorism is understandable. In a study of Armenian terrorism, Tololyan (1985) argues that terrorists are socially produced and can be understood only in terms of a specific cultural context. He finds the 'projective narratives' of the culture critical to this understanding: stories of the past that instruct individuals on how to live and die so as to symbolise collective values and identity. The times and places that are relevant and meaningful to the terrorist may be in the distant past or the promised future, not the temporal present. The past constitutes a mediating force between the individual and the reality which he or she experiences. Narratives convert historical facts into guides for political action, but the individual is not conscious of representing a symbolic model because these values have been thoroughly internalised.

Tololyan cites the importance of religion and literature, emphasising that terrorist writings both allude to and are continuous with mainstream social discourse. All Armenians share a collective memory of injustice, experienced as families and as a nation. In confrontations with injustice specific patterns of action are both prescribed by narratives of resistance and understood as such by wider Armenian society. The particular cultural reality which nourishes Armenian terrorism stems from the Middle Eastern diaspora, in countries such as Syria and Lebanon where assimilation is the exception. Two elements of the cultural experience dominate: the Genocide and the heroic legend of Vartan (fifth century AD). The model thus established of resistance and martyrdom is incorporated into an ethnonational identity. A willingness to accept risk and violent death is essential to faithfulness to properly Armenian values. Social and self-approval are thus inscribed on people's minds in these terms. Through terrorist actions, individuals can give their lives meaning by linking them symbolically with cultural myths. Terrorists can think of themselves as heirs to a noble tradition that others have forsaken. Failure in the present does not exist; the only failure is not to live up to the past. The individual terrorist's death may be necessary for the salvation of a political collectivity that has no other representation. Through this sacrifice traditions and narratives are reanimated, made continuous with the present, and given political relevance.

Tololyan contends that cultural narratives that dictate regulative autobiographies stem from centuries of accumulated tradition. Yet relatively recent events may raise behavioural models to the forefront of consciousness. Myths or scripts may also be deliberately created to serve political purposes, as may social traditions. The case of Irish terrorism illustrates this proposition and demonstrates the often paradoxical effects of religion. Irish nationalism and Catholicism have become synonymous, but this coincidence is less than a century old. Early leaders of rebellion against British rule were often Protestant, and their models of rebellion derived more from the French Revolution and continental republicanism than from Irish history. In the late nineteenth century this political and social rebellion was joined by a specifically cultural revival. While the IRA as a successor to the Irish Republican Brotherhood incorporated a mysticism, idealism, and asceticism that had religious overtones, its violence was condemned by the institutionalised Church. The image of martyrdom stemmed as much from the Easter Rising of 1916 as from Catholicism.

The religious derivation of Protestant terrorism is as strong as that of Catholics. Ulster Protestants also have a merged religio-political identity, with roots dating from the seventeenth century and the victory of the Orange over the Green, a victory annually celebrated in symbol and ritual. That a modern war of religion continues unabated in Northern Ireland cannot be explained by the specific attributes of either Catholic or Protestant faiths. Right-wing terrorists in the USA also claim allegiance to fundamentalist Christian principles.

It is reasonable to propose that just as one would not hold Christianity accountable for the terrorism of the IRA, Protestant paramilitaries, or American right extremists and anti-abortionists, one should not blame Islam for Shi'ite inspired terrorism in the contemporary Middle East. The legends of the Assassins of medieval Islam and the history of Shi'ism as a source of revolt against dominant political élites notwithstanding, religion acquired its modern relevance under specific political conditions. The defeats of 1967 and 1973 and the failure of the newly-oil-rich states to reap political benefits equivalent to their monetary wealth could not be explained by a secular nationalist or socialist ideology. Modernisation and secularisation did not lead to political power but to moral corruption. With the impetus given by Khomeini's ascent to power in Iran, the answer to these troubles seemed to lie in a return to a purity of faith. That religious fundamentalism has emerged among both Shi'ite and Sunni persuasions (and has taken form on both the left and the right, in conventional political terms) shows that terrorism is not an exclusive province of Shi'ism.

Religious justifications for terrorism were analysed by David Rapoport (1984), who studied 'sacred terrorism' in the cases of the Thugs of India, the Assassins of medieval Islam, and the Hebrew Zealots. He found that although these groups took their transcendent justifications from the parent-religion, their beliefs were deviant and represented distortions of the doctrines on which they were based. Nethertheless, divine sanction was a prerequisite for terrorism and determined the forms it took. Religion established the boundaries of permissable violence.

Rapoport noted that both Islam and Judaism provided strong millenarian doctrines which can become sources of terrorism. In other research (1985, 1986) he argued that messianism, which is a component of all revealed religions, may lead to terrorism: 'once a messianic advent appears imminent, doctrine guides the expectations and the actions of believers, doctrines which, for the most part, are the creation of . . . such orthodox religious cultures as Judaism, Christianity, and Islam' (Rapoport, 1986, p. 36). Terrorism may result when the millenium (conceived of as total liberation or historial transformation from a world of suffering to one of complete harmony) is thought to be imminent, when believers think that they can act so as to hasten its coming, and when violating the rules of the old order becomes imperative as a demonstration of faith. Millenarians may also believe in the necessity of withdrawing from secular or profane society to create a separate community of believers. These beliefs can contribute to the 'politics of atrocity', or deliberate abandon of restraints, symbolic of the individual's depth of commitment to destroying the old and adhering to the new. All ties to the present must be severed so that there can be no return. Integrative world-views tend to divide the world into 'good' and 'evil' camps. No mercy can be shown evil; the righteousness of the good is absolute. Believers need not be convinced that their actions will actually bring about the millenium, because the righteous can be saved through personal actions regardless of political consequences. Setting a personal example of sacrifice of oneself or another may be sufficient. The full achievement of the organisation's external goals is secondary. Any action in the service of the cause can be interpreted as a success. There can be no failure if all violence, whether its consequences are intended or unintended, brings the millenium nearer.

Secular ideologies which also embody traces of millenarianism are often identified as sources of terrorism (see Wilkinson, 1986). Contemporary terrorists often present themselves as followers of Marx, Lenin, Mao, Guevara, Fanon, Sartre, or Marcuse. Theories of revolution, anarchism, and fascism have been claimed as inspiration by practitioners of political violence in Western societies since the second half of the nineteenth century.

It is difficult, however, to separate the influence of ideology from that of indigenous traditions and historical experiences, even in modern societies without ethnic cleavages. While the myth of resistance to an oppressive foe is strong in ethnic separatism, it is also influential in countries like West Germany and Italy. It cannot be pure coincidence that the Western societies most afflicted by terrorism in the 1970s were also those with a legacy of fascism in the 1930s and 1940s. The need to redeem the past and to act appropriately where the previous generation had not was a theme for both the RAF and the Red Brigades. Horst Mahler, a member of the RAF, explained their violence in terms of a need to redeem the past, to make up for their parents' failure to resist evil, and to break the bonds of identification with Hitler (Billig, 1985, pp. 36–7). In Germany, the identification of existing élites with the Nazi leadership and the search for an external reference group, revolutionary movements in the Third World, symbolise the influence of the past. In France, where actual resistance to the Nazis was more developed than in either West Germany or Italy, and where identification with the resistance is part of political culture, indigenous terrorist groups have followed a different, less destructive course.

The historian Gordon Craig (1982, pp. 210–12) found evidence of older cultural influences in terrorist activities. He traced the historical roots of terrorism to the Romanticism of the early nineteenth century. Both terrorist and Romantic movements, their members drawn from the educated middle class, were based on a profound cultural pessimism. The modern rebels, terrorist and non-terrorist, shared with their predecessors of the nineteenth century and Weimar period three other characteristics: a flight from the real world into one of their own creation, a hostility toward theory and reason and a reliance instead on instinct, and a firmer grasp of what they disliked about the present than what they proposed for the future. The retreat of modern terrorists from the world was more drastic and their contempt for reason more pronounced. Craig adds:

> What is important to note is that the idealization of violence that was characteristic of the political Romantics of the 1920s was not only adopted by these middle-class rebels in the Federal Republic but made more consequential. For, if the terrorists had a guiding principle, it was that the use of the ultimately irrational weapon,

violence, directed randomly at individual targets, would infect
society with such unreasoning fear and anxiety that it would
become paralyzed and inoperative and therefore ripe for a revolution that would destroy the false democracy and create a new
society in the interest of the people and the working class
(Craig, 1982, p. 212).

Further evidence for the claim that ideology is no stronger a
motivation than cultural influences lies in the observation that
although modern terrorists adopt ideological terminology, most are
practitioners, not intellectuals or theorists. Emphasis is always on
action rather than talking. Many terrorist groups break away from
larger revolutionary or nationalist organisations precisely because
their members think too much time is spent debating ideas rather
implementing them. To Ulrike Meinhof, discussion appeared vain
and useless, a product of lethargy rather than intellectualism (*Textes
des prisonniers*, 1977, p. 37). Carlos Marighela (1971, pp. 30–1) referred
to the 'profitless discussion' of other radicals in contrast to his
organisation's focus on 'action: solely and exclusively revolutionary
action'. Through debates in 1969 and 1970 ETA's development con-
solidated a trend exalting the strategy of armed conflict to the point
of converting it into an end in itself rather than a means of obtaining
political objectives. Anti-colonialist ideology became only a device
for legitimising violence. All doctrinal and theoretical debate was
paralysed as the military faction enforced 'the absolute priority of
praxis and activism over theory and doctrine' (Bereciartu, 1985,
p. 19).

The West German terrorist organisations are often considered the
most ideological of contemporary terrorists. Yet a detailed study
(Fetscher and Rohrmoser, 1981) concluded that ideology was part of
their rhetoric but not a motivation. German terrorists were eclectic,
selectively appropriating what suited them from contemporary
leftist ideologies and excluding the more realistic components of
ideology. In fact, ideology may have served the useful function of
removing terrorists from an increasingly incongruent reality.

Rohrmoser, the coauthor of the German study, tried to find a
hidden logic in fragmentary terrorist ideological pronouncements
and to invent for them a synthetic and plausible ideology. He felt
that terrorist beliefs could be linked implicitly to modern Marxist
interpretations such as the Frankfurt School, Marcuse, Sartre, and

Lukacs. The terrorists, in Rohrmoser's view, were Utopians who regarded historical facts as deception. The future they sought was the source of their conception of their own rightness and popular legitimacy, as Craig (1982) says it was for their Romantic predecessors. Their conception of 'the people' was imaginary. To them, as for adherents to millenarian beliefs, present reality was irremediably evil; only in its destruction could there be personal fulfilment. Nothing existed between good and evil; compromise was betrayal.

Rohrmoser argued that terrorists sought out Marxism–Leninism and its revisionist modifications to buttress preexisting beliefs. Ideology accorded them automatic virtue as part of a preordained class struggle. They could not have persisted in their self-image of a revolutinary vanguard without the Marxist concept of true-versus-false consciousness, which allowed them to think that the masses were deluded by capitalist ensnarements of consumerism and materialism. Their acts of terrorism represented an effort to compel reality to fit the image they had of it, for example, to shape the German government into a Nazi model. Terrorism also enabled them to think of themselves as saviours of the true Marxist inheritance that had been betrayed by the orthodox left. (A sense of betrayal by the left, particularly political parties, was also felt keenly by the Red Brigades.)

This analysis suggests that terrorism is not a product directly of particular patterns of political thought or ideas. Instead terrorists may first develop beliefs and then seek justification for them through the selection of fragments of compatible theories. The ideas that are most attractive include millenarian narrative structures that justify individual violence. Terrorists may seek in the ideas of others elements of confirmation for incompletely conceptualised beliefs and images. Ideology is used to articulate these beliefs to an outside audience who might otherwise dismiss the terrorist conception of the world as illusory. Perhaps for similar reasons of external justification, most separatist terrorist organisations also adopt Marxist terms of discourse. Furthermore, in the modern world it is difficult to distinguish ideology from culture. Marxism in particular has become part of twentieth-century political education. Its terms and concepts may be part of the internalised value-structures of both terrorists and publics.

In sum, the political and the non-political environment shapes terrorist behaviour, and many elements of this environment are non-political. In specific conditions individuals deliberately or unconsciously assimilate models of appropriate action. These symbols, myths, or narratives have deep historical roots and are embodied in the institutions and cultural realities of a given society, but they may also be of recent creation. From family traditions, religious observances, art, and literature the individual learns how to live a life that will become meaningful in terms of the past and the future. The immediate political or personal consequences of terrorist actions may be less important then their transcendent and personal significance. Explicit political ideologies may play more of a role when strong cultural narratives are not present, but the two sources of belief interact. To terrorists, ideology may be secondary or even superficial but it represents an important reinforcement of extremist beliefs, making them easier to sustain in the face of an unpleasant reality. Rather than an uncritical borrowing of theories, terrorist beliefs may represent a selection of what is psychologically and politically useful.

PSYCHOLOGICAL FUNCTIONS OF TERRORIST BELIEFS

Few of the people exposed to the same reality – religion, literature, history, ideology, current events – choose the path of terrorism. Receptivity to cultural and political influences is highly uneven. Although most psychological analyses of terrorism are in agreement on the premise that there is no single terrorist personality or specific set of identifiable psychological traits (see Crenshaw, 1986), the individuals attracted to terrorism may possess characteristics that make them comfortable with extremist belief systems and violence. Beliefs serve individual psychological needs. Particular belief-systems may also be necessary to help to relieve the negative effects of the guilt and stress terrorists' experience.

Emotional predispositions to terrorism, if there are such, are not in most cases pathological, although there is some evidence that terrorists of the right suffer more mental disorders than do those of the left (Ferracuti and Bruno, 1981). Nor is the answer so simple as an attraction to violence or aggression *per se*. For one thing, the violence involved in terrorism is deliberate and premeditated and thus less likely to be emotionally satisfying to the impulsive personality. In addition, Knutson (1981) argued that many terrorists are actually ambivalent about the use of violence. This internal conflict may explain why it is necessary for terrorists to believe that they have no choice and that the enemy bears ultimate responsibility for violence. If Knutson's argument is correct, then the avoidance of responsibility and shift of attribution common to terrorist belief-systems (at least on the left) and the self-image of a victim rather than an aggressor may be important to personality integration. Belief systems that justify violence in terms of divine or secular necessity may reflect the terrorist's inability to accept his or her own violent tendencies. The act of violence is seen not as individual choice but historical determination (see also Knutson, 1980, and Böllinger and Jäger, respectively, 1981).

Role differentiation in terrorist organisations is relevant to the psychological functions of beliefs. The distinction between leaders and followers may be critical. It is important to remember that most followers are young. Leaders – particularly the imprisoned founders of the 'first generation' – are older. The cognitive and emotional states of the adolescents or young adults who turn to terrorism may be in a state of transition. Their personalities may not yet be integrated or stable. Immaturity may heighten vulnerability to extremism. Knowing the age at which individual terrorists were recruited and how long they have been socialised into the organisation is important to understanding their beliefs.

The structure of the terrorist belief system, portraying an all-powerful authority figure relentlessly hostile to a smaller, powerless victim, may possibly reflect early relationships with parents, particularly sons with fathers. (Certainly Feuer, 1969, felt that terrorism was a psychological reaction of sons against fathers, an inevitable part of adolescent rebellion.) Some individuals may need to see the world as hostile, shaped as a confrontation between good and evil in which only the child and the father are important figures. Their beliefs may actually reflect feelings of inferiority, low self-esteem, and helplessness. The need to be engaged in a fantasy war may also be a delusional means of self-aggrandisement. Kaplan (1978), for example, argues that the self-righteousness of terrorist beliefs reflects personal insecurity.

The terrorist image of the enemy may also result from projection, reflecting a lack of integration of the different elements of the personality. The young child is unable to accept the fact that he or she may be both good *and* bad. All the bad characteristics of the self-aggressive impulses, for example, are projected onto an external figure.

Erikson's (1963 and 1968) theories of developmental psychology, centred on the concept of identity, may also help explain the individual's attraction to terrorist belief-systems. Failure to establish basic trust, the first developmental hurdle the child confronts, might make the individual hostile and suspicions, prone to see the world as threatening and filled with enemies. Erikson also notes that for adolescents, ideologies serve a functional role as protectors of a still-precarious identity. Because adolescents need to believe in something unambiguous outside themselves, they are susceptible to ideologies which provide certainty. The emphasis on the future provides both hope for escaping an uncomfortable present and meaning for one's actions. Erikson also points out that the individual who has been deprived of something in which to have faith – disappointed by parents and the previous generation, for example – experiences an anger that is likely to gain outlet in ideologies that justify violence.

Böllinger (1981), who studied eight West-German terrorists, tentatively supports this view. He found the terrorists who agreed to be interviewed to have suffered developmental setbacks because of lack of familial and social suport at critical periods. In particular, the failure to acquire basic trust prevented them from integrating aggressive impulses. Later failure to develop personal autonomy created additional destructive tendencies. The child's world developed as a constant struggle for power with unresponsive parents. As young adults, these people were attracted to ideologies that posited inevitable hostility between a repressive government and a weak opponent. The child's rage at his or her helplessness was projected onto authority figures. Böllinger also claimed that belief systems based on violent resistance to an omnipotent enemy permit a process of collective identification both with victims and aggressors.

Erikson's concept of negative identity has also been used to explain terrorist behaviour. In such cases, individuals who have been unable to find a positive, socially acceptable identity adopt roles which have been presented to them as most undesirable or 'bad'. Essentially the adoption of a negative identity is a rejection of family and society. Knutson's (1981) research buttressed Erikson's further contention (1968, p. 303) that members of minority ethnic groups are especially susceptible to the acquisition of a negative identity because they are likely to internalise the prejudicial image of themselves held by the majority. They adopt a 'bad' stereotype.

Explaining terrorist motivation through the concept of negative identity is problematic, however. Knutson notes that the assumption of a negative identity is a painful and difficult process, often a result of a severe disappointment in life that cuts off the route to a positive identity. She admits that the negative identity of national separatists (such as Croatians) is not complete rejection of the social values of the relevant majority. In minority communities the majority holds traditional nationalistic values. Terrorists from these cultures perceive their role as guardians of a threatened national identity, rather than as the personification of traits rejected by family and society. In traditional cultures seeking to preserve old ways against the encroachments of modernity, the rebels against family and society are those people who assimilate, not those who resist absorption.

Perhaps the concept of negative identity is more applicable to radical groups in non-divided industrialised societies, such as West Germany or Italy. Post (1984, especially p. 243) has argued that there is an important distinction between 'anarchic-ideologues' and 'nationalist-secessionists' in terms of their respective mindsets. The difference is between terrorists who seek to destroy their own society, the 'world of their fathers', and those whose intention is to uphold traditions. Terrorism may be 'an act of retaliation' against parents for some, but for others it is an act of revenge against a society that harmed parents. Terrorism can represent dissent toward loyal parents or loyalty to parents who dissented from the regime.

However, rebellion against society may not symbolise rebellion against parents even in non-divided societies. In practice revolutionary terrorism in homogeneous societies may develop from obedience to the ideals of one's parents (which may not have been fulfilled) rather than rebellion. In Italy, West Germany, and the USA it has not been uncommon for terrorists to be the children of social critics (as Post, 1984, p. 246, also notes in the case of Italy). The motives for terrorism may be contradictory, reflecting the emotional conflict which the child feels. In Germany, terrorists may have felt a need to redeem the country's past because their parents were opponents who did not resist enough, rather than because they were Nazis. The sense of a mission left unaccomplished may have motivated their violence.

Another important function of the belief system for terrorists is the neutralisation of guilt. People who become terrorists may experience guilt for the commission of violent acts, so the belief that someone else is responsible and that normal standards of moral behaviour do not apply to them is comforting. The possibility that victims may be innocent must be excluded from consideration. The need to ward-off guilt, the prompting of the conscience or super ego, may also necessitate the legalistic and military imagery inherent in terrorist beliefs. Terrorists conceive of their role as agents of higher authority – soldiers or administrators of justice – rather than as independent persons, acting out of free will.

There are sources of guilt other than the commission of violence. The child feels guilty and anxious for hostility felt against the parent or authority-figure, so that erecting an ideological structure that justifies a violent challenge against a wholly bad enemy is attractive. Terrorists may also experience survivor-guilt when their comrades are killed or imprisoned. Thinking of the deaths of fellow-terrorists in terms of sacrifices for a long-term transcendental goal may be an essential means of coping with guilt assumed by having lived when friends died. The need for a meaning beyond life also grows from the fear of death, a realistic prospect for the terrorist.

In conclusion, what terrorists believe is derived not only from their surroundings, through processes of socialisation or deliberate adoption, but from inner emotional needs. For reasons having to do with the development of the personality, some people need to rebel against a hostile world. This resistance, however, might not take the form of terrorism if external justifications were not present. The individual is motivated to seek out certain types of beliefs or to feel comfortable with them if they are imposed on him. However, in arguing this premise, one should be realistic about how terrorists are recruited. Not all terrorists become so through choice. Accident, personal relationships, and growing commitment to a group identity are also reasons for participation in terrorist organisations.

RESISTANCE TO CHANGE IN TERRORIST BELIEFS

The unrealistic abstraction of terrorist beliefs and the persistence with which believers cling to them encourage misperception. Terrorists seem to maintain their commitment to a subjective reality in the face of overwhelming amounts of disconfirming information.

Theories of cognitive consistency imply that terrorists confront serious challenges to their beliefs, inconsistencies that require resolution if belief is to be upheld. The problem is why and how terrorist belief-systems resist change.

This persistence may not be unusual. In general, psychological studies show that belief systems, once established, are resistant to change. One reason for the stability of beliefs involves cognitive processing. The way in which the human brain processes information tends to reinforce preexisting beliefs and attitudes.

Robert Jervis (1976) proposed a set of theories concerning the cognitive sources of misperception and the effects of misperception on foreign policy behaviour. His hypotheses about government decision-making can be adapted to the processes by which terrorists make choices. Jervis argued that the principle of cognitive consistency implies that individuals resist information inconsistent with what they already believe to be true. Information is absorbed selectively, because people tend to recognise the familiar and thus isolate from the range of available facts only those that support their views. Selectivity prevails when the pattern demonstrated by the facts is ambiguous and difficult to interpret. Contradictory information will be ignored or reinterpreted as compatible with one's beliefs. When the facts are clear, the source of negative information may be discredited in order to permit disbelief.

Terrorists would thus in all honesty deny that there are innocent victims, despite objective evidence to the contrary. Claims of accidental victims would probably come from the government or the establishment press, so the source would be automatically devalued. Terrorists tend to believe only information from sources they trust, and the only trustworthy person would be someone who shared their beliefs. Leaders exercise a dominant influence. For example, a Tupamaro upon being asked if the movement had been destroyed by a government offensive that resulted in 2000 captured revolutionaries, replied that these were 'incorrect ideas' which clearly came from counter-revolutionaries, allies of the enemy, or defeatists who could think only in terms of quick solutions to historical problems (Kohl and Litt (eds) 1974, p. 303). The RAF contended that 'terrorism' was what the German state practised against the masses. 'Urban guerrilla' activities, in contrast, were directly exclusively against the state apparatus, on behalf of, and never against, the masses. Therefore, any reports of RAF actions that harmed or endangered 'the people' were part of a government campaign to discredit the resistance. If obliged to accept the fact that casualties among 'the people' had occurred, RAF leaders dismissed these actions as provocations performed by government agents (*Textes des prisonniers*, 1977, pp. 112–13).

Individuals avoid value conflicts in their choices. Leila Khaled (1973, pp. 133–4), an early member of the PFLP, for example, was able to deal with the presence of children on the plane she hijacked by turning her thoughts to Palestinian children and pushing the idea of the potential consequences of the hijacking out of her mind. She admitted that she felt uncomfortable thinking of innocent victims and had to 'rationalise' her distress. She was able to avoid coping with the conflict between two contradictory values because past injustice provided an alternative focus for her thoughts. Other means of ignoring the conflicts inherent in choices may lie in beliefs that one's actions are determined by historical forces or that the blame for violence lies with the enemy.

These ideas are based on assumptions about how people think and process information with the aim of reducing dissonance between beliefs and fact. Other studies emphasise the motivational factors that cause decision errors and misjudgements. They, too, can be adapted to explaining the inflexibility and persistence of terrorist beliefs. For example, Janis and Mann (1977) argue that making any consequential decision involves serious emotional conflict. The need to reduce anxiety and to avoid fear and shame means that people often strive to avoid the acceptance of new information that might require innovation. Rather than adapting creatively to warnings that a present course of action should be changed, they engage in 'defensive avoidance'.

For example, ego-involvement in prior commitments is always strong. The deeper the commitment to a given course of action, the greater the anticipated cost of changing it. The individual fears of peer- or reference-group disapproval or loss of self-respect if a commitment is abandoned. Violating a set of beliefs and expectations in which a person has invested time and ego is psychologically costly. In addition, when confronted with information that indicates that a decision must be made, people are strongly tempted to act immediately in order to relieve stress rather than to continue a search for more satisfactory alternatives. Little judgement will be exercised. Stress is especially acute when the individual must choose between two unpleasant alternatives – for example, surrendering to a government or dying with one's hostages. The perceived magnitude of the losses which a person anticipates from a choice also increases the intensity of emotional discomfort. The 'unpleasant-ness' of these emotions impairs the ability to search for options and appraise the consequences of choices. In the face of serious threats, individuals who have insufficient time to find an alternative to a no longer feasible course of action are likely to fall into a condition of 'hypervigilance', or panic. Isolation from social support systems and enforced inactivity (such as terrorists experience in barricade and seizure incidents particularly) also increase the likelihood of hyper-vigilance. People then make hasty judgements which they may later regret, since the drawbacks or negative consequences of the alternative have been ignored in a frantic rush to escape disaster. On the other hand, when *no* escape route is perceived, the person may collapse into fatalism and indifference.

Holsti's (1972) work on decision-making during the First World War also notes the importance of time-pressures in increasing psychological stress, which in turn impairs realistic and efficient decision-making. He also alludes to the tendencies of decision-makers in crisis situations to avoid assuming responsibility for unpleasant choices. As events led inexorably to war in 1914, each national leader felt that the responsibility for averting war lay with his enemy. Having lost control, he felt nevertheless that the adversary *could* change if he *would*. That he did not meant that he did not wish to, and thus that hostilities were inevitable and defensive action jus-tified. The pressures under which terrorists act make it necessary to cast responsiblity for violence onto the government, perceived as 'in control' and capable of determining outcomes.

Terrorists, particularly in hostage seizures, are involved in making decisions that involve momentous consequences. Not only do they accept personal risk, but the fate of the organisation and the beliefs to which they are passionately committed is at stake. Their lives and personal reputations as well as the status of the organisation and the security of its members will be affected by the consequences of their choices. Surely the emotional conflict they experience is acute. They might reasonably be expected to fall back on the simple decision rules dictated by their beliefs rather than debate alternatives until the least costly is selected. Beliefs will bind them to the commitments they have already made, and decision errors resulting from misper-ceptions will be frequent. They will be emotionally pressured to act precipitously rather than to spend painful time calculating conse-quences. Isolated in a hostage-taking episode they are likely to lash out destructively if they perceive that time is running out. The premises of the popular 'Stockholm syndrome' - that with the passage of time terrorists will feel an emotional affinity with their captives and become reluctant to harm them - are false if the decisional conflict theory is accepted. As stress intensifies, so may the irrationality of terrorist behaviour. The cost of changing beliefs or courses of action promotes continuity to the point of counter-productiveness.

Michael, or 'Bommi', Baumann, a recanted West-German terrorist, explained (1977, p. 98) that 'the group becomes increasingly closed. The greater the pressure from the outside, the more you stick together, the more mistakes you make, the more pressure is turned inward - somewhere you have to even things out.' There is 'total pressure' until someone collapses. Only in collapse is there failure. To avoid the humiliation of collapse, terrorists may bring about their own violent demise - and with it that of their hostages.

Objections have been made to the general theory that individuals must cope with cognitive dissonance or that consequential decisions cause emotional distress. There is evidence that unconventional beliefs are not fragile but extraordinarily persistent and that individuals do not experience difficulty in holding them (Snow and Machalek, 1982). Disconfirming facts may not challenge beliefs at all; people may not perceive the warnings or signals that indicate that their pressent course of action should be changed. The content of beliefs may make them resilient. The most resilient belief-systems are both the least systematic and the least empirically relevant. Logical consistency and specificity are drawbacks. Ambiguity about expectations is an advantage. When beliefs are so abstract as to be unfalsifiable, disconfirming evidence is irrelevant. There is no need to acknowledge disparity and therefore no need to employ cognitive coping mechanisms or to suffer emotional distress. Social scientists expect their subjects to engage in the same reality-testing procedures as they do, when actually belief is more natural than disbelief. Beliefs that are remote from reality exempt their holders from testing them. The abstract quality of terrorist beliefs, as well as the inherent distrust of any information coming from outside the group, may make it easy for terrorists to sustain their subjective reality.

An example of incontrovertibility of belief comes from the Tupamaros (Kohl and Litt (eds) 1974, pp. 301-2). Tactical defeats, according to the Tupamaro interviewed, were actually proof of 'real advances' because they indicated a new level of struggle. Serious defeat at the hands of the Uruguayan army was actually evidence of the 'state of war' necessary for a qualitatively new political position, which moved the confrontation from its previous state equilibrium. That the popular struggle should be repressed was a sign of the historically irreversible nature of the revolution. Bloodshed only demonstrated the correctness of the road chosen.

GROUP PSYCHOLOGY AND BELIEF SYSTEMS

In addition to psychological dependence on beliefs, the dynamics of interaction within the terrorist organisation prevent members from challenging collectively-held belief systems or for the group as a whole to change. In particular, the tendencies toward cohesion and solidarity present in all primary groups lead to the suppression of dissent and the internalisation of group standards and norms. Individuals become extremely dependent on the group. Deliberate organisational strategies may be designed to enforce uniformity and to insulate the group from reality. Dissent is dangerous to underground conspiracies. Challenges to orthodoxy are threats to individual identity and group existence.

The importance of group explanations to terrorism is central. As in religious cults, the existence of a social infrastructure provides essential emotional support. The need to have other people agree with one's beliefs is also shown in the proselytising drives in which many groups engage, an activity common to millenarian movements. In hostage seizures, terrorists often expend a great deal of effort in trying to convince their captives of the righteousness of their cause.

For the individuals who become active terrorists, the initial attraction is often to the group, or community of believers, rather than to an abstract political ideology or to violence. Baumann (1977, p. 14) explained that his recruitment into a counter-culture group came first, and that 'things became political later'. In their search for identity and personality integration, terrorists may seek a substitute for a family they may never have had. A substantial number of West-German terrorists seem to have come from incomplete or broken family structures. They seek to belong and to maintain a collective identity that is more comfortable for them than trying to maintain autonomy. Terrorist organisations in this sense form counter-cultures, or cults, with their own rules of behaviour drawn from an unconventional belief system. They usually require the total obedience of members to group norms, which often dictate behaviour in non-political realms such as sexual practices. The Weathermen, for example, attempted to ban monogamy. Members of terrorist organisations are often required to accept not only a set of political beliefs but systems of social and psychological regulation. Political beliefs become part of a more comprehensive web of social and ethical rules.

Immensely strong forces promote cohesion and uniformity in such primary groups. Having entered a world of conspiracy and danger, the members are bound together before a common threat of exposure, imprisonment, or death. Theirs is truly a common fate. Each is responsible for the survival of the others and the group. Exposure to danger increases solidarity, as shown in Janis's (1968) studies of soldiers in combat. Leaving the group or denying its doctrines not only risks provoking rejection by the only community the individual respects, but it endangers the lives of the remaining members.

Knutson (1980) found that perceptual distortions and lack of objectivity led to a form of 'groupthink' that hampered the individual terrorist's ability to test reality. Peer pressure was exerted on the individual to assume an ideological role and conform to group standards. She quotes (pp. 213–14) a terrorist's statement that 'We were increasingly losing our grip on reality' and that a 'group personality' had emerged, isolated but with an internal drive of its own. Individuality disappeared. Knutson (1980, p. 214) explains:

> In such an atmosphere, group actions take on a predetermined, fatalistic quality in which *responsibility* for the occurrence of specific actions is progressively shifted onto the opposition players in government, general social forces, or an inactive populace, and terrorist players come to experience themselves as guided by an externally perceived necessity.

Group leaders, who are the guardians and interpreters of doctrine, also work to maintain the loyalty and collective identification of the membership. Internal conflict is deflected to the outside, toward the enemy, the only acceptable target, for aggressive drives. Deviations from the group's way of thinking are seen as signs of lack of faith and commitment. Betrayal of the organisation is punishable by death.

Despite these pressures for cohesion, disagreements exist within terrorist organisations. In the case of the Red Brigades, the divisive issues seemed to concern tactics and internal power struggles rather than doctrine, except for the question of whether or not the terrorist underground should maintain contacts with larger protest movements. Attempts by the central leadership to control the autonomous city 'columns' and disputes between the 'historical nucleus' in prison and the outside leadership seemed to dominate endless and bitter discussions. All members of the Red Brigades agreed on the priority of the armed struggle and on a central core of beliefs; according to Enrico Fenzi, this coherence distinguished them from the rival organisation, Prima Linea.[3]

The question of dissent has not been systematically studied, but it seems plausible that when disagreements remain internal to the terrorist organisation or even to the broader resistance movement, they are based on different conceptions of the best way to achieve ends with which all agree. Fundamental objectives remain unquestioned. When terrorists come to doubt these core beliefs, especially if they perceive that the armed struggle is doomed to failure and that its destructiveness is pointless, they abandon the struggle. One of the Italian *pentiti* explained that he decided to dissociate himself from terrorism both because he became aware of the harm done to his family and to innocent victims and because he realised that armed struggle would fail (Moran [ed.] 1986, p. 87, quoting Massimo Cianfanelli). The kidnapping and murder of Aldo Moro and of Roberto Peci, the brother of the first 'repentant', disillusioned many Red Brigadists (see Fenzi's testimony in Moran [ed.] 1986, pp. 121–228). The effect of this disillusionment for some was absolute. There can be no compromise in the terrorist belief-system. Continuing to believe is necessary to maintaining identity and commitment.

POLICY IMPLICATIONS

American policy toward terrorism has been generally consistent since 1972, when in the aftermath of the Palestinian attack on Israeli athletes at the Munich Olympics, President Nixon first created the Cabinet Committee to Combat Terrorism. Its first principle is 'no concession to terrorist demands'. This insistence does not preclude negotiations in the event of a hostage seizure, but it does mean that no major political concessions are allowable under any circumstances.

The reason behind this operational goal is long-term. The interest of the USA in preventing terrorism in the future can only be served by resisting it in the present. The assumption is widely accepted that submission to today's terrorist demands only encourages future terrorism. Yet in hostage situations, this goal often comes into conflict with the humanitarian objective of saving the lives of innocent victims.

Because passive resistance, even coupled with extensive protective security, has neither halted terrorism nor enabled the USA to safeguard the lives of its citizens, the American government has moved to an active stance. Policy measures include military rescue attempts when hostages are seized and efforts to strengthen deterrence against terrorism, a policy based not only on denying reward to terrorists (and encouraging other states to follow suit) but also on punishing aggression. Threats of retaliation or preemptive attack increase the potential cost of terrorism to its perpetrators. The apprehension and punishment of terrorists also serves the purpose of making the cost prohibitive, as well as the goal of upholding international law and the norms of international society.

American policy is based on explicit standards of rationality. It presumes that denial of reward coupled with a credible threat of high cost will affect the terrorists' value calculus. The terrorist (or the government that supports the terrorist) will understand that terrorism does not pay. But terrorists may not think in terms of this framework of costs and benefits.

The circumstances of a terrorist group – isolated from society, constantly threatened, deprived of reliable information sources and channels – and their extreme dependence on abstract and often fantastical beliefs about their relationship to the world suggest that the terrorist's ability to adapt to reality is limited. Terrorists are as likely to act in terms of internal drives and motivations as in response to government offers of reward or threats of punishment. They are not uniformly capable of evaluating a full range of alternatives or correctly anticipating the consequences of their choices. At the extreme, terrorists may exist in a state of collective delusion. The high cost of changing beliefs impairs creative adaptation to changing environmental circumstances. The terrorist organisation, as a collectivity, is likely to be over-confident about successes and insensitive to failures, as well as impervious to evidence that contradicts central beliefs.

The lessons of this analysis of terrorist behaviour are cautionary. Terrorism is difficult to understand, much less to predict. Governments must try to influence the decisions which terrorists make without fully comprehending the determinants of those choices. Misperception, miscommunication, and mistakes may unfortunately be the rule rather than the exception. The depth of distrust which terrorists have for the state will distort any political message from authorities.

Yet it can only help government decision-makers to understand the view of the world that terrorists accept. Sensitivity to the particular subjective reality of the adversary is essential to appropriate policy responses. There are also two particular uses for this understanding. One lies in attempts to change terrorist beliefs, the other in the management of hostage-seizures.

The level at which the government can act to change terrorists' beliefs is that of the individual, not the group. There is little indication that the group as a collectivity will change. Yet governments should strive to avoid reinforcing the subjective reality of the terrorist. Their actions should not confirm the terrorists' stereotypes of the enemy of their self-image as heroes or as victims. Describing terrorism as a form of war fulfils the terrorists' most ambitious expectations. Contradictions between information about the world and terrorist belief-systems should be stressed; it is thought that in order to affect beliefs, disconfirming information should be obvious and preferably come all at once, so that the impact of incongruency is overwhelming (Jervis, 1976, pp. 308–10). Belief systems are unlikely to change if the evidence of their lack of fit is not compelling. The least important components of images are likely to change first, while the most fundamental attributes of beliefs will be most resistant. If beliefs are logically inconsistent, however, then changing one component will not necessarily produce a comprehensive change of outlook in the terrorist. Government communications to terrorists should stress three things: that terrorism causes innocent victims, that it fails as a tactic and that alternatives to violence can work in bringing about political change.

This prescription does not underestimate the difficulty of convincing terrorists that their strategies have failed. The more closed the belief system, the more unfalsifiable its predictions, and the less realistic its assessments, the more likely it is that terrorists can ignore disaster. If what matters to the individual is action that will win personal redemption rather than affect an outside audience, then evidence that external circumstances have not changed will not be significant. Yet a hopeful sign is that defections may result from the perception that the strategy of terrorism has failed.

The second application of this analysis is in dealing with hostage-seizures. Governments should recognise the dangerous effects of time pressures. Perceptions of lack of decision-time are likely to force terrorists toward impulsive actions. They are also more likely to take rash steps when they see no acceptable way out of an intolerable situation. It is up to the government both to reduce time-pressures – not to issue ultimatums, for example – and to offer an attractive alternative to killing hostages. The government must exercise great care in structuring and defining incentives to compromise. If there is to be successful bargaining, a common interest must be established. A settlement point must exist that is preferable to no settlement at all. In this respect, we should consider a question raised by game theory. Is a hostage-seizure basically modelled on the prisoner's dilemma, or on the game of chicken? In a prisoner's dilemma game, there are different outcomes, one of which will provide both sides with more gains than the worst possible outcome. The question is when parties to a conflict will choose it. In a game of chicken, the side most able to bluff – and perhaps the most irrational – wins. This preliminary analysis suggests that whatever the game, the players come to it with preconceived biases, derived from cultural, ideological, and psychological sources. Mutually comprehensible rules of the game may not exist.

Government leaders should also remember that forcing terrorists to accept the falseness of their beliefs (if this is possible) or denying them any way out of a threatening situation may lead to emotional breakdown. Panic may result in complete passivity and hopelessness, or in frantic unreasoning activity. As Baumann (1977, p. 99) explained, at the point of desperation 'there's no more sensibility in the group'. In either case, hopelessness or hyperactivity, extreme destructiveness may result. If terrorists cease to care about the outcome, restraint will disappear.

Government decision-makers in their turn should also avoid misperceptions and unrealistic expectations. Decision-makers often mistakenly think that an adversary will back down and are consequently surprised by the enemy's resolve (Lebow, 1981, pp. 270–9). There is a tendency to assume that a desired outcome is feasible because it is so badly wanted and that since one's own side cannot back down, the other side will have to do so. Because American policy-makers know that political concessions to terrorism are not possible, they may think that terrorists also understand this determination and recognise the necessity of compromise. They may also react to crisis in terms of fixed preconceptions about terrorist behaviour, when it is important to remain open to new information during a crisis, to learn as events proceed, to revise prior analyses in light of a changing situation, and, especially, to be alert to individual defection. It may be wishful thinking to suppose that terrorists will react to evidence of the government's determination to resist and to punish when they are actually driven by internal motivation, not external opportunity. Perhaps the most reasonable position is to start with the assumption of subjective rather than objective reality.

Notes

Author's note: I wish to thank Richard W. Boyd, Khachig Tololyan, and the editors of this volume for their comments on this manuscript.

1. The terrorist organisations to which I refer are autonomous and clandestine groups, acting to bring about radical political change through violence against established authority. Their reliance on terrorism – symbolic violence that exceeds the limits of what society considers legitimate in order to shock and intimidate rather than to destroy – is a distinguishing characteristic. I use the term terrorist to include all members of such organisations.
2. J. Bowyer Bell observed to the author, in response to the question of why the IRA does not seize hostages, that 'armies don't'.
3. The testimony of the Red Brigades' *pentiti* provided in Moran (ed.) (1986) deals extensively with the internal disputes that wracked the organisation, especially after the kidnapping of Aldo Moro in 1978. These conflicts appeared to be both time-consuming and lethal, because the contenders for power within the organisation tried to demonstrate their superior revolutionary prowess by carrying out ever more sensational actions, such as the kidnapping of General Dozier in 1981.

References

Alpert, J. (1981) *Growing Up Underground* (New York: William Morrow).

Baumann, M. (1977) *Wie Alles Anfing – How It All Began: The Personal Account of a West German Urban Guerrilla* (Vancouver, Canada: Pulp Press).

Begin, M. (1977) *The Revolt* (Los Angeles: Nash) revised edn.

Bereciartu, G. J. (1985) 'The Political Violence in the Basque Country'. Paper prepared for presentation for the International Political Science Association, Paris, France.

Billig, P. (1985) 'The Lawyer Terrorist and His Comrades', *Political Psychology*, 6, 1, pp. 29–46.

Böllinger, L. (1981) 'Die entwicklung zu terroristischem handeln als psychosozialer prozess: begegnungen mit beteiligten', pp. 175–231, in H. Jager *et al., Lebenslauf-Analysen*, vol. 2 of *Analysen Zum Terrorismus* (Opladen: Westdeutscher Verlag).

Conrad, J. (1963) *The Secret Agent* (Harmondsworth: Penguin).

Craig, G. (1982) *The Germans* (New York: Putnam).

Crenshaw, M. (1986) 'The Psychology of Political Terrorism', in M. Hermann (ed.) *Political Psychology* (San Francisco: Jossey-Bass) pp. 379–413.

Erikson, E. H. (1963) *Childhood and Society* (New York: W. W. Norton) 2nd edn.

Erikson, E. H. (1968) *Identity: Youth and Crisis* (New York: W. W. Norton).

Ferracuti, F. and Bruno, F. (1981) 'Psychiatric Aspects of Terrorism in Italy', pp. 199–213, in I. L. Barak-Glantz and C. R. Huff (eds) *The Mad, the Bad and the Different: Essays in Honor of Simon Dinitz* (Lexington, Massachusetts: D. C. Heath).

Ferracuti, F. and Bruno, F. (1983) 'Italy: A Systems Perspective', in A. Goldstein and M. H. Segall (eds) *Aggression in Global Perspective.* (New York: Pergamon) pp. 287–312.

Fetscher, I. and Rohrmoser, G. (1981) *Ideologien und Strategien*, Vol. 1 of *Analysen zum Terrorismus* (Opladen: Westdeutscher Verlag).

Feuer, L. (1969) *The Conflict of Generations: The Character and Significance of Student Movements* (New York: Basic Books).

Gergen, K. J. and Gergen, M. M. (1983) 'Narratives of the Self', in T. R. Sarbin and K. E. Scheibe (eds) *Studies in Social Identity* (New York: Praeger) pp. 254–73.

Himmelweit, H. T., *et al.* (1981) *How Voters Decide* (London: Academic Press).

Hoffman, B. (1982) *Right-Wing Terrorism in Europe*, N–1856–AF (Santa Monica: Rand).

Hoffman, B. (1986) *Right-Wing Terrorism in the United States* (Santa Monica: Rand).

Holsti, O. R. (1967) 'Cognitive Dynamics and Images of the Enemy', in J. C. Farrell and A. P. Smith (eds) *Image and Reality in World Politics* (New York: Columbia University Press) pp. 16–39.

Holsti, O. R. (1972) *Crisis Escalation War* (Montreal: McGill-Queen's University Press).

Hopple, G. W. and Steiner, M. (1984) *The Causal Beliefs of Terrorists: Empirical Results* (McLean, Virginia: Defense Systems, Inc.).

Horowitz, I. L. (1983) 'The Routinization of Terrorism and its Unanticipated Consequences', in M. Crenshaw (ed.) *Terrorism, Legitimacy and Power: The Consequences of Political Violence* (Middletown, Conneticut: Wesleyan University Press) pp. 38–51.

Jacobs, H. (ed.) (1970) *Weatherman* (New York: Ramparts Press).

Janis, I. L. (1968) 'Group Identification under Conditions of External Danger', in D. Cartwright and A. Zander (eds) *Group Dynamics: Research and Theory*, (New York: Harper & Row) 3rd edn, pp. 80–90.

Janis, I. L. and Mann, L. (1977) *Decision-Making: A Psychological Analysis of Conflict, Choice, and Commitment* (New York: Free Press).

Jenkins, B. M. (1979) *The Terrorist Mindset and Terrorist Decision-making: Two Areas of Ignorance* (Santa Monica: Rand) paper no. P-6340.

Jervis, R. (1976) *Perception and Misperception in International Politics* (Princeton: Princeton University Press).

Kaplan, A. (1978) 'The Psychodynamics of Terrorism', *Terrorism: An International Journal*, 1, pp. 237–54.

Khaled, L. (1973) *My People Shall Live: The Autobiography of a Revolutionary* (London: Hodder & Stoughton).

Knutson, J. N. (1980) 'The Terrorists' Dilemmas: Some Implicit Rules of the Game', *Terrorism: An International Journal*, 4, pp. 195–222.

Knutson, J. N. (1981) 'Social and Psychodynamic Pressures Toward a Negative Identity: The Case of an American Revolutionary Terrorist', in Y. Alexander and J. M. Gleason (eds) *Behavioural and Quantitative Perspectives on Terrorism* (New York: Pergamon) pp. 105-50.

Kohl, J. and Litt, J. (eds) 1974) *Urban Guerrilla Warfare in Latin America* (Cambridge, Massachusetts: MIT Press).

Laqueur, W. (ed.) (1978) *The Terrorism Reader: A Historical Anthology* (New York: New American Library).

Lebow, R. N. (1981) *Between Peace and War: The Nature of International Crisis* (Baltimore: John Hopkins University Press).

Marighela, C. (1971) *For the Liberation of Brazil* (Harmondsworth: Penguin).

Moran, S. E. (ed.) (1986) *Court Depositions of Three Red Brigadists*, N-2391-RC (Santa Monica: Rand).

Post, J. M. (1984) 'Notes on a Psychodynamic Theory of Terrorist Behaviour', *Terrorism: An International Journal*, 7, pp. 241–56.

Rapoport, D. C. (1985) Why does messianism produce terror?' paper prepared for the American Political Science Association, New Orleans.

Rapoport, D. C. (1984) 'Fear and Trembling: Terrorism in Three Religious Traditions', *American Political Science Review* 78, 3, p. 658–77.

Rapoport, D. C. (1986) 'Messianism and terror', *The Center Magazine*, 19, pp. 30–6.

Salvioni, D. and Stephanson, A. (1985) 'Reflections on the Red Brigades', *Orbis*, 29, pp. 489–506.

Schmid, A. and de Graaf, J. (1982) *Violence as Communication: Insurgent Terrorism and the Western News Media* (Beverly Hills: Sage).

Sheehan, T. (1981) 'Myth and Violence: The Fascism of Julius Evola and Alain de Benoist', *Social Research*, 48, pp. 45–73.

Sidanius, J. (1985) 'Cognitive Functioning and Sociopolitical Ideology Revisited', *Political Psychology*, 6, pp. 637-62.

Snow, D. A. and Machalek, R. (1982) 'On the Presumed Fragility of Unconventional Beliefs', *Journal for the Scientific Study of Religion*, 21, pp. 15–26.

Textes des prisonniers de la Fraction armée rouge et dernières lettres d'Ulrike Meinhof (1977) (Paris: Maspero).

Tololyan, K. (1985) 'Cultural Narrative and the Motivation of the Terrorist', paper prepared for the American Political Science Association, New Orleans.

Wilkinson, P. (1986) *Terrorism and the Liberal State* (New York: New York University Press). Rev. ed.

Wilkinson, P. (1983) *The New Fascists* (London: Pan Books) revised edn.

3 Goals and Objectives of International Terrorism
Alex Schmid

INTRODUCTION

The term 'international terrorism' has become a catchword whose use often clouds more than it explains. Not long ago David Lange, the Prime Minister of New Zealand, labelled a French secret service sabotage operation against Greenpeace's *Rainbow Warrior* 'an act of international terrorism.'[1] A former Dutch Minister of Defence used the same label when referring to this act (which killed one Dutch citizen) and stopped just short of asking whether it would be appropriate to demand the extradition of the ultimately responsible French Minister of Defence. I consider the label 'terrorism' as inappropriate in this particular instance for reasons which become apparent when one analyses the targeting of terrorists. The incident with the *Rainbow Warrior* was of course 'international' as are, in a trivial sense, all incidents of a political nature where the nationalities of victims and perpetrators differ or when an act of violence is intended to influence another nation. For many, international terrorism has become a psychological codeword for international communism. While not denying that the USSR arms and trains liberation movements and that members of such movements frequently have recourse to acts of terrorism, the search for evidence linking incidents to masterminds in the Kremlin has not produced conclusive results. Preoccupation with the role of the USSR can blind us to the fact that it explains at best only a very small segment of international terrorism. This is not meant to belittle Soviet meddling abroad. My study of 'Soviet Military Interventions since 1945' documents a steady growth of Soviet involvement in the Third World and virtually one military intervention for every year since the Second World War (Schmid, 1985).

In order to examine the goals and objectives of international terrorism, it is critical to define the 'targets' of terrorism. Terrorism involves targets both direct and indirect. Focusing attention on the wrong target, or on only one target, may cloud our understanding of the actual objectives of the terrorist act. First, there are *targets of violence* – random or symbolic victims usually sharing class or group characteristics (e.g. passengers for Israel at an airport) which form the basis for their selection. Through previous use of violence, or the credible threat of violence, other members of that group or class are put in a state of chronic fear. This group becomes the *target of terror*. The overall purpose of terrorism is either to immobilise the target of terror (in order to produce disorientation and/or compliance) or to influence the *targets of demands* (e.g., governments) or *targets of attention* (e.g. public opinion).

The first objective of terrorism – on which everything depends – is the production of 'terror' defined as an 'extreme form of anxiety ... followed by frightening imagery and intrusive, repetitive recollection'.[2] What makes terrorism so different and complex is that the terrorist actor can move or remove the target of violence, while also freezing or immobilising a target of terror, impacting on a target of demands and manipulating a target of attention. It is this multiple and diverse target population which makes terrorism so perplexing, particularly to those who see it only as 'senseless violence' or the wanton taking of 'innocent lives.' There is a method behind terrorism, whether or not the method works and brings about intended results. I start from the assumption that most 'international terrorists' are basically rational actors. While some terrorist acts are not goal-directed, the majority seem to be based on a rational choice and therefore remain open to rational analysis. Yet, at the same time, it is difficult to see the rationale behind all terrorist acts: the relationship between more or less accidental victims and the goal of victimisation are often impossible to determine on the basis of sources at our disposal to analyse terrorist incidents. The incident-list of terrorist and quasi-terrorist acts developed by A. J. Jongman is mainly newspaper-based and, containing thousands of events of the 1980s alone, is not sufficiently detailed to permit definitive judgements on many occurrences of political violence. This forms an important caveat when it comes to linking targeting with the goals and objectives of terrorists. The problem is not unique to this particular chronology of incidents.

One major problem of academic studies on terrorist strategies is that, except for terrorist movements of a more distant past, we have to rely on public data and, in most cases, on media accounts. As Philip Schlesinger et al (1983) have pointed out, the media more often than not reflect the *official perspective* on insurgent terrorism: that is, the set of views and policy suggestions advanced by those who speak for the state. Depending on whether it is an authoritarian, communist, or democratic state, the published data are slanted often in one way or another. Since the state is generally a party to the conflict with the terrorists, the facts made available to the public media are not infrequently instruments in the contest for the allegiance of the public. The *oppositional perspective* of those who perform acts of political terrorism against what they view as a repressive state or in favour of national liberation are less well covered in the mass media or not covered at all in countries where censorship is taking place. Some media, especially the 'yellow press', offer a *populist perspective* on the subject of terrorism, a vigilante view pleading for order without due process of law in the 'war against terrorism'. Such media are sometimes also outlets of (dissident) official voices. The last perspective distinguished by Schlesinger, the *alternative perspective*, refers to the set of views and policy suggestions advocated by those who dissent from the official view of terrorism without accepting the legitimacy of violence within liberal democracies. This particular alternative perspective, which, in my view, should be the point of departure of academic research has few media to provide data of an independent nature. By and large, academic researchers have to work with data provided by official perspective sources counterweighted only to a minimal extent by the written output of the non-state terrorists themselves. This data situation leads to an incomplete data set for an objective picture of terrorist strategies. It is a limitation from which few can escape. My discussion on targets, objectives, and goals of terrorism is mainly based on two sources: the views of colleagues in the research field of terrorism which I approached in connection with a sequel to my *Political Terrorism: A Research Guide to Concepts, Theories, Data Bases and Literature*, and the chronology of terrorist acts developed by A. J. Jongman for the period 1980–4.

TARGETS, OBJECTIVES, AND GOALS OF TERRORISM

Terrorist goals might not be different from those of other political actors: independence, self-determination, revolution, a better society. However, what distinguishes the terrorist is a desire to reach goals faster and at a higher cost. The means, rather than the proclaimed goals, of terrorists are unusual. In terms of strategy, the question is whether the means lead to the envisaged objectives (short-term aims) and goals (long-term aims). By 'means' I am not referring to the instruments of violence but to the targeting of terrorism. Most important is the relationship between targeting of terrorists and the terrorist objectives and goals. It is striking how many purposes terrorism is apparently able to fulfil. Depending on the way the actual victims of terrorist violence are linked to the target of terror, the target of demands or the target of attention, different objectives can be achieved. By activating the interplay between the three target groups, terrorism can create multiple secondary effects which serve a variety of purposes. An unanswered question is 'how can effects be planned with any degree of precision?'

We also have to take into account the variety of terrorist actors. On the side of state actors a distinction can be made between communist and non-communist state actors. On the side of the non-state actors, distinction can also be made between left- and right-wing, vigilante and ethnic/nationalist terrorists. When we think of international terrorism we have been conditioned to think of left-wing terrorism. The important point to make is that all terrorist actors – not just left-wing terrorists – can and frequently do become international terrorists. Some are more likely than others to be served by the broadening of a conflict into an international issue in order to put extra pressure on an opponent. Even vigilante terrorists are at times acting as international terrorists, especially when xenophobia plays a role. Yet right-wing terrorists are not by definition less international in their targeting. Recent increases in anti-American agitation by right-wing nationalists in the German Federal Republic are evidence of this internationalism. Acts of terrorism against American military personnel and installations are no longer the privilege of the violent left (see Bundesminsterium des Innern, 1984). In the 1970s one could already notice the strange pilgrimages of the left- and right-wing German extremists to Palestinian training camps in the Middle East. The first group was driven by 'anti-imperialism' while the second was attracted by anti-semitism. Both are now targeting American personnel and objects in Germany, the one for nationalist and the other for internationalist reasons.

State terrorists have also become more international. In fact, historically they were the first to do so as they were the first to have adequate means. Today, state actors use instruments of terrorism to reach *émigré* communities abroad which are considered dangerous. The long arm of Colonel M. Gaddafi has reached out to Libyan students and dissidents in Italy, Germany, Greece, Egypt, Austria, Cyprus, Great Britain and even the USA. Indirectly, through supporting non-state actors, Libya, Syria, and Iran and other states, have recently developed their own brand of 'gunboat diplomacy'. Among the most visible international terrorists are ethnic and left-wing organisations. Since both fight against the presence of foreign troops and representatives on soil which they consider exclusively theirs, their terrorism is almost by definition international although local collaborators of the opponent are also a favourite target.

CATEGORISING TERRORIST TARGETS, GOALS AND OBJECTIVES

The targeting of terrorist organisations, both state and non-state left and right, ethnic and vigilante, shows some similarities as well as dissimilarities. I have attempted to draw a composite picture of the targeting practices of the various types of terrorists, concentrating not solely on the international dimension. The roots of international terrorism are generally national and subnational conflicts and any categorisation scheme omitting these origins is of limited utility. It is important to point out that generalisations on each of the various types of terrorism are bound to be inaccurate if attributed to specific movements. Real-life movements are not ideal-types and might fall between categories exhibiting, for instance, traits of both nationalist and left-wing movements. For related reasons it is also necessary to stress that this classification scheme is less helpful for a theory of the development of terrorist groups. Nevertheless, such a classification can have a practical as well as heuristic value. In terms of 'response' to terrorism, it can be helpful in identifying and protecting likely targets. From an academic point of view it can be useful in differentiating our thinking on the subject of international and domestic terrorism and might, in turn, inspire hypothesis formulations for researchers.

Vigilante Terrorism Targeting

The targets of vigilante terrorism are alleged law-breakers including terrorists, people with 'deviant' habits, aliens, and others considered to be of subordinate races and classes, or any other representatives of forces of change who threaten the status of the group whose interests are defended by the vigilantes. The targets of terror are members of the same group or class as the victim, or potential supporters of the target of violence. It is for their intimidation that the example has been set. In vigilante terrorism there is often no direct target of demands. The warning to the target of terror is the message and the demand is implicit: 'know your place.' Sometimes the government is a target of demands, because it is considered too inefficient, forcing the vigilantes to 'take the law into their own hands'. The fourth target group, the target of attention, is usually not terrorised and plays a less significant role in vigilante terrorism.

The goal of vigilante terrorism is to maintain or restore group dominance, demoralise opponents, revenge acts of the 'enemy' which went unpunished by the government; in short, to assert social control and repression of groups challenging the 'natural' order of society. The acts of terrorism are at the same time meant to convey an image of strength which should facilitate disciplining, controlling or dissuading the target group. The American Ku Klux Klan epitomises this goal in stating that their actions are designed to maintain the supremacy of the white man by means of terror.

The link between targeting and objectives is visible in vigilante terrorism. Terrorism appears as a cost-effective method to freeze the challenging group in its place. Anyone who challenges the *status quo* is likely to become a possible target of vigilante violence. The process of leadership formation among the opponents can be seriously disrupted. Since vigilante terrorism has no goals beyond the enforcement of non-democratic order, the problem of a large gap existing between targeting and objective is absent. The international dimension of vigilantism is most visible when local death squads kill foreigners considered to be agents of (democratic) change. In practice, it is often difficult to establish whether a vigilante death squad is acting on its own or with the knowledge or even encouragement of the government. One incident of this type is the killing of the American priest Rev. S. Rother in Guatemala on 28 July 1981.

It is likely that international vigilante terrorism will increase in the future. The influx of legal and illegal immigrants and political refugees into the Western democracies has created tensions which have already produced acts of xenophobic terrorism.

Non-Communist State Terrorism Targeting

The distinction between vigilante terrorism and non-communist state terrorism is unclear, as Ted Gurr (1986) has observed when he asks whether or not such terrorism occurs with the implicit or explicit approval of authorities: 'If terrorist acts are patterned and persistent, if they are directed at opponents of a regime, and if authorities make no substantial efforts to stop them, the acts are *prima facie* state terrorism.' It is the sort of terrorism that we see in places such as Central America where both mass- and middle-class spokesmen challenge long-established forms of oligarchic rule or illegal military usurpations of state power. Targets of violence of authoritarian state terrorists are those who most eloquently by revolutionary or reformist methods challenge the legitimacy of the ruling élite: the representatives of democratic and socialist parties, progressive professionals, intellectuals, liberals, trade unionists and other dissidents. While the challengers of the regime target the élite, the authoritarian state primarily targets this counter-élite. Ethnic, religious, or other minorities (or majorities in minority positions) also constitute favourite targets. The targets of terror are all the other non-members of the ruling élite, the populace and in particular the actual and potential opponents. There are generally no targets of demands and attention. Attention is something about which state terrorists are wary. Hence the recourse to various forms of censorship, one of the more recent examples being the South African apartheid regime's prohibition of violence-related news coverage.

The goal of terrorist activities in these states is repression of opposition in order to maintain state power in the hands of the threatened (minority) élite. Regime terrorism, which often takes the form of torture and the maintenance of concentration camps, serves to enforce obedience by creating a climate of insecurity. The elimination of leaders of opposition movements, both current and potential, prevents others from rallying behind these, thereby consolidating the regime's rule. A classic practitioner in this field, Adolf Hitler, expressed this objective with singular candour:

I shall spread terror through the surprising application of all means. The sudden shock of a terrible fear of death is what

matters. Why should I deal otherwise with all my political opponents? These so-called atrocities save me hundreds of thousands of individual actions against the protestors and discontents. Each of them will think twice to oppose us when he learns what is awaiting him in the [concentration] camps
(Rauschning, 1940, p. 82).

Governance by terrorism, as has occurred in Guatemala almost uninterruptedly since 1954, represents a method of rule where insufficient normative and material power instruments are available to allow for a less brutal form of rule. Guatemala alone has seen about ten times as many victims of authoritarian state- and state-tolerated vigilante terrorism as there have been victims of so-called 'international' terrorism.[3] Authoritarian state terrorism also has an international dimension in which political leaders in exile are subjected to assassination and kidnapping attempts (e.g. the killing of Orlando Letelier by Cuban exiles of the OMEGA 7 Group, commissioned by the Chilean DINA of General Pinochet). However, only when such incidents evoke sharp chronic fear of sudden victimisation among the opponents of a regime is it appropriate to speak of terrorism, or international terrorism, where exile communities are targeted.

Given that the majority of nations remain authoritarian (roughly 100 nations, as contrasted with some thirty democracies and twenty communist regimes), there is ample room for extended international terrorist activities. Until now, it has not caught the eye of researchers.

Right-wing non-State Terrorism Targeting

The right-wing terrorists' targets of violence are often non-specific. Bombs are exploded in public places such as railway stations (the massacre in Bologna in August 1980 with eighty-five killed and 203 wounded) or a passenger train (e.g. the bombing of the Naples–Milan train 904 in December 1984 which killed seventeen and injured several dozen) (see *Intelligence–Parapolitics*, 1985, p. 1). The notion is widespread that left-wing non-state terrorists are more discriminate in their targeting than right-wing terrorists – if only because the élites are smaller than the masses. This might not hold in all cases. In a comparison between German terrorist groups on the left and right of the political spectrum. Friedrich Neidhardt (1982) found that both exercised goal-directed terror; that is, they were not aiming at arbitrary killing. On the basis of his limited material on right-wing groups, he found no evidence for massacre theories (Neidhart, 1982, pp. 467–8). However, less evidence exists to support such a theory for Italy where there were several massacres since the Piazza Fontana Massacre of 12 December 1969 (see Drake, 1984, p. 281).

Some of the specific targets of right-wing terrorism are left-wing leaders, intellectuals and traitors. The targets of terror are the supporters of leaders, regime opponents and society at large. Where there is a target of demands in right-wing terrorism, it is often the military which is informally invited to stage a *coup d'état*. Sometimes acts of terrorism by right-wing actors have been staged in such a way as to create the impression that left-wing forces were behind bomb attacks. The purpose was also to bring the security forces to the point of taking state power. Targets of attention are sometimes the government, the middle class or the conservative elements of the working class and other ultra-right groups abroad. The media and potential sympathisers among the populace also figure as targets of attention. Generally, the search for public support is less explicit than with left-wing terrorism because of the élitist authoritarian orientation of right-wing terrorism.

The long-term goal of right-wing terrorism is a change in the political system and the seizure of state power. The goal is an authoritarian regime. The short-term objectives are the discrediting of the existing government, the elimination of leftist influences, and the silencing of the opposition. Through random violence, generalised fear is created in the hope that the population accepts demands for a strong regime which can restore order. The creation of a climate of collapse and the undermining of legitimacy seem to have been the main objectives in the 'strategy of tension' practised, for example, by right-wing extremists in Italy in the period 1969–74. The long-term goal is a nationalist, anti-communist, non-democratic regime which tolerates no liberalism or pluralism.

Right-wing terrorism, by targeting the populace rather than the regime in power, is not directly aimed at seizing power. The restoration of a more conservative government, preferably through a military *coup* by friendly forces, is often considered sufficient by right-wing terrorists. In this respect it covers some of the same ground as vigilante terrorism.

The international dimension of right-wing terrorism has never been adequately documented, to my knowledge. The existence of an

International Neo-National Socialism is mentioned in the annual report of the German Ministry of the Interior on espionage and extremism. It has links in France, Belgium, Austria, Switzerland, but also in Ireland, Spain and the USA where much of the printed material appears to originate. Linkages between German neo-Nazis and Palestinian circles, the report holds, appear to be continuing (see Bundesministerium des Innern, 1984, pp. 162–7). The degree to which such links are only ideological or involve operational elements is unknown. An organisation such as the Turkish Grey Wolves appears to be able to operate internationally, in parts thanks to the Turkish immigrants in many West European countries. The terrorist Ali Agca, who attempted to assassinate Pope John Paul II on 13 May 1981, had close links with the neo-Nazi National Action Party (*Ulkuculer*, known as Grey Wolves) in Istanbul, a party also assumed to be involved in drug-trafficking with Western Europe (see Friedlander, 1984, p. 3). It is doubtful whether the true story behind Ali Agca's assassination attempt on the Roman Catholic Pontiff will ever be known. In one of his many and contradictory statements to the Italian interrogators he said 'My terrorism is not red OR black, it is red AND black' (Friedlander, 1984, p. 5). The dominant thrust of interpretation in the West has stressed the red or Bulgarian connection over the black neo-Nazi one. An extraordinary amount of time and money have been devoted in both the USA and Italy to proving Soviet implication without conclusive evidence. In January 1986 an Italian court had to drop charges against six Bulgarian alleged fellow-conspirators.

Ethnic/Nationalist Terrorism Targeting

The targets of ethnic and nationalist violence are members of the dominant or alien political authorities, especially the security forces, and other representatives and tools of the ruling regime. Sometimes members of the dominant ethnic population are targeted as are multinational-enterprise personnel and other foreigners, including tourists. Other targets include members of the same ethnic group, especially leaders who are either considered to be collaborators with the dominant regime or moderates. The targets of terror are generally those who deny the nationalist/ethnic goals. The dominating government and its allies can most often be identified as the target of demands. The targets of attention are the ethnic or national group itself, of which the terrorists see themselves as *avant garde*. The media and, through them, world opinion are the targets of attention.

If we examine the targeting of one particular ethnic terrorist movement, the Basque ETA (see Table 3.1) we find that the widespread notion that terrorists target primarily civilians and those who are unarmed, does not hold. It is for this very reason that ETA does not regard itself as a terrorist movement.

Table 3.1   Persons murdered by ETA between 15 October 1977 (date of the last amnesty) and 30 March 1981

	1977	1978	1979	1980	1981	Total
Civilians	–	24	28	49	3	103
Armed and Municipal police	3	19	16	17	2	57
Armed forces	1	4	11	5	2	23
Guardia Civil	3	20	20	27	–	70
TOTAL	7	67	75	98	7	254

Source: *Cambio*, No. 487, 30 March 1981, p. 23

ETA, founded in 1959 as a breakaway from the Basque Nationalist Party, has claimed more than 400 victims. Its international dimension is primarily with France, whose government has, until 1984, tolerated the operation on its territory of an estimated 200 Basque separatists. When the French policy finally changed, ETA began to target French economic interests and property on Spanish soil (e.g. in August 1984 bombs went off in two showrooms of Citroen, the French car company, in San Sebastian; in May 1984, a gasoline bomb was hurled into a French school, also in San Sebastian). Lately, ETA members have become internationalist in a different manner; they have been spotted in sizeable numbers in Central America and Venezuela and it is not clear what they are planning there.

We also see the international dimensions in the case of terrorism in Northern Ireland. While the majority of the roughly 2500 murdered and more than 25 000 wounded since 1969 have been local people (it has been estimated that about half of these were victims of Republican groups, more than one quarter of Loyalist groups and about one eighth of the security forces, with the remainder not clearly attributable to one side or another), foreigners are occasionally victimised. On 16 March 1980, for example, a West German citizen was killed by IRA members in Belfast. Faced with the difficulty of entering the British mainland, Provisional IRA terrorist attacks have been carried out on British army targets in West Germany in February and March 1980.

The short-term objective of the IRA campaign of terrorism is to raise the costs of occupation for the British army and to bring the British public and ultimately the British government to the point where it is tired of making further sacrifices in support of an intransient Protestant majority. The limited accord reached between the British and Irish governments in November 1985 can perhaps be interpreted as a partial outcome of this strategy. For the first time in history, the Dublin government is given a say in the affairs of Northern Ireland. However, this is unlikely to satisfy the Provisional IRA and the Irish National Liberation Army (INLA) terrorists. Their long-term goal is the reunification of Ireland (see Price, 1977, pp. 60–1). Since it is unthinkable that the Protestant majority would accept that, a civil war between the majority and minority populations would have to be fought; a war which Catholics cannot win. One cannot help wondering whether organisations like the IRA care to look far enough into the future. The Provos in Northern Ireland have apparently not learned from the sequence of events since 1974 in the British–EOKA confrontation in Cyprus, when the Turkish armed forces intervened and undid all the dreams of Enosis (see Price, 1977, p. 64). The separatist Catholics of Northern Ireland might end up without help from the Republic of Ireland when the showdown with the Protestants comes. This has already brought us to the question of goals and objectives.

In general, the short-term objective of ethnic/nationalist groups appears to be the mobilisation among the terrorists' own reference group. Sometimes the provocation of repression from the dominant group is deliberately sought. It is hoped that indiscriminate retaliation against their violence polarises the dominant and the minority groups. Through acts of disruption and destruction of property, the costs of a continued presence are raised to levels which must be unacceptable to the dominant regime. Sometimes, as in the case of ASALA (the Armenian Secret army for the Liberation of Armenia) the objective seems primarily to be revenge for historical injustices. The long-term goals are self-determination, independence, sovereignty, or at a minimum, a greater degree of autonomy.

If the terrorists succeed in portraying themselves as liberators of a 'subdued nation', and awaken a sense of separate identity, the likelihood of mass support is present. Given the greater attraction of nationalism over class-based identity, ethnic/nationalist terrorists can frequently marshal more local resources than can social-revolutionary terrorists. Since they are carrying out what they consider to be a sacred mission of their forebears, continuation of terrorist activity across generations is also more likely.

The international dimension of ethnic and nationalist terrorism is generally strong since the goal – the creation of a new nation – is likely to affect the international system. For this reason they can often count on the support of other nations interested in a restructuring of the international system. More than 100 nations have achieved political independence in the past forty years, trebling the number of nation-states to some 160. However, Murdock's *Atlas of World Cultures* (1981) lists no fewer than 892 major ethnic groups in the world, ranging from the Armensians and Kurds to Sikhs, Tamils, and Moluccans. It is impossible to say how many of these ethnic groups will succeed in their struggle for nationhood; it is equally difficult to say whether their search for identity will lead them to the use of terrorism. It is, however, safe to predict that ethnic and nationalist terrorism is likely to cause greater problems than social-revolutionary, class-oriented terrorism. A case in point is that of the Indian Sikhs who want a separate state in the Punjab. In 1981, one of the leaders stated:

> We finished with the organizational stage and are now involved in propaganda. Next will come direct action and then, finally, full-scale confrontation. Like the PLO, we are seeking inter-national recognition and at home we are preparing to use terror, the political language of the 20th century
>
> (Jongman, 1983).

Shortly afterwards, an 82-year-old Hindi newspaper editor who had written critically of resurgent Sikh separatism was killed. Since then, we have seen the killing of Indian Prime Minister Indira Gandhi by two Sikh bodyguards. In the meantime, more than 300 victims of Sikh extremism could be counted on the Indian subconti-nent. The bomb explosion on board an Air India Boeing 747 over the Atlantic in June 1985 more than doubled this death toll and only luck prevented the downing of another aircraft over the Pacific. In both cases, Canadian Sikhs have been accused of these indis-criminate acts. The purpose of such an act of non-focused violence is probably retaliation, in this particular case against the storming of the Golden Temple in Amritsar. A cruel irony was that a majority of the 329 passengers in the aircraft appear to have been Sikhs, which is not likely to contribute to the long-term goal of an autonomous state for the Sikhs. It is difficult to see what particular short-term objective such an act serves beyond 'raising the political temperature'. It does provide publicity which, whether positive or negative, is often considered an asset. It also polarises a situation which is already critical. Yet, ultimately, it is not likely to amount to more than providing the perpetrators and those who identify with their cause with a sense of power. We shall return to this theme of identification in a subsequent section of this chapter.

Communist State Terrorism Targeting

The targets of communist state violence are dissidents, mainly those at home. Potential as well as actual regime opponents have been targeted, almost independent of class background of the victims. In fact, social-democratic workers and rival groups challenging the legitimacy of the regime on class grounds have been frequent targets of violence. The targets of terror are the domestic public and the *émigré* communities abroad. In cases of divided countries, such as Korea and Germany, political figures on the other side of the fence have been targeted. One of the most serious recent incidents occurred in Burma, where on 9 October 1983 a plot carried out by North Korean Army officers led to the deaths of sixteen members of the presidential party, including four ministers, at the site of a wreath-laying ceremony also to be attended by the South Korean President Chun. There was no specific and explicit target of demands or target of attention apart from the target of terror itself.

The goal of communist state terrorism is to paralyse potential opposition so as to be able to continue indefinitely party control over society. The objective is to silence opposition at home and abroad. Attacks by Bulgarian, Romanian, and Cuban secret services on *émigré* dissidents are a recurring phenomenon. An example would be the incident on 4 February, 1981 in France in which two Romanians, P. Goma (a dissident writer) and N. Penescu (a former minister), received parcel bombs in hollowed-out books. In turn, a French explosives expert was injured. Foreign broadcasting stations, where emigrants are sometimes attached, can also become targets. On 21 February, 1981, the headquarters of Radio Free Europe–Radio Liberty was the target of a bomb attack causing damage amounting to $2 m. In that particular instance, responsibility was claimed in a letter written in Polish by a group called Armed Secret Execution Organisation.

Large-scale overt mass terror of the Stalinist variant has been on the decline in practically all Communist countries. Draconian punishments for minor offences and milder individual control measures have been taking the place of the Red Terror to eradicate the resistance and to immobilise forces of dissent. Large prison-camp systems presumably still act as a deterrent for dissent. The people in the camps can be said to be targets of violence with the remaining population as targets of intimidation or terror. In the late 1970s the camp population in the USSR was estimated to number between 1 and 4 million people, while in the worst of the Stalinist era some 9 million people were imprisoned.

The international dimension of Soviet state terrorism has become visible in the imposition of the same system of social control on the subdued countries of Eastern and Southern Europe, where deportations and labour camps were introduced and maintained for nearly a decade. The war tactics of the USSR in Afghanistan, resulting in the death or expulsion of one quarter of the population and the impoverishment of the rural population through scorched-earth policies can also be seen as a form of international terrorism. However, like Kampuchea, it is a borderline case: where the purpose of regime violence is not the control but the extermination of large parts of the population, genocide becomes a more appropriate term.

Left-Wing Terrorism Targeting

The literature treating terrorist targeting generally emphasises left-wing terrorists, thereby creating the impression of a greater variety of left-wing targeting. The targets of violence of left-wing non-state terrorists are representatives of the state apparatus from ministers to judges and policemen, government employees and military commanders, diplomats and civil and religious leaders. In addition to such representatives of the political power-structure, businessmen, especially those associated with multinational corporations, and managers from the military–industrial complex have been targeted. Journalists considered influential and opposing the methods and/or goals of the terrorists are also targets, as are moderate leaders who are draining support from the extremists. Favourite targets include buildings where government officials congregate: ministries, embassies, police stations. A second category of targets consists of those who can be considered to be under the protection, or falling within the responsibility of, a government. This would include passengers of naval and air carriers, trains and buses, school buildings and even tourist resorts. Those dependent on the government, but at the same time being least protected by it, are targets because of easy access and vulnerability.

Targets of terror are all those who share victim characteristics ('It might have been me', 'Will I be next?') or who strongly identify with the victim (e.g. a president whose daughter has been kidnapped). This can include large sectors of the public who are demoralised by seeing their representatives fall victim to faceless forces. The target of demands of left-wing terrorists can be the media which are expected to report certain statements (as appears to have been the case, at least in part, at the occupation of the Columbian Supreme Court by a commando of M–19 in November 1985), wealthy individuals (e.g. Armenian entrepreneurs who are expected to pay for the activities of one or other of the two Armenian terrorist groups), and the government (which is expected to release prisoners, grant safe passage, change domestic or foreign policy). Demands are also made on sectors of the public (factory owners, political parties, prison officials, etc.). The most frequent target of demands are local or foreign governments. Targets of attention are groups or classes for which the terrorists purport to fight – the international proletariat, the poor, the imprisoned. Sometimes the targets of attention are legal left parties who are not considered to be sufficiently activist. In addition, the media and public opinion, both national and international, are major targets of attention of left-wing terrorists.

Most striking about left-wing terrorism is that the target of terror is often the least important of the four kinds of targets. It is not so much the creation of terror in one specific target group as the utilisation of the act of violence for political blackmail and propaganda that seem to matter. The emphasis on these aspects also helps to explain the wide variety of possible targets.

The long-term goals are generally identified as the imposition of a Marxist state. In their own vision it is the liberation of the proletariat from capitalist exploitation, creation of a regime based on social justice, and replacement of parliamentary democracy or authoritarian rule by some more popular form of government.

The short- and mid-term objectives vary greatly, and include: publicity; raising the level of consciousness of the masses; the creation of fear and instability; the humiliation of the power-holders; obtaining ransoms through extortion; discouragement of industrial investment in an area; mobilisation of apathetic sectors of the public; creation of a revolutionary situation where none exists; disruption of the law-enforcement process; intimidation of witnesses, and provocation of government repression which is intended to rally the population behind the terrorists and/or cause for which they stand. Sometimes the aim is to immobilise the security apparatus by tying up large numbers of agents for the protection of targets identified on death lists or for the protection of buildings. In this context, one aim is to demonstrate the vulnerability of the government and shatter the image of strength and legitimacy surrounding it. The bombing of electric-power supply-lines is frequently attempted. The attrition of the opponent through countless needlepoint attacks is another objective. Where the victims of violence come from the terrorists' own ranks, as in the execution of alleged informers and traitors, the objective is clearly the enforcement of discipline and conformity. Yet other objectives are the creation of division among the 'enemy' camp, breaking-up alliances, and setting opponents against each other. Acts of terrorism are often portrayed as punishment for alleged or real crimes against the populace or the terrorist movement. Here revenge plays a major role. Another very important objective is 'propaganda by the deed', the purpose of which is the acquisition of popular support and winning recruits for the terrorist movement. Where the targets of attention are the terrorist movements of their sympathisers, daring acts against the enemy serve to build morale.

The international dimension of left-wing terrorism is especially pronounced as its practitioners regard themselves as international by vocation. They also regard the international environment as one shaped by international capitalism as the dominant economic power. As the hegemonic power, the USA and its citizens abroad have become prime targets. Diplomats, embassies and airlines are major targets of violence and terror as is evidenced by the data in Table 3.2.

At one point during the 1984 the US Government was receiving about 100 threats a week against embassies and other installations in foreign countries. In recent times, a shift in targeting from property

Table 3.2 Targeting of US government personnel and facilities, January 1984 to January 1985

Country	Number of incidents
West Germany	11
El Salvador	8
Lebanon	7
Colombia	5
Spain	5
Italy	4
Portugal	2
Sri Lanka	2
Peru	2
Australia, Belgium, Bolivia, Bulgaria, Ecuador, France, Greece, Guatemala, Honduras, India, Iran, Japan, Jordan, Namibia, Nicaragua, Sudan, Thailand	1 each
TOTAL	63

Source: *Federal Times*, 13 May 1983, p. 13

to people, and from individuals to groups, has been detected. NATO officials, soldiers, and installations have become favourite targets for terrorists in Western Europe. According to one set of statistics, American citizens and property were the target of 41 per cent of the terrorist attacks around the world in 1983. While this is certainly an exaggerated figure, the USA is widely seen as a supporter of repressive local regimes and thereby as a legitimate target. Striking at the USA is also a way of gaining publicity. Somewhat illogically perhaps, journalists and media are also major targets, despite their supporting role of drawing attention to a particular grievance or cause which is deemed to require immediate world attention in the eyes of transnational terrorists.

Conclusion

This basic classification of six types of terrorism covers most of the ongoing international activities. Some analysts might dispute the usefulness of making a distinction between communist and non-communist authoritarian actors, arguing that ideology is not an important factor for considerations of terrorist targeting. Other analysts might wish to include more categories. It is indeed possible to expand it to include other categories and two in particular seem appropriate. One type covers *fanatic religious political terrorist actors*, as we witness them among Islamic fundamentalist and Sikh extremists. While many of their activities can be placed under the rubric 'ethnic' or 'vigilante', closer investigation is needed to determine whether the differences are more important than the similarities. A second category places a distinction between authoritarian and democratic non-communist states. There are at least two ways in which constitutional democratic states can turn terrorist. Internally, security forces might create carefully delimited zones of terror which only affect violent minority groups. The treatment of the Black Panthers by the FBI in the USA between 1967 and 1972 has been labelled 'terrorist' by various authors (see Duvall and Stohl, 1983). Externally, democratic states have taken recourse to terrorist tactics in their colonies and spheres of influence, e.g. Algeria or Vietnam. However, when the sporadic, punctuated terrorist acts become very frequent, the context changes so much that other labels (like counter-insurgency) become more appropriate. Yet it is well to remember that democratically governed states are *not* by definition non-terrorists. Democratic governments can engage in tactics of terrorism particularly when under threat and especially abroad where distance makes control by publics and parliaments difficult.

Some general remarks can now be made about targeting practices among the six types of terrorism. While all types require a target of violence to set the mechanisms of terror into operation, the degree of discrimination varies. Mass slaughters without previous coercive bargaining are generally more associated with the right than with the left non-state terrorists. However, a trend towards greater casualties seems to be taking place in several of the categories. Not all types have an explicit target of demands; only left-wing and ethnic/nationalist terrorists normally direct explicit demands to local and foreign regimes and the media. Targets of attention can be identified only with non-state terrorism.

The following observations can be made about goals and objectives. The long-term goals range from the maintenance (or restoration) of the *status quo* (*ante*) to a change of regime, from local self-determination to indefinite party rule. They also include the destruction of imperialism through countless needlepoint attacks. Predominant, however, appear to be the short-term objectives which can be divided into mobilisation and demobilisation. On the one hand, we find objectives such as education of the masses by 'propaganda of the deed', collection of ransom monies to increase resources, etc. On the other hand, we find the enforcement of obedience and the disciplining and elimination of potential opponents. In some cases the objective seems to be to induce a calculated reaction by the opponent which serves the perceived objectives of the terrorist actor. There seems to be little point in engaging in further elaborations on the foregoing categories of goals and objectives. Rather than continuing at this level of abstraction, we shall turn our attention to a concrete case in an effort to come to a better understanding of the relationship between terrorist targeting and terrorist goals and objectives.

GOALS AND TARGETS OF THE ABU NIDAL GROUP

Our typology has only dealt with non-coalition actors. As terrorism has come of age, we increasingly find alliances between state and non-state actors. The creation of ententes between terrorist states, between non-state organisations and between states and non-state actors represents a new trend. A state like Libya maintains its own terrorist organisation and supports foreign terrorists. Support can be on several levels: rhetorical, logistical and operational. Support, even on the operational level, is different from control. Non-state terrorist movements can move from one sponsor to another. Perhaps the most outstanding example of this present state of affairs is the Abu Nidal group. It operates under many names: Al-Asifa ('the storm' – which is also the name of the military wing of Al Fatah, from which Abu Nidal distanced itself in late 1983), Black June (used when attacking Syrian targets), Fatah – the Revolutionary Council (used when attacking Israeli targets abroad), Al-Iqap ('the punishment' – used in its first anti-Saudi attack in 1973), the Egyptian Revolution or Revolutionary Egypt (used when attacking Egyptian targets), Revolutionary Organisation of Socialist Muslims (ROSM – used when attacking British targets), and Revolutionary Arab Brigades (RAM – used for attacks against smaller Gulf states). Other names behind which the Nidal group has hidden include the Palestinian National Liberation Movement (PNLM and Black September. Abu Nidal is, in line with the above, also a *nom de guerre.* The man behind it is the Jaffa-born, 50-year-old Sabri el-Banna, son of one of the richest families driven from Palestine.

The Abu Nidal group was first formed in Iraq in 1973, where el-Banna acted as Yasser Arafat's representative until he decided to break ties with the PLO and work in conjunction with Iraq. The attacks that have been traced back to the Nidal group in these first years were relatively few; until 1980 there were never more than five per year. The Iraqis were not his only sponsors. Already, in 1973, he worked together with the Arab Nationalist Youth Organisation ANYO, a Libyan-operated group) in arranging the hijacking of a Dutch KLM airliner. In 1980, Nidal moved from Baghdad to Damascus and found a new sponsor in Syria. The rate of recorded actions rose steeply: from five in 1980 to six in 1981, eight in 1983, ten in 1984 and thirty in 1985. In that year, Abu Nidal left Syria for Libya. If we look at Abu Nidal's targeting over this whole period since 1973, the breakdown shown in Table 3.3 emerges.

Table 3.3   Targets of violence of Abu Nidal Group, 1973–86
(in percentages, N =94)

Israel an occupied territories	0
Members of own group	3
West European and American	15
Israeli and Jews abroad	18
Palestinians and individual Arabs	24
Arab States	38
Other	2

Source: Calculated on the basis of a chronology by Melman (1986).

Given the deep cover of the Abu Nidal group, it is more likely that this calculation is based on an incomplete data set. However, certain trends emerge. The official PLO, after having gained world-wide attention through its international attacks, generally refrained after 1974 from anti-Western attacks in order to concentrate on attacks on the borders of Israel. Meanwhile, Abu Nidal's group, which until the late 1970s had mainly attacked 'treacherous' or unresponsive Arab individuals and states, shifted its attention increasingly to anti-

Western targets. The territory of Israel and the occupied territories on the West Bank were conspicuously absent from Abu Nidal's targeting. Also noticeable is a recent shift from focused assassinations to indiscriminate slaughters. The question is whether Abu Nidal was his 'own man' when selecting his targets in three continents and in almost twenty states. Melman (1986, p. 12), the author of a study of Sabri el-Banna, attributes to him a 'certain independence in choosing targets and goals' despite the fact that his group is supported by four different states – South Yemen, Iraq, Syria, and Libya. Given the basically identical or parallel goals, this is not surprising.

What are his goals? His self-proclaimed long-term goal is a Pan-Arab confederation based on the ancient Syrian empire and led by a Greater Syria consisting of present-day Syria, Lebanon, Jordan, parts of Iraq and Palestine. Attacking Israel on its present borders makes little sense to him:

> Neither the Palestinians nor the PLO will ever be in a position to achieve a military victory over the Zionists. The victory over the Zionists can only be achieved by a panarab strategy, in which all Arabs have to take part. As long as the Zionist entity remains, Arabs will be forced to unite to counter this danger. We, the Palestinians and Lebanese, shall be the ignitors for the struggle of all Arabs against the Zionists. We shall start the big fire in the Near East
>
> (Der Spiegel, 1985, pp. 204–5).

One of the targets of violence of Abu Nidal was the Israeli ambassador to the UK, Shlomo Argov, who was gunned down (but survived, though paralysed) on 3 June 1982. This assault offered the pretext for Israel to invade Lebanon, an attack which destroyed most of the military infrastructure of the Palestinians in that country. On the face of it, the assassination attempt on Argov backfired. However, for Abu Nidal this mattered less than the subsequent difficulties met in Lebanon by Israel, France and the USA. It brought Syria one step deeper into Lebanon and, perhaps, one step closer to a Greater Syria. Nidal's sponsor in this attack was Iraq (the weapon used, a Polish WZ63 sub-machine-gun which travelled from Baghdad to Warsaw and London in an Iraqi diplomatic pouch), probably had another goal – a cease-fire on honourable terms on the Iranian front 'necessitated' by Israel's attack. Terrorism is a highly unpredictable weapon. However, this does not seem to deter its practitioners. Abu Nidal, when asked whether he had come closer to his goal by his policies of assassinating Arab and Palestinian moderates, answered:

> For me this is not the question. If someone commits treachery against his country, his people, his nation, he gets the corresponding answer. That's the way all resistance fighters have acted. What has the French resistance done with its traitors?
> (*Der Spiegel*, Vol. 42, no. 39, 14 October 1985, p. 200).

Among the victims of Nidal were not only 'traitors' but also Jewish children in Antwerp and handicapped British tourists in Athens, as well as 122 passengers of a Gulf Air plane – hardly targets which the French resistance would have chosen. This is a difference of which one should not lose sight.

SOLDIERS, GUERRILLAS AND TERRORISTS

Many, if not most, acts of non-state terrorism appear to be aimed at tactical objectives such as punishing 'traitors' or the liberation of imprisoned colleagues through extortion. As acts of revenge and deterrence, terrorist killings can undoubtedly be effective in achieving short-term objectives. The question is whether long-term goals can be reached by terrorism alone. Paul Wilkinson (1984, pp. 213–15) has concluded that beyond this tactical level, non-state terrorism is not likely to achieve strategic goals such as national liberation. He has noted the few major exceptions to this rule: Aden, Algeria, Cyprus and Israel – new nations created with terrorism as the main, though not sole weapon. Other analysts like Thomas Thornton (1964, pp. 74–5) have also pointed out that 'the military function of terrorism is negligible ... it is a small-scale weapon and cannot in itself have any appreciable influence on the outcome of military action.

Some terrorists do see what they do as military activity. They certainly use military language as reflected in the choice of their names (Red Brigades, RAF, Irish Republican Army). They see themselves as soldiers or guerrillas, not as terrorists. This point deserves closer attention.

It is important to make a clear conceptual distinction between terrorism and guerrilla warfare. To confuse the two creates a basis for moral legitimacy which terrorists are eager to exploit. There is a distinction between a soldier and a guerrilla but the distinction between the latter and the terrorist, or 'urban guerrilla' as he frequently calls himself, is more significant. A soldier is required to identify himself by his uniform, carry arms openly and observe the laws of war. He has to respect the immunity of non-combatants from direct, intentional attack, and respect the principle of proportion between means and ends. A guerrilla fighter might wear no uniform but in many other respects emulates the soldier. He is fighting a 'little war' as part of an indigenous fighting unit against regular armed forces. His targets are the military and other security forces of the opponent, not the non-combatants. He is fighting predominantly *counterforce*, while the terrorist attacks predominantly *countervalue.*

Some of the operational techniques employed in guerrilla wars – such as the use of small, lightly armed units harassing the opponent intermittently while deliberately avoiding decisive battles, can also be found among terrorist movements. What is different, however, is the widening of the targets considered to be legitimate objects of threat and destruction. 'Collateral damage' affecting non-military and non-combattant parties and objects is not something which terrorists attempt to minimise. On the contrary, it seems that their main targeting is in this area. Terror is created among the civilian population, not just among the armed forces of the opponent. In addition, there appears to be a lower degree of protection granted to one's own reference group. This is a function of the relation of the armed group to the reference group. Guerrillas are generally direct indigenous representatives of the reference group and fight on their native soil. They generally enjoy the tacit support of major sections of the population. On the other hand, insurgent terrorists are often self-appointed champions of a reference group which has yet to be mobilised for the 'cause'. Therefore, the *deliberate* exposure of the reference group to government repression is sometimes used as a mobilising device.

In terms of targeting insurgent terrorists tend to attack individual exponents in the government camp, unarmed people or armed forces not in combat situations; third parties which are neutrals, bystanders, non-combatants. The treatment of prisoners also differs between terrorists and guerrilla fighters. The latter often grant them privileges consistent with the Geneva conventions while terrorists only claim such privileges for themselves without granting these to people held by them for coercive purposes. While guerrilla forces may occasionally take recourse to the lawless applications of violence which are more characteristic of terrorism (e.g. hostage-taking, torture, assassination of non-combatants), insurgent terrorists are generally unable to employ guerrilla tactics as they lack strength to do so (see Schmid, 1983, pp. 46–7).[4]

In reality, such distinctions are admittedly difficult to make. Several yardsticks can be used for labelling terrorists versus guerrilla forces: the extent to which armed men live among the people and are supported by them; the techniques of combat used; internal dis-ciplining within the movement for transgressions of codes of conduct; the nature of the opposing regime; and the human rights record of the opposing regime. It is important that the labelling should not be based on the self-declared long-term goals of the violent actors. 'Freedom fighters' should be assessed on the basis of their level of conduct as fighters, not on their love of freedom, self-determination or anti-imperialism.

At the same time, one has to judge a violent movement or state on the basis of the overall record, not on the basis of incidents which might be atypical. On this basis one could label Mujahiddin fighters in Afghanistan as guerrillas. The National Union for the Total Independence of Angola (UNITA), in Angola, represents a more terrorist-oriented movement as is part of the Contra movement in Nicaragua. Analysts, including this author, have referred to terrorism as a 'method of combat', conceptualising the phenomenon in a 'war model'. In an earlier study (Schmid and de Graaf, 1982), I tried to use a communication model of terrorism. Brian Jenkins has used the concept of terrorism as 'theatre' to refer to this paramilitary dimension. If we go back to the sources of modern insurgent terrorism, little more than a century ago, we find conceptualisations of terrorism as 'propaganda by the deed' and 'exemplary deed' (see Schmid, 1983, p. 220). Martha Crenshaw has also stressed the role of violence as communication without abandoning the terrorism as revolution model. Paul Wilkinson has contended that the 'richest theoretical insights into political terrorism are to be gained from an analysis of terrorism as a distinctive model of unconventional psy-chological warfare' (Schmid, 1983, p. 219). I believe that a merger between the war- and communication-models of terrorism is indeed a very fruitful approach to the study of sub-state though *not* state terrorism. The choice of model is more than an academic exercise. Murray Edelman (see Eidlin, 1980, p. 166) once said that 'political debate is commonly misunderstood as a struggle about facts or among competing values, when what really is at stake is how to conceptualize an issue'. The choice of the concept determines also the extent of possible knowledge.

In the following section, a case-study of the origins of what has been called Euroterrorism is presented, making use of the psychological–warfare model. While concentrating on the goals, objectives, and targeting of one particular group, the Red Army Faction (RAF), I would also like to introduce the concept of *identification* which, in my view, stands central to a key process of terrorist strategy.

CASE–STUDY: FROM HUNGER-STRIKE TO EUROTERRORISM: THE PSYCHOLOGICAL WARFARE STRATEGY OF THE GERMAN RAF

In recent months NATO installations and American personnel in Western Europe have been frequent targets of terrorist groups. While not entirely new, the list of attacks is impressive (see Visser, 1985, p. 29). In December 1981, James Lee Dozier, an American General, became a kidnapping victim of the Italian Red Brigades. In September 1981, US Army Commander F. J. Kroesen was attacked by members of the RAF as was Alexander Haig who, in June 1979, had nearly become a victim of an assasination attempt in Belgium. Since 1981 there has been a clear intensification of anti-American, anti-NATO attacks in West Germany and elsewhere. In Portugal, the Forcas Populares 25 do April attacked the Iberian Command of NATO, near Lisbon, in December 1984. In January 1985, three NATO vessels were attacked by mortar-fire in Lisbon. In Greece, the National Front group exploded a bomb in a bar at Gylfada near Athens in February 1985 wounding seventy-eight people, many of whom were American soldiers. In Belgium, the Fighting Communist Cells (CCC) sabotaged the NATO pipeline system at six different places in December 1984. In January 1984 the same group launched a bomb attack against a NATO building in Brussels. In the German federal Republic a bomb attack on a NATO school at Oberammergau failed in December 1984. In April 1985, a NATO pipeline in West Germany was sabotaged by an RAF commando. In January 1985 the German RAF and French terrorist group Action Directe announced a joining of their respective movements in a West European guerrilla whose purpose was to fight against NATO.

This list, which is far from complete, could be taken as an indication that a war is being waged in Western Europe against NATO and, in particular, against American troops stationed there. For the victims of this violence – so far limited – this is true. However, in an important sense this is war described by Franco Ferracuti (1982, pp. 137–8) as a 'fantasy war':

> Terrorism . . . is fantasy war, real only in the mind of the terrorist. Fantasy war, of course, is only partial war, real for only one of the contestants who then adopts war values, norms, and behaviors against another larger group . . . Fantasy war becomes real only if acknowledged by the 'enemy', and becomes terrorism when, unable to compel the enemy to accept a state of war, it must limit itself to harassing and destablizing the enemy through the utilization and diffusion of fear.

Fantasies can live a life of their own. One place where such fantasies are conceived are in German high security prisons. The minds who cultivate them are those of the second, third and fourth generations of German terrorists. On 4 December 1984, two German terrorists, Brigitte Mohnhaupt and Christian Klar, announced during a court session, the beginning of a hunger-strike. In the two months which followed, more than fifty acts of violence and sabotage occurred in Western Europe, all linked to this announcement. In France, General René Audran was killed and in Bavaria Ernst Zimmermann, an important figure in the military–industrial complex, was fatally wounded. Echos of this hunger-strike – the ninth of the RAF – were registered as far away as Cairo. In the Netherlands, the Germany embassy and consulates were occupied for a short period of time and an inter-city Amsterdam–Munich train was brought to a halt by young people who wished to inform the passengers about the hunger-strikes of the RAF members in German prisons. For a while, so much publicity was generated in and around Germany by the hunger-strikes and their supporters that those millions of people who suffered real hunger involuntarily in Africa became less newsworthy than those thirty-four terrorists and activists in German prison cells who had followed the appeal of Mohnhaupt and Klar.

How were these hunger-strikes linked to the terrorist actions in Western Europe? One RAF position paper (*Knipselkrant*, 1985, p. 646) analysing the effects, noted after the hunger-strikes were over:

We have utilised the political effects, the mobilisation which has picked up the momentum thanks to the strikes of the prisoners, and we have developed the entire dynamism to the point of breakthrough of the West European guerrilla.

In order to understand the full implications of this statement we have to turn for a moment to previous hunger-strikes and their utilisation as weapons of psychological warfare.

Hunger-strikes have not been confined to non-violent political activists like Gandhi. Sergei Nechaev (1857–82), the nihilist prototype of the modern terrorist, went on hunger-strike in late 1877, after four years of solitary confinement, in order to obtain books not in the prison library. Two years earlier, political prisoners in the same Russian prison went on a long hunger-strike. When some of them died from the consequences, the head of the police section was assassinated as revenge. In 1879, through a hunger-strike during which they resisted efforts to be fed by injection, political prisoners in the Fortress won the right to have visits from relatives every fortnight (see Sharp, 1973, pp. 365–8). Some of the themes of these nineteenth-century hunger-strikes recur in the nine waves of hunger-strikes launched in West German prisons by RAF terrorists. Yet these hunger-strikes were much more complex, thanks mainly to the communication revolution which greatly enlarged the size of the target of attention. The short-term objective of these strikes was to improve the conditions of confinement, conditions that were enviable by the standards of the Peter and Paul Fortress. The German terrorists had radios and often television in their cells and they were allowed to have numerous books at one time. They could, in the beginning, obtain practically every item they wished from the liberal Germany authorities. In Stammheim they were allowed to read books by Marx and Lenin and other works which carried titles like 'German Armoury Journal', 'Military Technique', 'Urban Guerrilla Warfare', and 'The Modern Explosive Expert'.[5] They were allowed up to four daily newspapers, two magazines per week and the use of a typewriter. They received more mail and visitors than ordinary 'non-political' prisoners and have generally been kept in small groups rather than in solitary confinement. Nevertheless, family members and advocates for these prisoners have been busy propagating an image of unbearable conditions of imprisonment in which words like 'isolation torture' and 'annihilation' play an important role. The latent functions of such accusations against the

German state become clearer when one turns to earlier campaigns of hunger-strikes.

The reconstruction of this hunger-strike offers a number of important insights into how idealistic young people can turn to terrorism. In addition, they show how terrorists devise a strategy in which the opponent is manoeuvered into a no-win situation. We also learn how the public media are involved and how psychological warfare is waged and, finally, how targeting is linked to objectives.

Background

The Rote Armee Fraktion (RAF), or Baader-Meinhof Gang, in the terminology of the German authorities, was an offshoot of the student movement and the anti-Vietnam protests. Their fight has been termed as 'six against sixty million' Germans by Heinrich Böll, the Nobel-prize-winning author. After one was killed by the police while trying to resist arrest, their romantic underdog revolt and image evoked considerable public identification. The Allenbach Opinion Survey Institute, in a poll conducted in July 1971, found that every fourth German below the age of 30 admitted to a 'certain sympathy' for the RAF. One in twenty of the sample indicated a willingness to hide an RAF member from the police for one night. 82 per cent of those polled had heard of the Baader-Meinhof group and 18 per cent held that the group was acting mainly from political motives (see Aust, 1985, p. 143).

By 1972, the imprisonment of the RAF leadership brought about changes in targeting by the group. Anti-American targeting (such as attacks on the headquarters of the 5th US Corps in Frankfurt in May 1972) shifted to anti-German state targeting. Until 1972, the RAF identified primarily with victims in Indo-China, the Vietnamese National Liberation Movement, and other liberation movements in the Third World. Once in prison, they offered their sympathisers – a different identification object – *themselves*. The underground RAF members were instructed to concentrate all their efforts on the liberation of their leadership (see Fetscher and Rohrmoser, 1981, pp. 124–5). Thus, the Vietnam war phase was succeeded by the 'prisoners' liberation phase'. After two hunger-strikes in early- and mid-1973, a strategy evolved which first took clearer shape in the third hunger-strike of imprisoned RAF members, lasting from 13 September 1974 to 5 February 1975. Ulrike Meinhof, the journalist-turned-terrorist, went on a hunger-strike after interviewing Gudrun

Ensslin for *Konkret* (a student magazine), indicating that she and her colleagues were determined to 'let the stone which the imperialist state has lifted against us fall on his own feet'. Three years later, on 9 May 1976, she committed suicide. Unable to victimise others in pursuit of their goal – the creation of a repression-free socialist society – they turned themselves into victims and placed the responsibility for their suffering on to the 'fascist' German state which they accused of torture. In terms of our previous distinction between targets of *violence, terror, demands,* and *attention*, the imprisoned RAF members portrayed the German state as terrorist and themselves as victims of violence, hoping to evoke empathy from audiences on the left – the targets of attention. Horst Mahler, the Berlin lawer-turned-terrorist through such a process, admitted after his 'second conversion' that the charge of torture as a propaganda lie meant to attract new members to the movement. The imprisoned terrorists 'terrorised' themselves with self-imposed hunger-strikes, the objective being to use the public echo as a recruiting instrument. In the words of Horst Mahler (*Der Spiegel*, 11 October 1978, p. 65), the weapon of the hunger-strike was used by the RAF 'as a whip against the Left to mobilise them for the interests of the guerrillas'.

The mobilisation of sympathisers for the goals of the RAF also appears to be the strategy of the ninth hunger-strike begun in December 1984. The mobilisation potential of hunger-strikes had earlier been demonstrated by the strike of Bobby Sands, begun on 1 March 1981, in the Maze prison in Northern Ireland. The self-imposed martyrdom of Sands and his nine colleagues, mobilised about 40 per cent of the Catholics behind Sinn Fein, the political wing of the Provisional IRA. In the same month, the RAF had launched its eighth hunger-strike in German prisons, which triggered a number of bombings against German and American targets. On the occasion of their ninth hunger-strike in December 1984, the RAF made an explicit reference to the Irish example (see Bundesministerium des Innern, 1985, p. 9).

The objective of the thirty-six German hunger-strikers was to raise the consciousness of the target of attention, the German and European left (see *Berliner Tageszeitung*, 1975). In this sense, the unlimited hunger-strike was an offer to identify with the cause. Some of the RAF members still at large worked to help to mobilise the responsive parts of the public. In a strategy paper discovered by the security forces in a so-called 'conspiratorial flat' in Frankfurt, the author Helmut Pohl (see *Volkskrant*, 1985) wrote: 'The practical approach we find best is that we – on the outside – open the offensive with assaults on the infrastructure of the military apparatus and that the prisoners do their attack with the HS [hunger-strike].' In his paper, Pohl expressed the hope that outside the prisons a level of activity could be generated such that the authorities would be forced to make the demanded concessions, namely the unification of RAF and other extremist prisoners into larger groups, a decrease of the surveillance, and a lifting of the limitations on contacts with the outside world. Had their demands been met, it would have transformed the prison cells into headquarters for further struggle outside the prisons, creating a liberated zone in the belly of the 'imperialist' beast.

An objective of the hunger-strike was to place the West German government in a no-win situation. The state would lose prestige if it granted the hunger-strikers what they wanted – namely, better conditions of imprisonment. The German government would also lose if the hunger-strikers had to be fed by forceful means. The state would thereby act against the manifest will of the prisoners. Finally, the state would also lose if it allowed the hunger-strikers to die since this would be interpreted as proof that the state was indeed pursuing an 'annhilation strategy', as the terrorists and their sympathisers had claimed. Either way, by feeding or not feeding the hunger-strikers, the German state would stand accused of torture or murder in the eyes of the unwitting public.

'Murder' and 'torture' call for revenge. One group emerging from the target of attention was the 'Knut Folker Commando' (the name was taken from one RAF hunger-striker). It announced that it would kill the Prime Minister and the Minister of Lower Saxony if one of the prisoners died in a prison on Lower Saxony. At about the same time, a 'Commando Holger Meins' let it be known that it had placed Helmut Kohl and Helmut Schmidt, the present and past Chancellors of the German Federal Republic, on its death list. These spontanteously emerging commandos were responding to the call issued by the imprisoned RAF members who, on 4 December 1984, stated that 'We want to . . . join with all those who have broken with this system and take as point of departure the revolutionary struggle against prison, state, imperialism, and reason of state' (see *Knipselkrant*, 1984). Outside the prison, a communiqué was distributed stating that 'all initiatives – demonstrations, propaganda actions, etc., are necessary to create the political pressure necessary to see our demands fulfilled'. The crucial word in this communique was 'etc.'. It could mean little else than what the RAF meant in 1977 when the call went out to 'work with all strength available for the liberation of the prisoners'. At that time, the objective was the freeing of the first generation of Germany terrorists, Andreas Baader, Gudrun Ensslin, Jan Carl Raspe, and Irmgard Moeller who had already been in prison for five years. The murder of the Attorney-General S. Buback, the banker J. Ponto, and the industrialist, H. M. Schleyer were the 'etc.'.

In 1985, only one prominent German, Ernst Zimmermann, fell victim to such violence. He was mortally wounded by gunshots at his house near Munich, on 1 February 1985. The murder, perpetrated by young people who called themselves the 'Patsy O'Hara commando' (after one of the Irish hunger-strikers), was taken as a signal for ending the hunger-strike. Their 'sacrifice' had produced a result weighty enough to stop without losing face. One group outside the prisons had called upon the hunger-strikers to end their fast. In its message, the group pleaded: 'We are asking you to terminate the strike. What this hunger-strike was able to achieve in terms of mobilisation, it has achieved' (see *Suddeutsche Zeitung*, 5 February, 1985).

If we examine this hunger-strike and murder in terms of the four targets of terrorism we find that one target of attention, the hitherto uninvolved sympathisers, turned into a perpetrator of violence and that the target of violence (Zimmermann) was sacrificed on behalf of the imprisoned RAF members who thereby were in fact the primary target of attention. If this interpretation is correct, the German government and public were only secondary targets of demands and attention. As the hunger-strike gained momentum, the likelihood of such a sacrifice to move the imprisoned RAF leadership increased. The drama of 'martyrs' slowly dying for a cause demonstrates a determination which invariably impresses onlookers. Part of the audience will interpret this willingness to die as proof that the cause is a good and just one. The success of the hunger-strikes will depend on the degree of publicity given to the fact that prisoners are on hunger-strike. Here the role of family members, legal representatives, and friends of the terrorists is crucial. As their identification objects are about to finalise their altruistic sacrifice, they are, for reasons which are understandable enough, driven to even more feverish activities to bring the public media to maximum coverage of the events. Solidarity gatherings are organised and people are invited to contribute all that is in their power to save the lives of their political prisoners. A number of these targets of attention will be moved to acts of arson, bombings and even murder as signs of protest, revolt and revenge.

One of the striking things about many acts of violence performed during the hunger-strike period is their amateurish nature. The bomb attacks showed a lack of expertise which seasoned terrorists would not exhibit. This is an indication that most of these acts were not performed by the fifteen to twenty RAF members who were still at large, but by their above-ground supporters (between 100 and 300 according to police estimates) and by sympathisers and newcomers who had no organisational links with the RAF. These people were drawn into the terrorist movement by the mobilising forces and devices of the hunger-strike.

In general terms, this process of recruitment has been described by Jerold Post:

> The path to joining a terrorist group tends to be slow and gradual, from sympathizer, to passive supporter, to active supporter, and finally joining the group itself. The decision to join often follows failed efforts at adaptation – socially, educationally, and at work. There is a tendency for marginal, isolated, and lonely individuals with troubled family backgrounds to be attracted to the terrorist group, so that for many, belonging to the terrorist group is the first time that they truly belonged, and the group comes to represent the family
>
> (Post, 1984, p. 254).

Post observed that the path to joining the terrorist group was quite similar for groups as diverse as the Basque ETA, the Italian Red Brigades, and the German Red Army Faction and he suggests that:

> The need to belong – the need to have a stable identity, to resolve a split and be one with oneself and with society ... is an important bridging concept which helps explain the similarity in behavior of groups of widely different motivations and composition
>
> (Post, 1984, p. 254).

In my view, the significance of the concept of *identity* can increase in its explanatory power when it is incorporated into the concept of *identification*. Together these concepts can help us to explain not only terrorist behaviour but also our own behaviour towards terrorism.

The search for the link between terrorist targeting and terrorist goals and objectives is most fruitfully conducted in the field of identification. It is for this reason that our attention now turns to the role of identification in terrorism.

The role of identification has not yet, to my knowledge, been the subject of substantive research in the field of terrorism. However, astute observers have recognised this dimension: 'an act will come to be seen as terrorist if people identify with the victim of the act' (Wardlaw, 1982, p. 7).

The term 'identification' has a variety of meanings. In psychoanalysis it denotes a process, conscious or unconscious, in which the subject has the impression that he thinks, feels or acts like the object. In social psychology, it refers to the more-or-less lasting influence one person can exert on the behaviour of another. For our purposes, a passage from a work by the Finnish social psychologist Karmela Liebknecht, is most helpful:

> Identification can mean at least two different things; a wish to become or remain like the other (individual or group), or a recognition of existing similarities, good or bad, between the self and the object of identification ... In a definition of a person's overall identity both of these meanings of identification have to be incorporated: a person's identity is defined as the totality of his self-construal, in which how he construes himself in the present expresses the continuity between how he construes himself as he was in the past and as he aspires to be in the future
>
> (Liebknecht, 1979, p. 43).

The use of the concept of identification is usually confined, in the terrorist literature, to identification with the aggressor – the positive attitude that some hostages show towards their captors. This has also been described as the 'Stockholm syndrome', a term coined when a female Swedish hostage fell in love with her captor. Yet other identification processes are also at work. The tremendous public interest in acts of hostage-taking seems to result from many members of the audience emphatically identifying with the fate of the victim. Some members of the public offer themselves as hostages in exchange for those already held. Where help is not possible, the empathiser experiences unpleasantness from which he might try to escape by 'freezing' himself psychologically. Other members of the witnessing audience, often the target of attention, will react differently, by identifying with the terrorist rather than with the victim. By identifying with the aggressor, an observer can take on the strength of the feared terrorist and reduce his own feelings of vulnerability.

Terrorism can be considered as a contest for identifications. Acts of shocking violence are staged with the objective of creating sharp fear and polarisations among targets. The outcome is strongly determined by the way in which the identification process goes. Its direction is not only determined by the attentive public's assessment whether or not the victim 'deserves' what he gets but by such factors as race, class, nationality, and party-membership. This identification process is not confined to terrorist atrocities; any act of violence with an irreversible outcome is likely to produce polarisations among witnessing audiences.

An act of violence can polarise audiences and produce identification processes with the victim among most of those sharing common characteristics while leaving others indifferent and yet others even satisfied. Guilt attribution apparently occurs along similar lines. The media provide us daily with identification offers and we more or less consciously take sides wherever conflict and violence along lines relevant to our own situation occurs. Identification with the winner or with the aggressor can make us feel powerful vicariously, while identification with the loser or victim can make us feel weak or revengeful. Do we share victim or victimiser characteristics? Is he one of 'us' or one of 'them'? Does the victim deserve it or not? When we do not approve of the means utilised in a conflict situation but share the goals of the 'aggressor' we are apparently much more apologetic towards an act of violence than we are when there is no goal consonance. When the perpetrator is 'one of us' we judge differently than when he is not. Most people appear to be terribly selective in their outrage against acts of violence. Acts of violence brought by television into the homes of hundreds of millions of people can stir some members of the witnessing audiences so much that they feel terrorised themselves. Others are incited to anger and in turn become violent actors by acts of imitation or revenge. In such a way, new terrorists can emerge.

In many ways, Trotsky provided us with a vivid description of the origins of terrorism:

> Before it was elevated to the level of a method of political struggle, terrorism makes its appearance in the form of individual acts of revenge. So it was in Russia, the classic land of terrorism. The flogging of political prisoners impelled Vera Zasuylich to give

expression to the general feeling of indignation by an assassination attempt on General Trepov. Her example was imitated in the circles of the revolutionary intelligentsia, who lacked any mass support. What began as an act of unthinking revenge was developed into an entire system in 1879–81 ... The most important psychological source of terrorism is always the feeling of revenge in search of an outlet

(Trotsky, 1974, p. 8).

Trotsky's observation also fits the German RAF and helps us to explain their past and present strategy. Their social consciousness was awakened by their identifiction with the victims of the Vietnam war and with the poor in the Third World. As Jilian Becker put it:

They got a regular stirring up from the media-pity and indignation roused on behalf of the story characters, existent or not. Learning about wars, exploitations, oppressions in the same way as they learned about the fate of fictional victims, they felt strongly not because they were a generation of visionaries but because they were a generation of televisionaries

(Becker, 1978, p. 63).

Horst Mahler, the co-founder of the RAF, admitted that the televised massacres in Vietnam and the passivity of the German government with regard to them drove them to acts of resistance and revenge:

It was our moralism which led us to terrorism ... The German nation again was passive. How could we escape from the society which once again mixed itself in a war: that of Vietnam? We had nothing to identify with in the West, so we identified with the Third World ... From that time on we no longer felt like Germans; we were the Fifth Column of the Third World

(Nagel, 1980, pp. 221–2).

Many of the first-generation RAF terrorists had middle- or upper-class backgrounds. They rejected their backgrounds and identified with the poor, the victims of war or with the German proletariat, or what they held for it. Today's third- and fourth-generation RAF terrorists are still in search of a proletariat to be moved to action. In one of their pamphlets they plead for a 'reconstruction of the European proletariat'. The RAF terrorists were in search of a 'revolutionary subject' whose awakening they could trigger with their acts of violence. Privileged as they were themselves, they chose to become spokespersons for those who had no voice. In his study of German terrorist careers, Schmittchen (1984, p. 273) found that these started generally with an identification with the powerless. Within the RAF there were various views about the prime revolutionary subject. Some thought more in terms of the German workers while others looked more toward the Third World. They were impressed by the Tupamaros and tried to copy their model of urban terrorism. They also identified with the Palestinian terrorists who triggered a massacre during the Munich Olympic Games. A dozen RAF members had already gone to Jordan two years earlier for six weeks of training in guerrilla tactics.

Identification leads to imitation and imitation leads to contagion. Hence the wave of terrorist incidents during certain periods. During the last hunger-strike of the RAF we see identifications with the RAF by other terrorist movements. In Portugal, the FP-25 dedicated some its acts to the RAF as did Action Directe in France. In January 1985, the RAF and Action Directe announced kind of fusion and the creation of a common political–military front in Western Europe (see *Knipselkrant*, 1985, p. 371). This Euroterrorism has been taken at face value by some observers as a sign that the terrorist threat has reached a new pinnacle. Whether or not this is true remains to be seen. It depends in part on the success of the last hunger-strike – on the number of new recruits it could mobilise. However, the unification of terrorist movements can be seen as a sign of weakness as well as strength, namely as a confession that they could not rally sufficiently large sectors of the population independently, despite the fact that there are millions of Western Europeans without work and many without hope. That they do *not* identity with the terrorists appears to be an encouraging sign.

CONCLUSION

The case-study of the hunger-strike by German RAF terrorists indicates that it has little in common with the image of international terrorism directed from Moscow. A closer look at the Abu Nidal group also reveals the relative greater importance of local and regional influences over those of the Kremlin. Clearly, the main root of international terrorism is not international communism.

Regional, national, subnational, group and personal factors are likely to give us a more realistic explanation of international terrorism than an abstract global perspective within a bipolar framework. There are, as I have argued, at least six different basic types of international terrorism and even more if coalitions between various actors are counted. Some of these have not even been studied. While there are a number of international terrorist data bases, most focus on terrorism of an anti-Western orientation. Since we also lack comprehensive data on domestic terrorism in the more than 160 nations, most analysts notice terrorism *only* when it becomes international.

As this chapter has tried to make clear, our knowledge of the targeting, objectives and goals of international terrorists is still woefully inadequate. Any better understanding of terrorist strategies presupposes more detailed data than are currently available from open sources. The role of identification processes in the dynamics of terrorism is even less well understood than targeting processes and deserves a research programme of its own. Even the conceptual problems – e.g. how to differentiate between small-group terrorism and insurgency-related terrorism – are not yet satisfactorily resolved. While the quantity of literature on terrorism is growing rapidly, the quality leaves much to be desired as few major empirical *academic* research programmes are actually being carried out.

Hannah Arendt once said that 'the danger of violence . . . will always be that the means overwhelm the end' (Arendt, 1970, p. 80). While this danger is epitomised by terrorism itself, it also poses itself in the anti-terrorist response. It is for this reason as well that open academic study of both terrorism and anti-terrorism is a democratic necessity.

Notes

1. As quoted by ZDF, the West German television, on 9 September 1985.
2. F. Ochberg, in response to questionnaire.
3. See van de Putten (1985:4), who speaks of up to 100 000 people killed and 38 000 'disappearances' for the period since 1954. On the other hand, or data base records 6500 terroristic incidents worldwide with more than 3500 people killed and about 7600 injured in the decade 1974–83.
4. See also Haluani (1982).

5. See Stefan Aust: *Der Baader-Meinhof Komplex* (Hamburg: Hoffmann und Campe Verlag, 1985) p. 461; Aust, in an interview with *NRC Handelsblad* (Rotterdam) 27 July 1985, p. 3 (*Zaterdagbijvoegsel*).

References

Arendt. H. (1970) *On Violence* (New York: Harcourt Brace Jovanovich).
Atlantisch Nieuws (1986) 1–2, p. 7.
Aust, Stefan (1985) Interview with *NRC-Handelsblad* (Rotterdam) July 27, 1985 (*Zaterdag-bijvoegsel*).
Becker, J. (1978) *Hitler's Children* (London: Panther).
Berliner Tageszeitung (1975) 5 December (taz).
Brien, W. (1985) 'Terrorism, What Should We Do?', in *This World*, Fall, no. 12.
Bundesministerium des innern (1984) Verfassungsschutzbericht, Bonn.
Bundesministerium des innern (1985) Terroristen im Kampf gegen Recht und Menschenwurde. Bonn.
Crotty, W. J. (1979) *Assassination and the Political Order* (New York: Harper & Row).
Der Spiegel (1978) 11 December, pp. 62–65; 17 August, p. 81.
Die Welt (1985) 26 January (Hamburg).
Die Welt (1985) 10 January.
Drake, R. (1984) 'Contemporary Italy', in *International Political Science Review*, vol 5, no. 3, p. 281.
Duvall, R. D. and Stohl, M. (1983) 'Governance by Terror' in M. Stohl (ed.) *The Politics of Terrorism* (New York: Marcel Dekker) 2nd edn.
Edelman, M. (1977) *Political Language: Words that Succeed and Politics that Fail* (New York: Academic Press).
Eidlin, Fred H. (1980) *The Logic of Normalization* (New York).
Ferracuti, F. (1982) 'A Sociopsychiatric Interpretation of Terrorism', *The Annals of the American Academy*, vol. 463, September, pp. 137–8.
Fetscher, I. and Rohrmoser G., (1981) *Ideologien und Strategien. Analysen zum Terrorismus*, vol. 1 (Opladen: Westdeutscher Verlag).
Friedlanger, R. A. (1984) *An Infinity of Mirrors: Mehmet Ali Agca and the 'Plot to Kill the Pope'* (Gaithersburg, Maryland: IACP).
Geissler, H. (1984) 'Der Weg in die Gewalt', in *Totalitarismus, Exterimismus, Terrorismus* (Opladen: Leske & Budrich).
Goren, R. (1984) *The Soviet Union and Terrorism* (London: Allen & Unwin).
Gurr, T. R. (1986) 'The Political Origins of State Violence and Terror: A Theoretical Analysis', in George Lopez and Michael Stohl (eds) *Govenment Violence and Repression: Agenda for Research* (New Haven: Greenwood Press).
Haluani, Makram (1982) *Gewaltpolitik, Eina Politikwissenschafliche Makroanalyse einse politischer kampfmittels und seiner Problematik in heutigen Lateinsamerika* (Munster: Westfalische Wilhelmus Universitat).
Intelligence–Parapolitics (1985) no. 62, February (Paris) p. 1.

Jongman, A. J. (1983) 'World Directory of "Terrorist" Organizations' in Alex P. Schmid (1983) *Political Terrorism, A Research Guide to Concepts, Theories, Dates Bases and Literature* (Amsterdam: North-Holland Publishing Co. and New Brunswick, New Jersey: Transaction Books).

Klein, H. (1979) *Ruckkehr in die Menschlichkeit, Appell eines ausgestiegenen Terroristen* (Reinbek bei Hamburg: Rowohlt).

Knipselkrant (1984) (Groningen).

Knipselkrant (1985)

Koestler, A. (1967) *The Ghost in the Machine* (London: Hutchinson).

Laqueur, W. (1977) *Terrorism* (London: Weidenfeld & Nicolson).

Liebknecht, K. (1979) 'The Social Psychology of Minority Identity: A Case Study of Intergroup Identification: Theoretical Refinement and Methodological Experimentation', (Helsinki: University of Helsinki).

Melman, Y. (1986) *The Master Terrorist: The True Story Behind Abu Nidal* (New York: Adama Books).

Merton, R. K. (1973) *The Sociology of Science* (Chicago: University of Chicago Press).

Murdock, George P. (1981) *Atlas of World Cultures* (Pittsburgh: University of Pittsburgh Press).

Neidhart, F. (1982) 'Linker und rechter Terrorismus. Erscheinungs- formen und Handlungspotentiale in Gruppenvergleich', in Wanda von Bayer-Katte *et al. Gruppenprozesse: Analysen zum Terrorismus*, vol. 3 (Opladen: West-deutscher Verlag).

Nieuwsblad van Antwerpen (1985) 30 January (Antwerp).

Post, J. M. (1984) 'Notes on a Psychodynamic Theory of Terrorist Behavior', in *Terrorism: An International Journal*, vol. 7, no. 3.

Price, H. E. (1977) 'The Strategy and Tactics of Revolutionary Terrorism' in *Comparative Studies in Society and History*, vol. 19, no. 1, January.

Putten, Jan Van Der (1985) 'Staatshoofd van Guatamala Vergoeilijkt moordpartijen', in *Volksrant*, 6 November.

Rauschning, H. (1940) *Gesprache mit Hitler* (Wien).

Schlesinger, P. G., Murdock, G. and Elliott, P. (1983) *Televising Terrorism: Political Violence in Popular Culture* (London: Comedia Publishing Group).

Schmid, A. P. (1985) *Soviet Military Interventions Since 1945* with case- studies by Ellen Berends (New Brunswick: Transaction Books).

Schmid, A. P. and De Graaf, J. (1982) *Violence as Communication: Insurgent Terrorism and the Western News Media* (Beverly Hills, California: Sage).

Schmid, A. P. (1983) *Political Terrorism: A Research Guide to Concepts, Theories, Data Bases and Literature* (Amsterdam: North-Holland Publishing Co.; New Brunswick: Transaction Books).

Schmittchen (1984). As quoted in Backes. Uwe and Eckhard Jesse (1984) *Totalitarismus, Extermismus, Terrorismus* Opladen, Leskeand Budrich.

Spiegel-Gesprach, (1979) 'Wir mussen raus aus den Schutzengraben', Bundesminister Baum und ex-Terrorist Mahler uber des Phenomenon Terrorismus, *Der spiegel*, vol. 33. no. 32, 31 December.

Suddentsche Zeitung (1985)

Thornton, T. P. (1964) 'Terror as a Weapon of Political Agitation', in H. Eckstein (ed.) *Internal War: Problems and Approaches* (New York: Free Press).

Trotsky, L. (1974) *Against Individual Terrorism* (New York: Pathfinder Press (reprinted from 'On Terrorism' in *Der Kampf* no. 1911).

Visser, Cees (1985) 'Het Westeuropese terrorsme. Oorlogsverklaring aan de Navo', *Intermediair* (Amsterdam) vol. 21, 24 May.

Volksrant (1985) (Amsterdam) 4 January.

Volksrant (1985) 10 april, p. 1.

Wardlaw, G. (1982) *Political Terrorism: Theory, Tactics and Countermeasures* (Cambridge: Cambridge University Press).

Wilkinson, P. (1984) 'Terrorism – Global Links' in *Rusi and Brasseys Defence Yearbook 1984* (New York: Pergamon Press).

4 Support Mechanisms in International Terrorism
Paul Wilkinson

INTRODUCTION

There are seven essential prerequisites for mounting terrorism. There must be some main *aim or motivation* among the perpetrators, even if it ultimately amounts to little more than an intense hatred of their perceived enemies or a desire for violent revenge against some alleged injustice. There must be *leaders* to instigate and direct the struggle. In any sustained and significant campaign, there will also need to be some degree of *organisation*, some *training* in the special skills of terrorism, and *cash* which helps to buy *weapons and ammunition* and other essential needs. Finally it is clearly vital for the terrorists that they should have *access to the target* country and the precise targets selected within that country. Of course, we know of numerous groups which possess considerable resources over and above those listed above. Some succeed in building up large numbers of supporters/ sympathisers among the general population. Many obtain the substantial advantages of sponsorship by one or more states. In certain circumstances, terrorists can attain sanctuaries or safe bases beyond the reach of security forces or opposing factions; for example, in the remote terrain of the interior.But these are bonuses for the terrorists. We know that the majority of terrorists operating in the contemporary international system do not have these advantages.

Exactly the same basic ingredients are required to mount a viable campaign of international terrorism. But unless the perpetrators restrict themselves to attacking foreign personnel and property within the terrorists' own country of origin, they will require significantly greater levels of organisation, training, expertise, cash and means of access to foreign states, to wage a full international campaign.

Let us identify some of the major types of support mechanisms involved in contemporary international terrorism:

(i) Cells of predominantly indigenous terrorist organisations

Very few cases exist of purely indigenous movements. Terrorism tends to have inherent tendencies towards internationalisation. Even groups with a strong and durable base of support in their target area, such as the IRA in Northern Ireland and ETA in the Basque region of Spain, inevitably tend to look across their international frontiers for sanctuary, sources of weapons and explosives and bases for training and planning. Often they establish cells specifically to mount attacks on their target-government abroad, or against the government of a neighbouring state. The IRA has launched attacks against bases of the British Army of the Rhine in West Germany. ETA has had cells mounting attacks in France, claiming to be punishing France for alleged collaboration with the Spanish authorities' repression of their movement. However, as with indigenous ideological terrorists such as the Red Brigades and the RAF, the vast majority of the attacks by these movements are concentrated within specific countries or localities.

Some of these indigenous groups remain extremely tiny and politically isolated. Others develop a 'movement' of political supporters and sympathisers which becomes a valuable source of recruits, cash and other practical forms of support. The larger and more successful terrorist groups can develop sophisticated bureaucracies, propaganda activities and leadership structures. At the other end of the scale are the tiny groups of activists in terrorist groups which may consist of no more than one or two four- or five-member cells. Some of the largest and most experienced indigenous groups sometimes develop strong bilateral contacts with other groups, to which they channel expertise, terrorist weapons and explosives. The Red Brigades often carried out such functions in the mid- and late-1970s. More recently the RAF and Action Directe have developed stronger links, and have formed a loose Euroterrorist alliance of extreme left groups. In the case of these groups there are two distinct targets; their own domestic governmental and legal systems, and NATO and defence-related targets in Europe as a whole. Sometimes the terrorist groups with entirely indigenous bases of support decide to attack foreign targets. For example, the Red Brigades kidnapped the US General James Dozier and assassinated US diplomat Leamon Hunt, head of the Sinai peace-keeping force. Presumably the terrorists believed that these attacks would help their cause in some way. Nevertheless, these incidents were a departure from the traditional targeting pattern of the Red Brigade.

It is a major feature of the well-established indigenous terrorist groups that they are relatively free of dependence on state sponsors or help from foreign-based movements. A group such as the IRA, for example, has become quite a successful capitalist organisation in its own right. As James Adams (1986) has shown in a pioneering study of terrorist finances, such movements can get most of the cash they need from armed robberies, ransom payments for the release of kidnap victims, so-called revolutionary 'taxes', racketeering, and 'legitimate' business activities. They also have the expertise and experience to provide all their own training in weapons, bomb-making and other skills.

(ii) Cells of terrorist groups in exile

These groups are utterly dependent on their international support bases because they have been forced by political circumstances or necessity to operate entirely abroad. Well-known examples are the Armenian terrorist groups, such as the Armenian Secret Army for the Liberation of Armenia (ASALA), and the Croatians scattered in many Western countries.

These groups can draw on invaluable local bases of support among sympathisers in the emigre populations of major Western cities. These provide sanctuary, fund-raising, sources of weapons and explosives: on the other hand, they are generally desperately conscious of their weakness in political and military terms, and find it impossible to gain state sponsorship. Few states wish to back a loser. They are also potentially vulnerable to police and political reaction by their hosts in the states to which they have migrated. They can be fairly easily identified, and they risk a backlash against their small communities if they make trouble abroad.

Far more difficult, from the point of view of the authorities, are those groups which have support bases *both* among exiles *and* in their country of origin, as is the case, for example, in Britain with the Kashmir Liberation Front, the Tamils, and Sikhs. The USA has many more exile groupings in this situation. The problem in such cases is complicated by the dangers of retaliation, counter-retaliation, and communal violence leading to inter-communal feuding and killing in the countries of exile.

All terrorist groups are prone to schisms and splits, sometimes over matters of fundamental aims and programme but more often on questions of leadership, organisation and tactics. But exile groups are vulnerable to this type of organisational fragmentation. Their militant supporters are often very widely dispersed around the cities of the Western world. Inevitably different leaders with their own views on how the struggle should be conducted tend to emerge in the various parts of the diaspora. And because few or none of them have any real power-base in their country of origin, it is plausible for any self-appointed leader in exile to claim that he offers the true path to the salvation of his people. Many exiled terrorist movements have been paralysed, or rendered virtually ineffective, by internecine conflict. For example, the Palestinian movement in exile suffers from a bitter split between the pro-Arafat and anti-Arafat factions, frequently spilling over into assassinations and revenge killings of Palestinian leaders based abroad. The Armenian Secret Army for the Liberation of Armenia (ASALA) has recently been exhausting itself in a conflict between the hard-liners and more pragmatic factions.[1]

(iii) Mixed Indigenous and Multinational Groups and Alliances

The mixing of indigenous and international terrorist support bases can be easily illustrated in relation to the Shi'ite fundamentalist revolutionaries. In Iran, in Lebanon, and the other major centres of Shi'ite populations there is a constant emphasis on achieving dominance of their religious ideas in their own societies. Yet simultaneously, and interdependent with these efforts, the Shi'ite movements, such as Islamic Jihad, are also consciously engaged in a wider 'holy war' to export Ayatollah Khomeini's ideas and practice to the whole of the Muslim world. For these wider purposes, the Shi'ite militants can call on an impressive support base in Iran in the form of religious ideas and propaganda, religious leadership, a fair degree of centralised coordination and organisation, cash weapons, and substantial training in the network of camps now dotted around Iran, and Iran's diplomatic and spying network.

Another interesting variant of the 'mixed' (i.e. indigenous and multinational) support base is the recently formed alliance of extreme-left terrorist groups in Western Europe against NATO and defence-related targets. It is clear that all the groups involved – Red Army Faction (RAF) in West Germany, Action Directe (AD) in France, and the Fighting Communist Cells (CCL) Belgium – on the one hand continue to wage their own private wars against the governments, law-enforcement systems and other key institutions in their respective states. Hence, the hunger-strike campaign of the

RAF in early 1985, aiming, without success, to intimidate the FRG authorities into relocating all RAF prisoners in the same gaol.

Yet on the other hand, those who study the evidence surely cannot doubt that a genuinely new, if loosely coordinated, international alliance of these groups is attempting to mount a West European campaign against NATO. They are not organisationally integrated under a centralised leadership. But it is clear from their communiqué of 15 January 1985 (see Appendix A) that they have common aims. They believe they are fighting for the cause of 'proletarian internationalism' attacking what they term the 'totality of the imperialist system' in its capitalist heartland. Of course they are not Communists in the Moscow mould. They are more like anarchist communists, more clear about what they wish to destroy than what they are for. All the groups in this alliance are bitterly anti-American, anti-capitalist, anti-NATO, anti militarist, and anti-Zionist. Their leaflets and slogans all use similar jargon and declarations. They have clearly coordinated uniformally on common targeting. In the case of the murder of General Audran in Paris, there is evidence of direct close operational cooperation between RAF and AD. And there is also some evidence that other groups, such as FP 25 in Portugal and November 17 in Greece, are imitating the RAF and AD line and see themselves as part and parcel of the anti-NATO alliance.

By operating as an international alliance, these groups give themselves more surprise and flexibility in attacks, exploit weaknesses in NATO's international response, and are exposing new vulnerabilities. So far, there is no evidence that they are currently receiving any physical assistance from possible state sponsors, such as Warsaw Pact countries. This may come if the Soviet Union comes to see real advantages in injecting clandestine state sponsorship/support to help disrupt NATO. Mixed indigenous/multinational alliance support bases of this kind are probably the hardest of all for the NATO democracies to counter. The internationalisation of their strategy in itself creates a wider support mechanism.

(iv) Indirect State Sponsorship, via Surrogates and Client Groups

Indirect state sponsorship occurs when a government decides to aid a particular movement or group on the grounds that it will serve the strategic and political interests of the sponsor.[2] It is generally adopted as a policy for one or more of the following purposes: to redress an international grievance, to export revolution, to hunt down and eradicate exiled dissidents or to intimidate them into silence, to weaken an adversary state, and as an auxiliary weapon in a wider war of intervention or international war.

In the course of the Arab – Israel conflict on the issue of the Palestinians, many states have intervened by giving indirect sponsorship and help to factions of the PLO. The major funds of the PLO groupings are derived from the contributions of the rich Arab oil states. And there is abundant evidence of the very substantial military support given to Al Fatah and the other main PLO formations since the mid-1970s. The Soviets were happy to use Yassir Arafat and his movement as a stalking-horse to try quietly to expand Russian influence in the Middle East. Documents captured in the 1982 war in Lebanon confirm also the substantial Soviet and Eastern European stake in training PLO members.[3] This undoubtedly helped Moscow to capitalise on the conflicts and to build closer links with the rejectionist front states, such as Syria. But in 1982, it became clear that indirect sponsorship also has heavy costs: they could not *control* the behaviour of their clients. Yet they did not wish to risk a full-scale intervention on behalf of Arafat's group in the siege of Beirut. Since 1982, they have seen the situation vastly complicated by the split of the PLO and the bitter struggles between the Musa and Arafat factions in Lebanon. They have found state sponsorship is a costly and unreliable weapon which may backfire badly. They too have had their diplomats targeted by terrorists in Beirut, and elsewhere.

Since 1984 a loose alliance of 'rejectionist' terrorist groups – that is, groups totally rejecting diplomatic negotiation or compromise as a means of resolving the Palestinian issue – has emerged with strong encouragement and indirect state sponsorship from both the Syrian and Libyan regimes. This new grouping includes such groups as the Abu Musa Faction, based in Syria and Syrian-controlled areas of Lebanon, and the Abu Nidal Group, which has offices in Damascus, Beirut and Tripoli. These groups have undoubtedly gained considerable benefits from the assistance of the secret services and diplomatic networks of President Assad and Colonel Gaddafi.

Intelligence gathered during 1985 and 1986 by the USA and Israel, and by various West European governments disclosed a pattern of continuing flagrant Syrian and Libyan abuses of 'diplomatic' facilities, the so-called Libyan Peoples' Bureaux, and Syrian embassies, together with Syrian and Libyan agents, to help to plan and assist terrorist attacks on Israeli and American targets in Western Europe and the Middle East. It cannot therefore have come as a complete surprise when Libyan 'finger-prints' were found in the December 1985 attacks on El Al ticket-counters at Rome and Vienna, and at the bombing of a night-club in West Berlin frequented by US troops. The evidence of Syrian involvement which engaged in the Hindawi trial was unusually detailed and damning. Nor can it have surprised Western intelligence services when, at his trial in London in October 1986, on charges of trying to plant a bomb on an El Al jet at Heathrow, Nezar Hindawi gave a detailed account of Syrian complicity in the crime. He claimed he was briefed by Syrian intelligence on how to set the bomb on the plane, that he was paid US $12 000 by Syria to undertake the attack at Heathrow, and that he was in touch with the Syrian Embassy in London.

Normally it is exceedingly difficult to establish beyond doubt the identity of a state sponsor indirectly implicated in this type of international terrorist attack. A major aim of the state sponsor is to remain covert, at the very least to be able plausibly to deny any involvement. The use of Tunisian passports by terrorists, documents clearly supplied by the Libyan regime, and the interception of incriminating messages relayed by Libyan Peoples Bureaux and Tripoli, provided convincing evidence of the Gaddafi regime's continuing role as a 'fairy godmother' to the groups.

But it should be noted that sponsorship takes many forms. Help and encouragement, even the provision of false documents and weapons does not necessarily mean that the state sponsor has total control over choice of target and method of attack. Many of the militant and experienced Palestinian groups, for example, are quite capable of running such operations autonomously, and providing their own logistics, if need arises. A further complication is that some of these groups have a number of state sponsors helping them simultaneously in various ways, and are able to establish safe havens and operational bases in several different countries.

A logical consequence of this complex form of alliance with multilateral indirect state sponsorship is that even if coercion or pressure succeeds in forcing one state sponsor to disengage from support, the terror group itself will still be able to continue its activities using other resources. Indeed they will probably intensify their use of violence to prove that they are still a force to be reckoned with and to convince any other state sponsor or potential sponsor that they are still an effective client. Hence, even if one state sponsor fears reprisals and *does* try to rein them in, it may not succeed.

(v) Direct State Sponsorship

Some state sponsors have tried to avoid the uncertainties and problems of indirect sponsorship by resorting to direct state-controlled international terrorism, using their own hit-squads to assassinate opponents or disrupt or undermine adversaries. The Libyan and Iranian regimes blatantly flout international norms and laws by such behaviour. For example, Colonel Gaddafi openly boasts of his intention to murder President Mubarak and Western leaders and his plan to hunt down and murder his exiled opponents, whom he describes as 'the stray dogs'. There is no evidence that Gaddafi has any intention of abandoning this weapon. In 1985 alone there were seven major incidents involving actual or abortive attacks by Gaddafi hit-squads on opponents of the regime abroad, including murders committed in Rome, Nicosia, and Bonn.

It should be noted that although diplomatic cover and facilities have frequently been utilised in recent years for direct state-sponsored terrorism, especially by Libya, Syria, Iraq and Iran, there are many other ways in which such attacks can be mounted. The assassination squads used by the secret services of terrorist states may be sent on their missions under many different types of cover. They may pretend to be 'students', 'businessmen' or even simply 'tourists'. These informal arrangements can be utilised, of course, even where no diplomatic representation or mission exists in the state where the target is residing. In the open and easily accessible societies of the West these hidden assassins are almost impossible to identify and apprehend. A glance at the complex organisational structure of the Soviet subversive *apparat,* for example, shows some of the many agencies and links that may be used by state sponsors.

AIMS, MOTIVATION AND IDEOLOGY: A VITAL ELEMENT IN THE SUPPORT MECHANISM

It is important to emphasise that *every* international terrorist movement or group requires an extremist ideology or belief-system of some kind to nourish, motivate, justify, and mobilise the use of terror violence. There is ample historical evidence that extreme movements have been led and sustained by what Eric Hoffer has termed *The True Believer*, and it is certainly important to take into account the social and psychological processes which create the basis for fanatical attitudes and behaviour. For example, in his pioneering portrait of the personality of the fanatic, Hoffer (1951) suggests that the factors which permit a spirit of self-sacrifice are: identification with a collective whole, make-believe, deprecation of the present and the inculcation of extremist doctrine. Among the key unifying agents at work in creating extremist mass movements, he identifies: the fanning of collective hatred, imitation, the use of coercion by the extremist movement and the systematic promotion of an attitude of suspicion and mistrust towards outsiders and exclusivism and dogmatic superiority within the extremist movement. In a remarkable passage, Hoffer (1951, pp. 142–3) describes the role of the fanatic in the development of the extremist movement:

> Without him the disaffection engendered by militant men of words remains undirected and can vent itself only in pointless and easily suppressed disorders. Without him the initiated reforms, even when drastic, leave the old way of life unchanged, and any change in government usually amounts to no more than a transfer of power from one set of men of action to another. Without him there can perhaps be no beginning ... Chaos is his element. When the old order begins to crack, he wades in with all his might and recklessness to blow the whole hated present to high heaven. He glories in the sight of a world coming to a sudden end. To hell with reforms! All that already exists is rubbish, and there is no sense in reforming rubbish. He justifies his will to anarchy with the plausible assertion that there can be no new beginning so long as the old clutters the landscape.[5]

The comparative study of political extremism ignores such insights into the role of the extremist personality at its peril. Clearly they suggest an important dimension for research into both the origins of political extremist movements and the factors which help to sustain them.

However, concentration on the personality traits of individual extremists is not sufficient as a basis for identifying extremist movements in whole political systems. For this purpose, it is clearly important to adopt a third approach, a method of identifying extremisms in terms of the political ideology they express in relation to liberal democractic values and institutions. Marxists like to lay claim to a monopoly of wisdom about ideology, claiming that Marx and Engels laid the foundations for a genuinely scientific study of ideas in their theory of dialectical materialism. But like Marxist

theory in general, the theory that class ideology or false consciousness emanates directly from the material mode of production has
been overwhelmingly rejected by modern social scientific research.

This does not mean that the concept of ideology has been dis-
pensed with: it has been found as vital to the study of politics and
society as, for example, the concepts of religion and culture. As one
influential American scholar defines them:

> [Ideologies are] articulated sets of ideas, ends and purposes,
> which help members of the system to interpret the past, explain
> the present, and offer a vision for the future. Thereby they
> describe the aims for which some members feel political power
> ought to be used and its limits. They may be deceptive myths
> about political life; they may be realistic appraisals and sincere
> aspirations. But they have the potential because they are
> articulated as a set of ethnically infused ideals, to capture the
> imagination. From a manipulative or instrumental point of view,
> they may be interpreted as categories of thought to corral the
> energies of men: from an expressive point of view we may see
> them as ideals capable of rousing and inspiring men to action
> thought to be related to their achievement. Values of this kind,
> consisting of articulated ethical interpretations and principles
> that set forth the purposes, organization, and boundaries of politi-
> cal life, I shall describe by their usual name, *ideologies*.

This brilliant brief characterisation of ideology by David Easton
(1965) in his *A Systems Analysis of Political* Life usefully reminds us
that ideologies do appear to minister to certain profound social and
individual needs. People do hunger for a sense of meaning and
purpose. There is a deeply felt need to understand the meaning of
human existence and history, and for some vision and collective
goal for the future. There is a sense in which all societies and social
groups require some basic doctrines or intellectual framework not
only for their own personal life and conduct but also to structure
their relations to their fellows and to provide some guidelines and
rationale for their modes of political and economic organisation. It
is a fact confirmed by many historians that these needs for meaning
and for hopes of salvation (in earthly terms) are felt all the more
intensely in periods of major social crisis inducted by dramatic
social and political changes, threats to survival or welfare, and
conflict.

The pretensions of political ideologies to fulfil these basic social needs, however false and dangerous they may prove to be in practice, undoubtedly go far towards explaining the continuing ability of ideologies to sustain the loyalty of their adherents and even to acquire fresh converts. Moreover, the inherently combative and crusading ethos of political ideologies in itself strengthens their hold on their activists and their organisational durability. Trotsky, in one of his many vivid insights into the nature of revolution, clearly recognised the importance of 'the struggle' as a means of strengthening the hold of ideological commitment.In *My Life* he observed 'For us the tasks of education in socialism were closely integrated with those of fighting. Ideas that enter the mind under fire remain there securely for ever'.

On the other hand, in recent history we have seen the devastating military and political defeat of one aggressive and totally evil ideology, Nazism, and at least the partial containment of the spread of another expansionist political ideology, Marxism–Leninism. And at the intellectual level, totalitarian political ideologies have failed to drive out alternative belief systems and values.

It is very important to remind ourselves that ideology is not a synonym for belief systems and philosophies of all kinds. Religions do have many features in common with political ideologies. Both tend to be universalist and millenarian. Religious movements also tend to have their fanatical and zealous proselytisers, their charismatic leaders, their scriptural texts and their authoritative 'codes' for personal action. Both tend to be resistant to fundamental changes in belief and yet are extremely prone to schismatisation. Religious fanaticism also provides the basis of terrorist violence by certain groups. Yet, despite these similarities, there are some crucial differences. The religious are concerned primarily with the spiritual rather than the worldly, with the after-life rather than with building the Kingdom of God on Earth, with saving souls rather than revolutionising international politics. It is a fundamental mistake to assume that religious faith automatically involves a commitment to active involvement in temporal affairs, political conflicts, and programmatic social and economic change. On the contrary, in most world religions, there are extremely influential elements promoting the idea of *withdrawal* from the distractions of the secular world.

Nor should we overlook the difference between the *Weltanschauung* or world outlook and the ideology proper. The *Weltanschauung* is a more general philosophy. It is far less explicit and less dogmatic than an ideology. It does not claim absolute authority. It is not generally embodied in any organisation or movement, and it certainly does not demand obedience among followers.

It is thus perfectly possible to develop systems of thought of many kinds which are free from the most negative and potentially repressive qualities of ideology such as dogmatism, exclusivism, and enforced political activism. If we adopt the concept of ideology outlined here, it is certainly possible to argue that it is possible for societies and individuals to live without any dominant or consensual ideology. Indeed one can argue that it is an essential condition for the survival of any genuine intellectual freedom that this should be so. A society totally dominated by any particular ideology is a prison-house of the mind.

It is important to avoid the temptation of regarding all ideologies as being equally dangerous and potentially destructive to freedom and justice. We can and must engage in an informed and searching critique of the ideologies which some groups and regimes seek to promote at the expense of other ideas and belief-systems. What is the precise content of their ideological message? What does this reveal about the ideologies involved and how they see the world? What normative evaluation can we make about the kind of political, social and economic order they wish to institute? Are their methods and tactics commensurate with their aims? Do their intended means appear likely to involve even greater evils for society than the wrongs they claim to be redressing? How do their ideological beliefs square with real historical experience and our knowledge of human life and conduct? We must seek to make these judgements in as informed and responsible a way as possible. Above all, we must seek to improve the quality of public education and debate on these important matters. It is crucial, if we are to improve our understanding of what causes and sustains terrorist movements, to increase our knowledge of terrorist belief-systems, aims, motives and attitudes.

We must always bear in mind that many violent extremist movements have made a serious bid to build political front organisations and mass movements. It would be extremely foolish to discount the possibility of extremist political ideas and movements gaining mass support. For example, most liberal democrats would have regarded Hitler's National Socialist Party under the Weimar Republic as an extremist party, yet in the July 1932 German election they gained 36.4 per cent of the vote, a larger percentage than the combined Socialist Parties achieved. Similarly, in Northern Ireland, the Democratic Unionist Party (DUP) and Provisional Sinn Fein (PSF) have both taken very considerable proportions of the popular vote in recent elections in Northern Ireland, yet there is abundant evidence that these parties represent extreme militant Protestant Unionist on the one hand and extreme Republican Nationalist on the other. And if one is going to adopt the proportion of votes gained in elections as a criterion of extremism, where should the threshold for 'acceptability' be fixed? Has Rabbi Kahane's Kach Party become respectable or diminished its extremist character in Israeli politics simply because opinion polls now show that over 10 per cent would consider voting for him in elections for the Knesset?

COUNTERING SUPPORT MECHANISMS OF INTERNATIONAL TERRORISM

Like most scholars who have specialised in the study of terrorism, I am deeply suspicious of claims by politicians, officials and armchair strategists that they have found the 'solution' to terrorism. Some apparently believe that if only we could alight on the appropriate formula for a diplomatic settlement or political reform, the underlying grievance or demand of the terrorist movement would be met, and violence would melt away. This idea appeals to those Utopian souls who believe there is a perfect rational solution to every human problem and that people will behave rationally enough to apply it if only you point them in the right direction. But let us take the intractable Arab–Israeli conflict: is it to be seriously believed that if Arafat and Hussein were to agree on a settlement with the Israeli government tomorrow concerning the establishment of an autonomous Palestinian enclave in the West Bank and Gaza, this would bring an end to Palestinian terrorism? The anti-Arafat 'rejectionist' groups would undoubtedly view any such agreement as a betrayal, and would intensify their terrorist campaigns in order to stop or sabotage any such settlement.

Others argue that the appropriate solution to terrorism is the use of overwhelming military force to eradicate the terrorists and their bases and to punish and deter states that support the terrorists. General Ariel Sharon and his colleagues in the Begin government in Israel undoubtedly believed in the efficacy of absolute military force against terrorism in their invasion of Lebanon in 1982. What actually happened was that the Israeli people became deeply divided over the justifiability of the war, the Israeli Defence Forces suffered heavy losses in a long terrorist war of attrition far worse than the terrorism before June 1982 which they were supposed to be eradicating, and Lebanon slipped still further into chaos and division into warring zones of factions, many of which are bitterly opposed to Israel. The invasion did not stop Palestinian terrorism and it did not make the northern border of Israel secure. Israel has again reverted to reprisal bombings of alleged terrorist bases in Lebanon.While it is true that these raids provide an outlet for Israeli outrage and anger against terrorist attacks, it would be foolish to claim, after years of Israeli use of this tactic, that such methods have 'worked' in reducing or eradicating terrorism.

This does not mean that political and military methods have no place in an effective strategy against terrorism. The important point is that they should be part of a more carefully considered long-term multi-pronged approach,[4] using many other key elements, such as well-chosen and effective legal, police and intelligence measures, and the skilful use of the mass media. Political reforms and initiatives can make a useful contribution to isolating the terrorist extremists and enhancing public support for the government. Selective use of specialist military units skilled in specific roles, such as hostage rescue, bomb-disposal and physical protection of key points can be an invaluable aid to the civil power. But the key point to be emphasised is that there are many pathways out of terrorism for democratic societies. They all take time and they are mostly extremely complex. We need to learn to use *all* the pathways, rather than place all our bets on one quick-fix solution which will probably turn out to be illusory.

Among the least glamorous and most neglected of these pathways are those involving the countering of the life-support systems on which terrorists depend. Effective measures attacking all the key elements in the support mechanisms – aims and ideas, leadership, organisation, training, cash, weapons and explosives, and access to target – could make an extremely valuable contribution. It is true that if they are to be really effective in undermining terrorism, they need to be applied by as many countries as possible. It is worrying to observe that although we have a number of multilateral and bilateral mechanisms for anti-terrorism cooperation among Western governments, little or no effort has thus far been put into this particular set of tasks.

The countering of the terrorists' key ideas and belief-systems should be concentrated at several levels. The very notion that terrorism is a legitimate weapon of last resort, provided the terrorists can claim they have a just grievance or cause, needs to be attacked. Western societies should enlist the mass media, the churches, and the other key social institutions as well as educationists in a major effort to show young people that terrorism, whatever its professed justification, is a basic crime against human rights and therefore an intolerable method of campaigning for a cause. Second, and just as important, democratic societies should also mount intensive efforts at civic and moral education designed to increase understanding of, and support for, the values and institutions of parliamentary democracy. Deeds speak louder than words in this matter. Above all, democratic governments need to be able to show by their actions that their political system is capable of meeting the basic needs and aspirations of the people.

The basic prerequisite for attacking and undermining the leadership and organisational structure of terrorist movements is high-calibre intelligence. If the identity of leaders and activists remains hidden, even from the security authorities, the society will experience continuing terrorist violence, or threat of violence.This good quality intelligence needs not only to be gathered efficiently and swiftly and analysed professionally: it must also be made available at the right time to those involved in policy and crisis management decisions on terrorist situations. This requires expert intelligence coordination. To date the US government still appears to have grave weaknesses in this area, not mainly because of lack of means of technical and human intelligence sources, but because of the profusion of agencies and constant involvement of other branches of government.

The second basic requirement for countering terrorist leadership and organisation is to have an adequate structure of law, law enforcement, and judicial and penal policy to deal with terrorist criminals once they have been identified. Some agencies, such as the FBI in the USA and the Metropolitan Police in London, have made great strides in developing professionalism and pioneering new techniques to deal with terrorism. Unfortunately, this expertise is not always available when needed at the provincial level. And many countries, even those with serious terrorist problems, lack it at national level.

However, by far the greatest weakness in this field is in law enforcement and judicial cooperation at international level. The usual device for bringing terrorist suspects to justice once they have fled abroad is extradition. But it is unfortunately all to easy to find areas where terrorists can safely rest, knowing that there is almost no chance of them ever having to face trial. This is because even many democratic countries do not have extradition agreements, and those that do have them often find that differences of national laws, jurisdictions, and procedures, effectively make extradition impossible.

To overcome this key obstacle, and to ensure that the arm of the law can be given a much longer reach, we need to strengthen the framework of international law. It is surely time that NATO governments considered instituting an international criminal code and court. This would have the advantage of being able to investigate, try, and sentence in cases of all serious international crimes including drug trafficking, war crimes, and slavery, for example, in addition to international terrorism. It is true that initially only a small number of democratic states would be likely to join in such a project. But as these pioneers, and other democratic states, came to see the immense advantages of overcoming the obstacles of national legal differences and calling on the power and prestige of an international criminal court to help them to confront ruthless international criminals, so the Court's membership would rapidly increase. There is already an excellent draft convention and statute setting up a court proposed by the International Law Association conference at Wingspread and Bellagio in 1972.[5] It deserves urgent consideration by Western governments.

In dealing with the use of the law against terrorist leaders and organisations, we should also remember the vital role of the prison systems. The gaols should be capable of implementing the degree of maximum security needed to prevent the formation of terrorist organisations within the prisons, and the establishment of links between gaoled terrorists and their comrades outside. Second, there must be a serious effort made to re-educate and rehabilitate the numerous medium-term terrorist prisoners so that we greatly diminish the danger of their returning to terrorism after release. There is an urgent need for research into the most promising ways in which this might be achieved. It will almost certainly need more resources and professional skills devoted to this area of the gaol systems.

Other strangely neglected pathways out of terrorism are countermeasures against the financial support systems of terrorist movements. As James Adams (1986) argues many of the larger terrorist movements have turned themselves into successful capitalists, operating budgets amounting to millions of dollars. Groups such as the IRA and the PLO, for example, have become so rich as a result of legitimate business activities, investments, racketeering and conventional crime, that they no longer need to depend on handouts from foreign supporters or state sponsors. If our intelligence services can identify the sources of these funds, governments should set about staunching the flow of cash that supplies terrorists with the means of murder; they should seize terrorists' assets, freeze their bank accounts, wind up their business operations and use the law to break up their rackets. Why have Western governments been so slow to take such obviously useful measures?

Last in our list of key elements in the support mechanisms of terrorism is access to targets. Western governments have declared their willingness to tighten visa controls, particularly where nationals of pro-terrorist states are involved. They have also improved intelligence-sharing at bilateral and multilateral levels. This has already shown some modest successes. But is it not extraordinary that we have not modernised the passport system in our Western states, despite the fact that international terrorists constantly make use of false passport documents to reach their target countries? It is high time we applied to the passport the kind of advanced technology we now take for granted in the plastic cards used by banking and credit companies. It should be possible to design a card which can be computerised, containing a coded biometric profile of some form, and which could therefore be used as a swift and efficient filter to stop international terrorists and other criminals when they try to cross our frontiers. Again this is an aspect of countering terrorism which deserves urgent attention by an expert working-group of the NATO countries.

So far as countering state sponsorship of terrorism is concerned, there are, in my view two particular sets of measures that would be very damaging to terrorist states such as Libya and Syria:

1. We must persuade all law-abiding states to join in a collective international measure to close down Libyan People's Bureaux and Syrian Embassies in their countries. These so-called 'diplomatic missions' are in reality command posts and transmission belts for international terrorist attacks. Reducing the size of these Bureaux, as some countries have agreed to do, is

simply not enough. So long as there is a Libyan People's Bureau of any size in a capital city, it will be used to further Gaddafi's policy of terrorism for domestic and foreign policy reasons. Therefore they should be shut down until Gaddafi abandons terrorism or is overthrown and replaced by a non-terrorist regime. Syria's diplomatic presence in Western cities should also be expelled until the Damascus regime alters its behaviour and abandons international terrorism.

2. There is a potentially highly-effective weapon against state sponsors of terrorism in the form of collective economic counter-measures by all the major industrial countries of the West. Dictators such as Gaddafi and Assad are highly dependent on Western markets, products, skills, and technology. It is an outrage that so many Western democracies are still doing business as usual with this sponsor of murder gangs. The USA would obviously welcome an economic boycott of such regimes. If all the other NATO states joined in, it would more effectively than anything else, undermine Gaddafi's power-base in Libya and weaken Assad's regime in Syria.

Legislators and public opinion in West European countries should be made aware that economic action to isolate Libya and Syria economically and diplomatically is being blocked by vested interests and 'fat cats', highly placed in the Mediterranean EEC states' governments. What is more important, the protection of those who have major personal financial interests in trade with Libya, and Syria, or carrying forward the international efforts to protect the rights of the innocent against international terrorism? Some West European countries have perhaps, unwittingly, become an important part of the terrorist states' support mechanism.

Appendix A

POUR L'UNITE
DES REVOLUTIONNAIRES
EN EUROPE DE L'OUEST

FÜR DIE EINHEIT
DER REVOLUTIONÄRE
IN WESTEUROPA

ACTION
DIRECTE

JANVIER. JANUAR 85

For revolutionary solidarity in Western Europe

We proclaim:
That it is both necessary and feasible today to open, in the centres of imperialism, a new phase in the development of an authentic revolutionary strategy; and that one of the conditions for this qualitative leap is the creation of an international proletarian combat organisation, its politico-military core: the Western European guerrilla.

We take this decision,
because of the global situation, viewed objectively:
The central role of Western Europe in the imperialist redeployment created by the opening of a breach in the unity of international power by the liberation struggles of the peoples of the periphery, resulting in a collision between the accretion of productive forces and the limits of the global market, leading to a political and military globalisation of the crisis in the gathering of imperialist countries.

on the basis of our experience:
The last few years have seen in the cities, the implantation and development of armed, revolutionary politics, just as at different points fresh theatres of liberation struggle have appeared. Because of these experiences, discussions have been held at the heart of the revolutionary movement, for the building of revolutionary tactics and strategy in the cities, the conclusions from which – from the communist perspective in Western Europe present themselves as undeniable.

To elaborate:
A war economy as one of the means to resolve the crisis.

The features of the domination of capital and of its ideology of 'well-being', 'the social contract', 'the right to work', are shattered by the brutality of the measures taken to reconstruct: the exclusion of millions of men from the .production processes by robotisation and the redeployment of industry to a global level.

The imperialist states from their substantial instabilities and from the gradual collapse of their legitimacy can only wish to demonstrate their will to rule. In fact today they are confronted by no longer benefiting from a passive consensus to impose their plans.

Political death-rattle.
That is the other aspect of their power. This agony – resulting from the antagonism that has been created at a worldwide level by the proletariat and by the downtrodden peoples in their struggle against imperialism – is the terrain on which the offensive of proletarian power in Western Europe must be based, the key factor for the spreading of the unrest and the deepening of the crisis of the system.

The attacks against the buildings of multinationals and of NATO, against their bases and strategists, against their plans and their propaganda are constituted as the first great mobilisation in view of the make-up of the proletarian political strategy in Western Europe in the changed political climate.

The absolute power which the bourgeoisie wishes to reconstitute by concealing all the contradictions created by national or economic aspects of this structure, which penetrates and determines all the areas of society, and for whom the solution of their global crisis is the generalisation of the war:

militarily:
— 'Roll back' against the victorious peoples of Asia, Africa and Central America through the creation of a unified 'blitzkrieg', interventions against the liberation movements of the periphery and concrete preparations for a war against the socialist countries of Eastern Europe. Imperialism fights and prepares itself to fight everywhere. To do that, it must tighten up and improve its forces, ever more aspects of this fighting and its preparation managed through a new partitioning of roles under the control of the US under the guise of a 'new politics for NATO', by the European states.
— The setting up of missiles although essential will not take more than a moment. The revitalisation of the West European Union, the creation in

France of Force Action Rapide, armament cooperation between the NATO allies (including France), discussions for a German participation in the French deterrent and its integration with NATO, the clearly expressed intention to intervene against liberation movements in the capacity of NATO..., these are the most concrete aspects of their capacity for military action.
— In other respects the counter-revolution ('counter-insurgency') as a common policy crossing the group of countries in the imperialist network in the capacity of an antagonism to and prevention of a revolutionary front able through a breach to throw into doubt their strategy, determines the objective reality which it must realise in the fighting of the revolutionaries.

economically:
to structure the European economy under the domination of the USA on concentrating on the strategic area of research, production, new technologies, electronics, armaments... in order globally to ensure the position of the imperialist bloc – the USA, Japan, Western Europe – and the conditions for stabilising the capital of the multinationals.

Consequent on the fact of the unification of imperialist strategy, the key tasks of the communist guerrilla in Western Europe, for the development of its historic project in the struggle against imperialism, are:

TO LEAD THE ARGUMENT FOR A REVOLUTIONARY POLITICAL FRONT, CREATING THE CONSTRUCTION OF UNITY IN THE OFFENSIVE AGAINST THE IMPERIALIST MACHINE.

TO INSTIGATE A DEVELOPMENT METHOD FOR CLASS POLITICS WHOSE DIALECTIC BRINGS TOGETHER DIFFERING STRATEGIES INTO A MOVEMENT AGAINST THE DESTRUCTION EXPERIENCED EVERY DAY.

TO CONSTRUCT A POLITICO-MILITARY FRONT IN WESTERN EUROPE, IN THE CAPACITY OF THE GLOBAL CONFRONTATION BETWEEN THE INTERNATIONAL PROLETARIAT AND THE IMPERIALIST BOURGEOISIE. THIS FRONT, AS THE DEVELOPMENT METHOD UNFOLDS, MOVES TOWARDS A JOINT ATTACK, WHICH WILL BE SHATTERING, ON THE CENTRES, THE IMPERIALIST STRATEGIC CORE BECAUSE IT IS HERE THAT THEY MUST BUILD MILITARILY AND ECONOMICALLY IN ORDER TO HOLD ON TO THEIR GLOBAL DOMINATION.

The central plan in the current phase of imperialist strategy is the fusing together into a homogeneous grouping, a firm bloc, of European states, which would integrate completely into the hub of imperialist power, NATO in the capacity of the most advanced structure of power here. This structural redeployment articulated politically, economically and militarily, is in the nature of a pulling back in the face of the earlier setbacks in the face of the pressure from liberation movements, their blueprint outlined here.

A mobilisation which strengthens itself in the nature of a battle against the system of exploitation and war, as was shown by attacks in Portugal, Greece, Belgium, Spain, West Germany and France...

In the face of all the ideological debate and theoretical 'internationalist' programmes we declare:
The strategy of the guerrilla is, through his resolution: a part of and a function of international class war, and by his actions: politically uniting the communists of Western Europe, the construction of the attack against the entire imperialist system, and the material transformation of the international proletariat which the present situation demands.

The true revolutionary strategy in Western Europe will deploy itself in attacks against the central aims of the imperialists: the collectivity and the coherence of the fighters, from their particular conditions and possibilities.

Unit, which in the destruction of the imperialist edifices conquers the ground on which the consciousness and power of the proletariat is nurtured.

THE WEST EUROPEAN GUERRILLA SHAKES THE IMPERIALIST CORE!

Appendix B

SUBVERSIVE APPARATUS OF A STATE SPONSOR – the case of the USSR

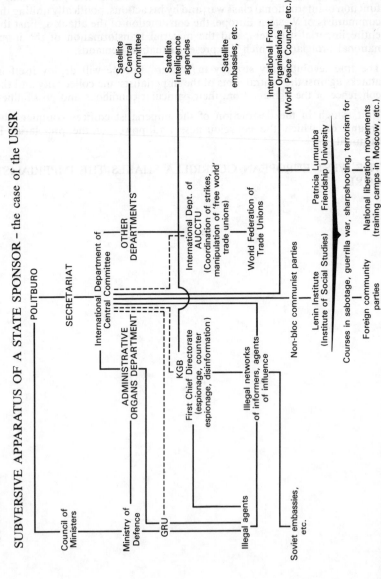

Appendix C

Training camps in Arab countries for foreign terrorists

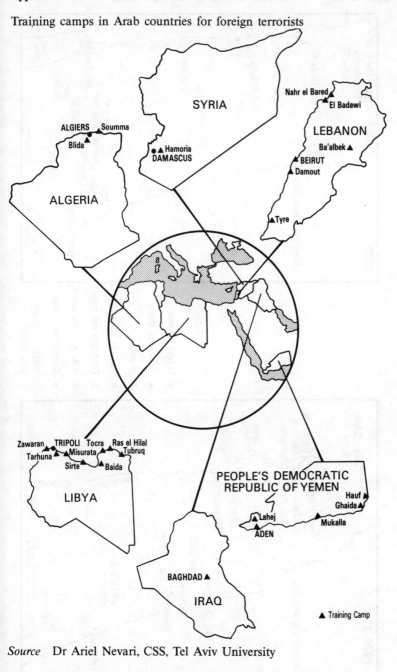

Source Dr Ariel Nevari, CSS, Tel Aviv University

Appendix D   **Terrorist attacks in Palestine/Israel**

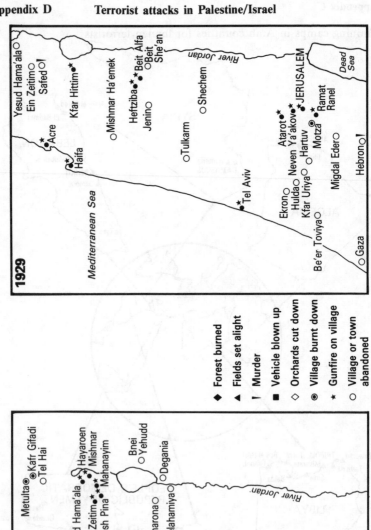

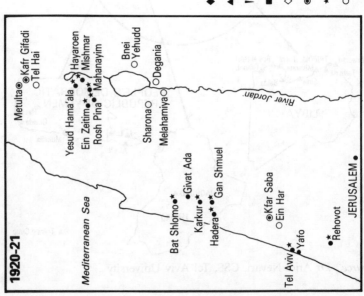

- ◆ Forest burned
- ▲ Fields set alight
- ▌ Murder
- ■ Vehicle blown up
- ◇ Orchards cut down
- ◉ Village burnt down
- ★ Gunfire on village
- ○ Village or town abandoned

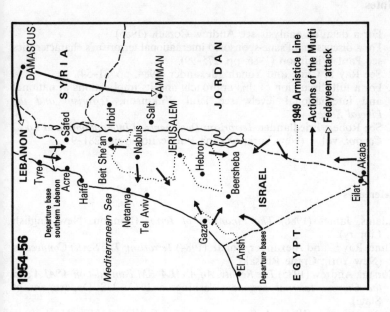

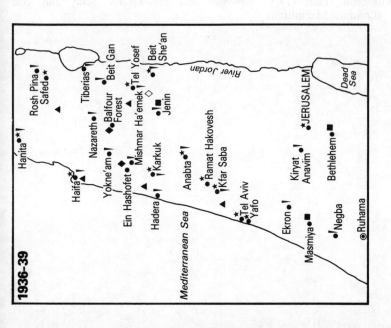

Notes

1. For a detailed analysis see Andrew Corsun (1985).
2. For a discussion of state-sponsored international terrorism's characteristics see Paul Wilkinson (1986, pp. 275–99).
3. See Ray S. Cline and Yonah Alexander (1984, pp. 31–54).
4. For a full discussion of this approach, and its implications at national and international levels, see Paul Wilkinson, *Terrorism and the Liberal State.*
5. See Robert Friedlander, *Terrorism: Documents of International and Local Control*, vol. 1 (New York: Oceana Publications) pp. 281–9.

References

Adams, James (1986) *The Financing of Terror* (London: New English Library).

Cline, Ray S. and Alexander, Yonah (1984) *Terrorism: The Soviet Connection* (New York: Crane Russak).

Corsun, Andrew (1985) *The Reality: An ASALA–RM Pamphlet on ASALA and the Current Internal Dispute* (Washington D.C.: US Department of State).

Easton, David (1965) *A Systems Analysis of Political Life* (New York: Wiley).

Friedlander, Robert (1979) *Terrorism: Documents of International and Local Control*, Vol I (New York: Oceana Publications).

Hoffer, Eric (1951) *The True Believer* (New York: Harper & Row).

Wilkinson, Paul (1986) *Terrorism and the Liberal State*, 2nd edn (London: Macmillan).

5 Empirical Research on Political Terrorism: The State of the Art and How it Might be Improved

Ted Robert Gurr[1]

A decade ago J. Bowyer Bell observed that 'terror has become trendy'. The same could be said of terror as the subject of an out-pouring of essays, monographs and symposia in which experts purport to explain and offer solutions for an elusive and threatening phenomenon. Bell went on to observe that 'the academic response to terrorism has been ahistorical, exaggerated, and closely associated with congenial political postures' (Bell 1977b, pp. 476, 477). The judgement of this chapter is a little less harsh. Many challenging questions and provocative theoretical ideas have been advanced in the study of terrorism since the mid-1970s (cf. especially Crenshaw, 1981, and the review in Schmid, 1983, Part II). Careful gleaning of the literature turns up some sound quantitative, comparative and his-torical studies of terrorist phenomena. But the fact remains that the research questions raised in the literature are considerably more interesting than most of the evidence brought to bear on them. With a few clusters of exceptions there is in fact a disturbing lack of good empirically-grounded research on terrorism. This essay reviews the current state of knowledge and systematic research on oppositional terrorism and asks how the enterprise might be improved, with par-ticular attention to the questions raised and the methods that are most suitable for answering them.

Let me make explicit several conceptual points which underlie the discussion to follow. First, I accept the essential accuracy and utility of Thornton's classic definiton of the subject matter: 'terror is a symbolic act designed to influence political behavior by extra-normal means, entailing the use or threat of violence' (Thornton,

1964, p. 73).[2] It is consistent with this conception to regard terrorist incidents as *tactics* used in political conflicts within countries and among them. Second, this essay is limited to research concerned with oppositional terror, which is to say the use of terrorist tactics by opposition groups against governments and other politically dominant groups. Oppositional terror is conceptually distinct from terror directed or sponsored by states against their own subjects and other governments, topics which only recently have begun to stimulate substantial empirical research (see Stohl and Lopez, 1984; Lopez and Stohl, 1986).

I also assume that terror as a tactic is not inherently or uniquely revolutionary and is in fact used in the pursuit of a great many different kinds of political and other objectives (see Gurr, 1979, for some relevant evidence). 'Terrorism' is a *doctrine* about the efficacy of unexpected, dramatic, and life-threatening violence for inducing political change, and a *strategy* of political action which embodies that doctrine. Particular opposition groups may rely exclusively on terror tactics – i.e. a strategy of terrorism – or use them occasionally along with other tactics, as many guerrilla movements do, or use them not at all. In conventional academic and journalistic usage a 'terrorist group' is any opposition group which uses symbolic violence against instrumental targets for political purposes. This obscures the substantial differences among violence-using opposition groups in their preferences about strategies and tactics. Some rely mainly on terrorist tactics, others do so only occasionally. The empirical research relevant to political terror thus extends to studies of the ideologies and strategies of terrorism; the incidence and consequences of episodes of terror; the nature and dynamics of groups which occasionally or recurrently use terrorist tactics; and the traits of individuals involved in such groups.

This essay begins with some general observations about the data and methods suitable for the empirical study of terrorism. These provide the basis for a more detailed examination of research issues and approaches at five different levels of analysis, ranging from the global to the individual. The conclusion is a set of recommendations for future research.[3]

I QUESTIONS, METHODS, AND DATA

The term 'empirical research' implies the use of the methodologies of the social sciences. Methodologies in conflict analysis are techniques for ordering information systematically and drawing inferences from that information about the patterns, trends, causes, processes, and outcomes of conflict. Since political terrorism is a type or strategy of conflict, the full armamentarium of techniques for conflict analysis are potentially applicable to it.[4] The appropriate methodologies are exceptionally diverse: they include psychological and biographical analysis of individuals, comparative case-studies of conflict episodes, econometric analysis of large sets of data on conflict and its causes, and simulations of conflict processes based on formal models. 'Methodologies' does not mean simply the analysis of quantitative data, although the most technically-sophisticated methods are those designed to generate and analyse quantified information. The term also encompasses systematic case-studies, that is, case-studies guided by an explicit theoretical argument or framework.[5]

Asking the Right Questions

Methodologies do not exist in abstract form. They assume the existence of an analytic question and a body of relevant information which bears on the question. The analytic question is logically prior: what kinds of ethnic and religious minorities are most likely to resort to oppositional terrorism? What is the relative importance of personal grievance and ideological commitments as motivations for joining terrorist groups? What are the effects of a 'no-concessions' policy on terrorists' later strategies? Given a specific question of this sort, a methodology is *designed* or *adapted* to guide the collection of relevant information and its analysis. This 'question first' procedure is in principle the preferred one in scientific and policy research because it maximises the likelihood that the researcher will get valid answers to the question.

Available Data

In practice the researcher often begins by confronting a body of previously-collected data. In this 'data first' situation, the nature of the data constrains both the questions that might reasonably be asked and the methods appropriate to the particular combination of information base and analytic questions. For example, the two major publicly-available compilations of global information on political terrorism are Edward Mickolus's ITERATE II dataset for 1968–77 (see Mickolus, 1979; Heyman and Mickolus, 1981) and the Rand Corporation's chronology of terrorist events from 1968 to present (see the bibliography to Cordes *et al.*, 1984). Both are restricted conceptually to incidents which have international dimensions.[6] Thus they cannot be used to answer questions about domestic terrorism or about possible linkages between domestic and international terrorism. And since the unit of analysis is the *incident*, it is very difficult to use these data sources to estimate the propensities for terrorist actions by different ethnic and religious minorities. To answer this kind of analytic question would require the researcher to merge information from a comprehensive databank on terrorist incidents (transnational *and* domestic) with information on a comprehensive data bank on minorities (which does not exist). This is not a criticism of ITERATE II or the Rand chronology. The point is that since they were designed to serve specific research purposes, particularly the analysis of trends and characteristics of incidents, they are not well-suited to the analysis of some other kinds of questions, in particular the analysis of political context and causations.

Methodological Determinism

Some of the empirical literature on terrorism aims to demonstrate the utility of a particular method or technique for studying the subject. Causal modelling and time-series analysis of data on terrorism and its context have been pioneered by Hamilton (1981) and Wright (1981). The uses of simulation techniques for research and training have been advocated by Gilboa (1981) and demonstrated by Sloan (1981). Others have shown the applicability of Markovian and Poisson probability models to the analysis of the distribution of terrorist incidents over time and space (Gleason, 1980; Midlarsky, Crenshaw and Yoshida, 1980; Heyman and Mickolus, 1981). No doubt formal expected-utility models of terrorists' decision-making calculus are in the offing, in emulation of Bueno de Mesquita's work (1985) on decisions to initiate international conflict. Of course such techniques have appropriate uses. But in the longer run basic and applied research on conflict are best served if the analytic question determines the choice of method rather than vice versa.

Thus there are two basic considerations which help to structure an intelligible discussion of systematic empirical research on terror and terrorism:

1. It is necessary to identify the kinds of analytic questions which are of greatest concern to scholars and policy-makers. The methods by which one might answer them follow from the nature of the questions. Parts II to VI of this chapter identify what I regard as the essential questions which should guide analysis, and discuss alternative research approaches.

2. Following from analytic questions and decisions about methods are implications about the kinds of substantive information and data which are needed. I am convinced by a review of the empirical literature on political terrorism that many, perhaps most, of the important questions being raised cannot be answered adequately with the kinds of information now generally available to scholars. The conclusion summarises the case for a more comprehensive system for gathering and codifying information related to oppositional terrorism.

In general one can distinguish five different levels of analysis at which questions are raised about political terrorism in its various manifestations: (i) global, (ii) national, (iii) group, (iv) incident, and (v) individual. The questions raised at each level of analysis are rather different: so are the appropriate methods for answering them.

II GLOBAL AND WORLD-REGIONAL ANALYSES OF TERRORISM

In this as in the following sections I begin by specifying the major analytic questions, then comment on the research approaches suitable for answering them.

Trends. What are the trends in aggregate levels of terrorist incidents, globally and by world region? What are the trends in characteristics of terrorism: the types of groups involved, their tactics and targets, their likelihood of success? What conditions or events lead to changes in the trends?

Diffusion. What is the evidence for diffusion processes, for terrorism in general, for particular kinds of episodes, or for particular tactics? What kinds of diffusion processes are at work: what is the relative importance of imitation, external encouragement and assistance, foreign direction?

The context of inter-state confict.   To what extent is terrorism an outgrowth or manifestation of larger conflicts among states? More specifically, to what extent is domestic or transnational terrorism centred on issues of North–South or East–West conflicts, rather than nationalism or specific internal political grievances?

To answer these kinds of questions presupposes the existence of a codified body of information on groups which use terrorist tactics, their ideologies and objectives: and data on incidents and campaigns of terrorism and their short-run outcomes. It is impossible to give reliable answers to questions on 'trends' and 'diffusion' in the absence of such data. The empirical literature offers examples of popular and official impressions about trends which are inconsistent with the objective evidence, as documented by Wardlaw (1982, pp. 51–2).

Graphic analysis is the simplest kind of trend analysis and has been widely applied to data on incidents in the ITERATE dataset and Rand chronologies, among others. Typically the graphs are used to summarise information, with accompanying narrative interpretation. One limitation of most such descriptive analyses is their failure to make sufficiently detailed distinctions among types and characteristics of incidents. One instructive exception is an analysis by Bass and Jenkins (1983) of trends in anti-nuclear incidents compared with overall trends in transnational terrorism. A different kind of exception is Hoffman's (1985) three-year study of trends in the location and targets of Palestinian terrorism. These two studies, like most other trend studies, make use of data on transnational incidents. It is clear from such studies that transnational terrorism has increased greatly in the past fifteen years, but is that also true of the total volume of domestic and transnational terror? Or has there been a shift, globally or in particular regions, from domestic to transnational terrorism, in other words an internationalisation of a pre-existing strategy of conflict? The comprehensive data on domestic terror which would be necessary to answer this kind of question have yet to be collected and analysed.

Trend analyses have looked at the distribution in time and space of particular kinds of terrorist tactics: bombings, hostage incidents, assassinations. Targets have been similarly studied. But I know of no analyses of trends in or the distribution of *types of groups* using terrorist tactics: nor of the changing relative importance of nationalist versus revolutionary objectives; nor of success rates. The neglect of these latter kinds of analyses, like the neglect of comparisons between domestic and transnational terrorism, is not due to oversight but to the lack of enough codified information.

Also missing from virtually all studies of trends are statistical analyses. If one wishes to project or forecast the future incidence of a particular kind of terrorist action the first step is to estimate a best-fit linear or non-linear equation to describe the trend in existing data. Analysts could also use statistical tests to determine whether the occurrence of a particular precedent-setting incident (such as the killing of Israeli athletes in Munich) or a dramatic innovation in response (the Israeli raid which freed hostages in Entebbe, the US bombing of Libyan targets) leads to significant changes in the level or trend of incidents. There are well-established techniques for dealing with such research questions in conflict analysis, including interrupted time-series analysis (Cook and Campbell, 1979; for applications see Lewis-Beck, 1980; Iris, 1983) and Box–Tiao intervention analysis (Box and Tiao, 1973; a recent application is Thompson and Rasler, 1986). The data are sufficient for some analyses of this sort: the problem is probably lack of familiarity with the techniques.

Interestingly enough, the processes by which terrorism diffuses have been studied with considerably greater methodological sophistication than trends. Three somewhat different approaches to diffusion analysis have been used:

1. One is the application of statistical tests of randomness: the question is whether incidents are randomly distributed in space and time, and if not, how their distribution is structured. Published studies of transnational terrorism demonstrate the significance of both contagious and hierarchical processes in the spread of incidents within regions and among them (Midlarsky, Crenshaw and Yoshida, 1980; Heyman, 1980; Heyman and Mickolus, 1981; Govea, n.d.).
2. A second, related approach uses the results of statistical analysis (Markov-chain analysis specifically) to construct *adjacency maps* which show graphically the national and regional concentrations and diffusion of incidents (Heyman and Mickolus, 1981). Both methods can be and have been applied to (i) and the aggregate of all recorded incidents and (ii) specific tactics such as skyjackings, kidnappings, and bombings.
3. The third, least-common approach uses mathematical techniques

to examine the cumulative frequency with which new terrorist and other conflict tactics are used. evidence from the analysis of success/failure rates in waves of skyjacking has been shown to be a function of the relative learning rates of parties to conflict (see Pitcher and Hamblin, 1982, and the references cited there).

Transnational terrorism obviously is conditioned by, and in some instances is, an extension of inter-state conflicts. Domestic terrorism may be similarly influenced by inter-state conflict. In fact, the intensification of East–West and North–South conflicts is responsible for internationalising some internal conflicts, just as the use of terrorist strategies internationally has a contagious effect on the tactics used in domestic conflicts. Empirically one can ask whether the emergence or intensification of particular East–West or North–South conflicts has altered trends in terrorism; or how they affect hierarchical diffusion patterns. An alternative approach would require the analysis of coded data (which do not now exist) on the motivations and ideological rationalisations of conflict groups, to determine whether they are influenced by shifts in the salience of current issues of international conflict.

III   THE NATIONAL LEVEL OF ANALYSIS: COMPARISONS ACROSS TIME AND PLACE

Global and world-regional analyses can provide general knowledge about the trends in terrorism and about the transnational processes which generate or contribute to them, but they are not likely to provide the more specific understanding sought by most scholars and policy-makers. Geology provides an analogy: knowledge of plate techtonics on a global scale explains why the areas along the San Andreas fault are unstable, but does not make it possible to predict the timing, location or magnitude of California earthquakes: that requires more precise and localised analysis. Cross-national and longitudinal analysis provide the first step toward more localised analysis of oppositional terrorism.

Distribution. In which kinds of countries is terrorism most prevalent? What are the nationalities most often targeted by terrorists?

Trends and diffusion. Within countries that have relatively high levels of terrorism, what are the trends and diffusion patterns?

National policies. What kinds of national policies appear most effective in minimising the onset of terrorism? Which policies work best in extinguishing episodes of terrorism after they have begun?

Political context. In what kinds of political systems are oppositional and state terrorism most likely? What are the relationships between the state's use of coercion and violence and the resort to oppositional terrorism? More generally, what kinds of conflicts are most likely to give rise to terrorist campaigns?

Consequences. What are the short- and long-run effects of terrorist campaigns, especially large ones, on the structures and policies of governments? What are their effects on public opinion and on popular support for regimes and their officials?

There are two different general approaches to the systematic analysis or these kinds of questions. One is *cross-national analysis* which applies a familiar set of methods for the analysis of domestic civil violence specifically to terrorism. The basic objective is to identify the socio-economic and political conditions which are associated with – theoretically, are causes of – terrorism. Some such studies use quantitative techniques: cross-tabulations, correlation, regression, and causal-path analysis. Typically the dependent variable is some property of terrorism such as the number and intensity of incidents. The causal variables used in Hamilton's prototypical study of this kind (1981) include the type of political system, level of economic development, the extent of group discrimination and regional separatism, and governmental oppression (sanctions). Hamilton is especially concerned with the connection between oppression and terrorism. His evidence supports the general argument that 'terrorism succeeds as short-term provocation, but succumbs to long-term oppression' (Hamilton, 1981, p. 236).

More numerous than quantitative analyses are interpretive studies using comparative materials to assess general causal factors. One example is Targ's systematic attempt to specify the kinds of societies in which political terrorism is most common: he suggests that terrorism decreases as societies move from pre-industrial to industrial, then increases again as they move on into a post-industrial phase (Targ, 1979). In an intra-regional analysis of black Africa, Welfling (1979) asks why political terrorism has been uncommon in most African countries. The answers have to do with the character of African regimes and patterns of political repression and exclusion. These two studies are instructive examples of the kinds of systematic analysis that can be applied to terrorism in the absence of large-scale data banks: they pose general theoretical questions, present suggestive information (tabulations of data, case-studies), then draw out the general implications of that information. Good cross-national data on domestic terrorism would make it possible to address the same questions with more precision and with more definitive results.

There is no reason in principle why the cross-national approach could not be extended to deal with other questions identified above. Whereas Hamilton focuses on the nexus between terrorism and government coercion, one could equally well examine whether blanket policies of no concessions versus negotiation and concession strategies have any bearing on the future incidence of terrorism. This is the question asked in a recent study by Reuben Miller (1985) of the effects of harsh versus soft policies on the success and incidence of international terrorism in six target countries. The study is based on 115 cases from the ITERATE II dataset. National differences in responses are evident but do not appear to have consistent effects on the recurrence of terrorism. The study points toward the kinds of systematic cross-national research which could be done on a crucial policy question.

This is one facet of the larger question of the political circumstances which affect the likelihood of various manifestations of terrorism. It is widely observed that transnational terrorism is most likely to occur in Western democracies, though not in the USA (see Gurr, 1979; Bell and Gurr, 1979; Mickolus, Heyman and Schlotter, 1980, 176; Cordes *et al.*, 1984, pp. 2–9). It is also the case that domestic oppositional terrorism is widespread in some autocratic and élitist political systems – though by no means all of them. The inference is that *different types of terrorism are likely to characterise different types of political systems*. Similarly, the specific characteristics of terrorist campaigns and their outcomes are likely to vary from one type of regime to another. Cross-national quantitative analysis is one –

though not the only – technique suitable for studying these questions.

Longitudinal analysis is appropriate to the study of all the above aspects of terrorism in those particular countries where terrorist incidents are common. There are many historical and interpretive studies of this sort. On the USA, examples include Clarke's (1982) comparative study of fifteen incidents of actual or attempted political assassinations (not necessarily 'terroristic') and more general interpretive analyses by Bell and Gurr (1979), Homer (1979), and Johnpoll (1976). Another is Weinberg's (1979) study of the targets and objectives of neo-fascist violence in Italy in 1919–22 compared with 1969–76. Such studies in effect are 'country case-studies'. Clarke's study is one of the few examples which uses an explicit analytic framework, in this instance about the socio-psychological characteristics of American assassins. Weinberg's study is also unusual in its use of systematic data on targets of neo-fascist terrorists.

Some country-specific data sets on terrorist incidents are reviewed in Schmid (1983, pp. 247–51). Wright (1981) has done a pioneering time-series analysis of data on sectarian and government violence in Northern Ireland from 1969 to 1976. It demonstrates the utility of several time-series techniques for the study of terrorism and, commendably, takes account of the complex relations between government coercion and oppositional violence. Unfortunately the study is inductive, rather than organised around a particular substantive or theoretical question, and as one consequence its results are very difficult to interpret much less apply. More tightly focused studies could use the techniques of interrupted time-series analysis and Box–Tiao analysis (cited above) to study the effects of particular government policies and actions on trends in terror. In general, the lack of systematic longitudinal analyses of terrorism in countries other than Northern Ireland can be blamed partly on the scarcity of reliable data, partly on scholarly inattention – but certainly not on lack of suitable methodologies.

The outcomes of terrorism is a subject on which little national-level research has been done, systematically or otherwise. The speculative assessments and studies of Northern Ireland and Argentina in Crenshaw (1983) are about the best the literature has to offer. (For studies of incident outcomes see Part V, below.) Political terrorism is, after all, a purposive political strategy and all parties concerned presumably have an interest in a more precise understanding of its past and potential consequences. Both cross-national and longitudinal techniques of the kinds cited above are applicable to the topic. One difficulty is that systematic evaluations of the outcomes of political violence in general are a relatively new subject in conflict analysis (see Gurr, 1980b, for a review). There are several distinct kinds of questions: whether the opposition group gains any of its objectives through violence; what kinds of policy changes (reforms, new coercive policies) are introduced in response to or in the aftermath of episodes of violence; and the more general effects of violence on society, economy and political institutions.

One of the rare cross-national efforts to assess the utility of *campaigns* of political terrorism is Mack (1981), who uses five brief case-studies. He concludes, *inter alia*, that anti-colonial terrorists have sometimes achieved their political purposes but that in Western democracies 'revolutionary terrorism strengthens the very forces it seeks to destroy' (Mack, 1981, p. 218). Another empirical approach is to look at the psychological effects of terrorism on its indirect or public targets. The nominal purpose of 'terrorism' is to induce changes in the attitudes and political behaviour of a wider audience: government officials, supporters of a regime, and larger publics. The question is whether it does so. Mack's analysis (1981) and case-study evidence suggests otherwise. Low-to-medium levels of terrorism in Western societies appear to generate public hostility toward the perpetrators and support for strong countermeasures, as in the USA and West Germany (see Pridham, 1981). In Northern Ireland most people have adapted to living with the risk of chronic terror. Crelinsten has proposed the use of opinion surveys to 'provide some measure of the extent of perceived terror, the effects of terror on basic values, and the effects of incidents on public pressure for government action' (Crelinsten, 1978, p. 121). Such studies would be most useful if carried out longitudinally, that is, at regular intervals during and after a period of substantial terrorist activity. And they could be paralleled by more in-depth studies of official attitudes about the degree of threat and preferred responses.

It is essential to recognise, as Fromkin pointed out in 1975, that terrorism is an indirect strategy 'that wins or loses only in terms of how you respond to it' (Fromkin, 1975, p. 697). This suggests again the need to examine carefully the effects of sustained terrorist campaigns on government policies, especially but not only in democracies. Crenshaw has specified a number of factors which condition the impact of terrorism: the organisational characteristics of the terrorists, the domestic and international situation in which terrorism occurs, and patterns of government response (Crenshaw, 1983, pp. 21–37). One can cite the Tupamaros' campaign of urban terrorism in Uruguay in the early 1970s which eventually led to the suspension of civil liberties and an end to democratic government – and the resort to new coercive policies that put an equally decisive end to the Tupamaros (see Sloan, 1979). Uruguay, however, offers the only contemporary case in which terrorism led to a *structural* change away from democracy. The prevailing response in Western democracies facing substantial terrorism has been to strengthen legal and police instrumentalities, not to suspend civil liberties or abolish democratic institutions.[7] In fact Dror concludes that 'until now democracies as a whole have been successful in containing and handling terrorism' (Dror, 1983, p. 81). Arrests and prosecutions of terrorists have tended to increase as a consequence; whether harassment of non-violent dissidents or other political abuses have also increased is a matter of dispute. This entire set of interrelated questions about the outcomes of terrorism is well worth careful comparative research, especially but not only in democratic societies. Figure 5.1

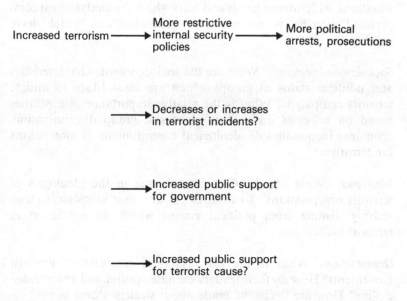

Figure 5.1

provides a basic causal model. Which of the final outcomes is likely depends on a variety of factors which need specification: What kind of regime, facing what kinds of internal opposition? What kinds of more restrictive policies, and against whom are they used? A set of comparative and longitudinal case-studies is the most promising way to begin research on the subject.

IV COMPARATIVE ANALYSIS OF TERRORIST GROUPS

Cross-national analysis (see Section III) makes it possible to identify the kinds of countries and conflicts in which terrorism is likely to be used. At the group level of analysis the research questions are more narrowly focused. They also require a shift in perspective away from the search for abstract patterns in quantitative data. It is necessary, when dealing with specific groups and comparisons among them, to take a close and unbiased look at their situations, beliefs, strategic decisions, and internal dynamics. In other words such groups must be examined on their own terms, not merely as 'security threats' but as organisations of real people, acting in concrete sociopolitical situations, with intense hopes and fears which the analyst must comprehend if s/he is to arrive at generalisations which have validity.

Socioeconomic origins.   What are the socioeconomic characteristics and political status of groups which are most likely to initiate terrorist campaigns? What is the relative importance of hostilities based on religious and ethnic cleavages, group discrimination, economic inequalities or ideological commitments as motivations for terrorism?

Ideologies.   What are the dominant themes in the ideologies of terrorist organisations? To what extent are their ideological views sharply distinct from political groups which do not resort to terrorist tactics?

Organisation.   What is the organisational structure of terrorist movements? How do their leaders exercise control and enforce discipline? How are decisions made about strategies and tactics?

International linkages. What kinds of external encouragement and assistance are received by particular terrorist groups? What are the effects of external support on groups' strategies, tactics, and persistence?

Dynamics of movements' rise and decline. What are the specific political circumstances in which groups choose terrorist tactics? Why do some groups persist in terrorist campaigns much longer than others? What conditions (concessions, repression, failure, exhaustion) lead to the disintegration of terrorist groups or basic shifts in their strategies of political action?

Comparative case-study is the ideal method for the analysis of these kinds of issues. By 'comparative' I mean studies which use a common framework to study and contrast a number of groups. It is necessary to study several groups – the more the better, within the limit of resources – to ensure that a particular observed pattern or relationship is a common one rather than idiosyncratic to one group. Since there are enormous differences among groups using terrorist tactics, a useful step prior to comparative analysis is to categorise groups. Wilkinson (1979, p. 104) proposes a fourfold categorisation that is a useful beginning-point:

1. nationalist or ethnic minority movements;
2. ideological sects with revolutionary objectives;
3. exile or *émigré* groups with separatist or revolutionary goals in their country of origin;
4. transnational groups with 'world revolutionary' goals.

We would expect that the origins, ideologies, organisation, and dynamics of groups would vary systematically among these types. Merari (1978) has proposed a typology based on groups' 'target population' and base of operations. Based on these distinctions he specifies how goals and modes of operation are likely to vary among groups. Comparative case-studies guided by such typologies could either be restricted to groups of one type (a 'most similar cases' research design) or include cases of several or all types ('a most different cases' design). The 'most similar cases' design is typified by Hoffman's (1982) comparative study of right-wing terrorist movements in Italy, West Germany and France. A 'most different cases' approach is Strinkowski's (1985) comparative analysis of organisational characteristics of the Irgun, the IRA and the Weather Underground. The general recommendation is that both kinds of study should be done in order to maximise knowledge about similarities within types *and* similarities/differences among them.

It should be obvious that case-studies can be only as good as the information (data) available on groups. There are also very substantial differences among case-studies, which range from narrative descriptions to rigorous theoretical analyses. Eckstein's 1975 essay on 'Case Study and Theory in Political Science' makes a strong argument about how to conduct theoretically-guided case-studies which should be required reading for anyone doing case-studies of terrorist phenomena. Two examples of theoretically-guided case-studies in conflict analysis are Wedge's comparative analysis (1969) of the causes of revolution in Brazil in 1964 and the Dominican Republic in 1965; and Dahlgren's retrospective study (1978) of the causes of the Chilean *coup* of 1973. Both studies made use of a theoretical model which required the authors to *make* (that is, to code or estimate) data on a number of variables. Good case-studies generally require more and better data than aggregate studies of patterns and trends.

The case-study literature on movements using terrorism is abundant. The narrative approach is prevalent: two informative recent examples are Sayari's (1985) analysis of generational changes among left-wing terrorists in Turkey (actually a kind of longitudinal case-study) and Sundberg's (1982) detailed account, based on trial records, of the establishment and disintegration of a German–Swedish terrorist group. Comparative case-studies which make systematic use of an analytic or theoretical framework are more rare. J. Bowyer Bell has written a series of excellent case-studies (Bell, 1974, 1977a, 1978, 1979), some of them comparative, which are widely acknowledged for their 'rare authenticity' (Schmid, 1983, p. 419). Bell knows his subjects well and communicates his understanding with great facility. But his studies also reflect an impatience with analytic frameworks and general theoretical questions, and as a consequence they contribute less than they could to cumulative knowledge and valid generalisations about terrorist movements. a contrasting approach is a recent, thus far unpublished study by Strinkowski (1985) of the organisational characteristics of three revolutionary terrorist movements. He relies on secondary sources for an analytic comparison of these groups' processes of recruitment, decision-making, intelligence-gathering, operational control, and maintenance of internal discipline (see also Pike, 1966; Bell, 1974; Wolf, 1978). Another example is a set of studies of the group dynamics of left- and right-wing German terrorist groups by Groebel and Feger. Data on 250 members of such groups are used to analyse the effects of such factors as emotional reinforcement and forced compliance in the recruitment and retention of members; the results are integrated into a process model of the motivations of group members (Groebel and Feger, 1982; Groebel, 1986).[8]

Much might be done to systematise information on terrorist movements:

1. *One approach is to collect and code information on all oppositional groups which have used terroristic tactics.* The intelligence community has some such information but it is not publicly accessible. Researchers relying on news sources have compiled lists of groups involved in political violence, some narrow and some broad (for example, Mickolus, 1979, pp. 170–6; Jongman, 1983). Mickolus's list consists of groups which claimed responsibility for incidents and categorises the incidents, but the published version provides no substantive information on the groups other than their names. Jongman's 'directory' is the most comprehensive, identifying some 1500 groups and parties which have been either initiators *or* targets of 'armed violence', but it is indiscriminately broad and relatively little information is provided (in the published compilation) on each group. Virtually none of the questions about terrorist groups at the head of this section could be answered using this compilation.

2. *A second, potentially complementary approach is to codify the information from chronologies and in-depth case-studies in accordance with a generaly analytic scheme that specified theoretically-relevant variables and coding categories.* The information bank might be structured similarly to the Human Relations Area Files – a codified set of information on world cultures derived from the field research of anthropologists. An information bank of this sort on terrorist movements would be far more selective than 'directories' in its coverage of groups, but would characterise each in far greater depth. A pioneering effort of this sort is under way at Rand and has thus far been applied to twenty-nine groups. The analytic framework employed indentifies 150 attributes of terrorist groups including aspects of their organisation, leadership, ideology, funding, and operations. Preliminary analyses have been designed to demonstrate the utility of such a data base, e.g. comparisons of groups according

to the lethality of their attacks and the probability that they will target Americans (Cordes, Jenkins and Kellen, 1985).

A major component in any comparative analysis of terrorist groups is a careful dissection of their ideologies. A useful categorisation of their ideologies is proposed by Lopez (1982, pp. 4–5):

(i)   minority nationalism,
(ii)   social anarchism,
(iii) revolutionary Marxism,
(iv)   'New Left' syndicalism,
(v)   reactionary neo-fascism.

Similar distinctions are used by Wilkinson (1979, cited above) to categorise groups *per se*. The nature of ideological appeals influences who is attracted to a group and its potential for gathering widespread support. For example, minority nationalism has considerably greater potential appeal and potential staying-power in most multi-ethnic societies than has, say, social anarchism. Since radical ideologies embody conceptions of the ideal society and identify those who stand in the way of its realisation, they structure the general strategies of conflict. The strategic and tactical elements of ideology also help to determine the way movements are organised and their choices of targets (see Merari, 1978). Evidence about these components of ideology can be found in most good case-studies of terrorist movements. The ideologies of left-wing terrorists in West Germany have been evaluated at great length in the first of five volumes on *Analysen zum Terrorismus* issued by the Minister of Internal Affairs (Fetscher and Rohrmoser, 1981). What is lacking is *systematic and comparative* content analysis of terrorist doctrines and how they affect support, persistence, organisation, strategies and targets.

There is also much that could be done using *cross-national analysis* to identify the kinds of groups most likely to initiate cycles of political violence generally and terrorism in particular. A number of empirical studies have shown that ethnic, regional, and religious minorities are disproportionately involved in rebellions, civil wars, and revolutionary movements (see Barrows, 1976; Gurr and Lichbach, 1979; Rebushka and Shepsle, 1972). This is particularly true of minorities (and subjugated majorities) which are the objects of more or less systematic discrimination by dominant groups. Some of these groups, not all of them, respond by mounting campaigns of terrorism. Cross-national research on the correlates of past and present conflict should make it possible to specify which kinds of minorities, in which kinds of socio-economic conditions, and in response to what kinds of political circumstances, have high potential for future terrorism. This research should have at least one result of direct policy relevance: it would make it possible to construct *profiles of potentially terrorist groups* which are analogous to individual-level profiles of potential skyjackers (Pickrel, 1977).

The dynamics of groups' involvement in terrorist activities pose a large set of questions, some of them summarised at the beginning of this section, which appear not to have been studied at all in the literature on oppositional terrorism. It is worth elaborating on them here. Only some groups with revolutionary or separatist objectives rely primarily on terrorist strategies, and many of them have a history of using other kinds of political action. There are non-violent as well as violent means toward these political ends, and also alternative violent means: *coup d'état*, urban uprisings, protracted guerrilla warfare. So in what circumstances are decisions made to use terrorism? Let me propose two sharply distinct etiologies: (i) relatively large, widely-supported groups involved in long-term conflict make strategic shifts from other modes of political action to campaigns of terrorism; and (ii) Small groups, newly established or breakaways from older groups – including many of Wilkinson's 'ideological sects' – choose terrorist strategies from the outset. The factors relevant to a general explanation of such strategic choices include the size and organisation of the groups, their ideologies, the extent of their potential public support, external influence and support, the results of their previous political actions, and the opportunities inherent in the policies and weakness or strength of the state.

The dynamics of group persistence and decline are equally complex. We need to know more about why terrorism is persistent and recurring among groups such as the Catholics in Northern Ireland, the Basques of Spain, and the revolutionary left in post-war West Germany, yet has been short-lived and easily suppressed among similarly-situated groups such as the Québecois in Canada, separatists in the South Tyrol, and the revolutionary left in the USA. Only part of the answer lies in government strategies of concession and coercion. The grievances, ideologies, and organisation of the groups are equally relevant; so are broad patterns of public support and opposition for their causes.

Parallel to this general analysis of movements is the need for more fine-grained study of sequences of actions and counteractions. Terrorist tactics, like all other kinds of political action, involve a learning process (see Pitcher and Hamblin, 1982). The issue for research is to determine how the consequences of particular episodes affect future tactics, including decisions about whether to persist with terrorism or to shift to other strategies. One beginning point for this kind of empirical work is Post's (1984, 1985) specification of the likely effects of retaliation on the dynamics of terrorist groups (see also Crenshaw, in chapter 2 of this volume).

In brief, to study the dynamics of the onset and decline of terrorist campaigns requires systematic research on almost all the more specific questions and issues raised at the group level of analysis.

V THE ANALYSIS OF INCIDENTS

Many aspects of the study of terrorist incidents have already been considered. The study of sequences of incidents in their political context is part of the analysis of the group dynamics of terrorist movements (IV, above). The study of the trends and diffusion of incidents in the aggregate is essential to the mapping of global and national patterns of terror (II and III above). At issue here is the information sought through the comparative analysis of specific incidents.

Targets. What are the most likely and vulnerable targets of terrorist incidents? How can they be 'hardened', or the risks to individuals minimised?

Incident outcomes. What are the outcomes of terrorist incidents? What kinds of outcomes or responses minimise the likelihood that incidents will be repeated or imitated?

Negotiations. What are the sequences of action in barracade and hostage-taking situations? What negotiating strategies by authorities minimise the risks to hostages?

The media. What are the effects of the mass media's treatment of terrorist incidents on public attitudes and on the contagion of terrorism?

These are among the most-thoroughly-studied questions in the empirical literature on oppositional terrorism. With regard to the study of targets, for example, Fattah (1981) has proposed a general typology, Shaw *et al.* (1977) discuss approaches to analysing the extent of threat, and Karber and Mengel (1978) develop a conceptual framework for the study of terrorism targeted at the nuclear industry (Karber and Mengel, 1978; see also Mullen, 1980). There are also a variety of technical studies aimed at enhancing the physical security of specific kinds of targets (for brief reviews see Wardlaw, 1982, pp. 166–70; and Mickolus, Heyman and Schlotter, 1980, pp. 176–7). Empirical research, however, is limited mainly to macroanalysis of types of targets in incidents of transnational terrorism (see II above) and to intensive microstudies aimed at protecting particular types of targets such as nuclear installations, commercial aircraft, and business executives. This leaves largely unstudied a broad middle range of questions. What kinds of targets are chosen by different kinds of terrorist groups? This issue is best studied at the national level of analysis, using data on both domestic and transnational incidents (III above). A more-narrowly-focused question concerns the ways in which existing terrorist groups have altered their choices of targets in response to changing opportunities and risks. This is a topic best examined as part of the comparative analysis of groups (see IV above).

The pioneering empirical research on outcomes has been carried out by Brian Jenkins and his associates at the Rand Corporation, including studies of seventy-seven kidnapping and barricade incidents between 1968 and 1975 (Jenkins, Johnson and Ronfeldt, 1977) and forty-eight embassy takeovers between 1971 and 1980 (Jenkins, 1980). The results make it possible to estimate the terrorists' likelihood of success and the results of various tactical responses. The former study is the source of the widely-cited observation that in nearly eight out of ten cases (more precisely 77 per cent) all members of a kidnapping team escape death or capture. The same study shows that all hostages were eventually released in 77 per cent of cases. Hostages were most likely to be killed either during rescue attempts or by kidnappers whose demands were rejected. These studies are limited to transnational incidents, however. Assessment of patterns in the outcomes of domestic terrorist incidents should be a key objective in future data-collection efforts.

At the micro-level there is a great deal of lore and expertise on the conduct of negotiations in hostage-taking incidents. Some of this is derived from Rand's comparative studies of incidents (above). Most, however, is based on close observation of a relatively small number of cases and consists of prescriptions about negotiating tactics. Miller's analyses are particularly well-grounded in case-studies and first-hand observation (Miller, 1979, 1980). Simulation is another approach, developed by Sloan (1980, 1981) to train potential negotiators to understand the dynamics of hostage-taking situations. The principal methodological criticism to be made of studies and prescriptions based on observation concerns the (non)representativeness of the cases from which the generalisations are derived. Clearly the effectiveness of different kinds of negotiating strategies depends on the psychological traits and political objectives of the hostage-takers. It is also influenced by the cultural backgrounds of perpetrators and negotiators. An obvious strategy for improved knowledge of hostage-taking situations is to carry out comparative studies (using information on real episodes and simulations) of a *substantial and representative sample* of incidents, domestic and transnational. Wherever possible such studies should develop information (by retrospective interviews) with actors on both sides of the incident, including hostages and perpetrators as well as authorities.

Methods and frameworks used for analysing the role of communications in the terrorism process are largely outside the scope of this chapter. The flow of information about terrorist incidents is relevant to a number of the levels of analysis considered here. There is first the immediate, incident- and group-specific level of analysis: how the media treat the actions and demands of perpetrators in a particular episode. A comparative analysis of the Western media's portrayal of terrorist incidents and purposes is Schmid and de Graaf (1982). One contingent question is what are the consequences of media treatment for mass opinion: the extent of public knowledge about the initiators, and affective changes – whether of sympathy or antipathy toward the perpetrators – or a more generalised state of fear or anger (see Jenkins 1981)? This kind of question is best treated at the national level of analysis using opinion survey techniques, as Crelinsten (1978) has proposed. A very different question concerns national and transnational contagion: the extent to which widely-publicised tactics and ideologies of terrorist movements strike a respondent chord among dissident groups or hostile loners elsewhere. Redlick (1979) has developed a conceptual argument about the transnational flow of information about terrorism and its effects on political action elsewhere. The statistical studies of diffusion, cited above (Part II), assume but do not test directly for the existence of such effects. For general commentaries on the communication of information on terrorism see Schmid and de Graaf (1982); Schmid (1983), pp. 219–24; and Wardlaw (1982) pp. 76–86.

VI THE INDIVIDUAL LEVEL OF ANALYSIS

Some research at the national, group, and incident levels of analysis rests on crucial assumptions about the psyches of people involved in terrorism or affected by it. Potential terrorists are usually assumed to be motivated by ideological beliefs and to make rationalistic choices about strategies and tactics. Hostage-takers are expected to respond in predictable ways to the strategems of negotiators. Audiences are assumed to be informed, angered, frightened, or perhaps merely titillated by news of terrorist episodes. The only direct way to test the accuracy of any of these assumptions is to gather information directly at the individual level. These are some of the crucial questions raised in the literature.

Recruitment and training. Which kinds of individuals, from what backgrounds, are most susceptible to joining organisations using political violence? How are they recruited and socialised into the group? How are the inhibitions against taking high risks and using personal violence overcome?

Motivation. What is the relative importance of perceived deprivation, rational choice, and appeals to group solidarity in motivating members of terrorist groups? What are the differences in the psychological traits, perceptions, and motives of leaders versus rank-and-file versus sympathisers?

Exit. Under what circumstances will individuals give up violent activities? What are the effects of repeated failure and the threat or actuality of sanctions on continued membership in terrorist groups?

Hostages. What are the psychological effects of being held hostage?

The motivational question is paramount because it underlies individuals' decisions about joining terrorist groups and their behaviour once they are members. It is necessary at the outset to abandon *a priori* assumptions that all terrorists are mentally unstable, or victims of oppression, or agents of international conspiracies.[9] Such ideologically-derived assumptions predetermine the choice and interpretation of evidence and as such are worse than useless guides to empirical research.

We should also be prepared to jettison some pet theoretical propositions, to the effect that all participants in political violence are motivated by discontent (Gurr, 1970) or the rational pursuit of self-interest (Tilly, 1978). It is more plausible, and fruitful for empirical research, to posit three general kinds of dispositions to political action:

1. a *reactive* disposition which is a response to perceived deprivation and threat;
2. a *normative* disposition which is a function of cultural experience, social beliefs (including ideologies) and peer reinforcement;
3. a *utilitarian* disposition which is based on calculated assessment of the potential gains and risks of alternative courses of actions.

The critical theoretical and empirical question is the relative importance of these kinds of dispositions for individuals in organisations using violence. The answers are variable: they will differ for any given individual in the course of his or her career in the organisation, and will be influenced by his or her position in the organisation. And the model dispositions (their relative importance as well as their content) will differ among terrorist organisations and at different points in their organisational life-cycles.

Methods for eliciting this kind of information are well established in the behavioural sciences but active members of violent political organisations are rarely willing to submit to systematic observation, structured interviews, or projective tests. Prospective and retrospective research is somewhat more promising. Survey techniques have been adapted to the study of samples of people with high levels of political activism, for example, riot observers and participants (in US cities in the 1960s; see, for example, Sears and McConahay, 1973) and student activists in contemporary West Germany (Schmidtchen, 1983; Muller and Opp, 1986). Such studies can provide information on the dispositions prevailing in groups from which violent activists are most likely to be recruited.

The most detailed and focused information on terrorists, guerrilla fighters, and other users of violence comes from personal statements, interviews and autobiographies. Occasionally active revolutionaries have been studied, for example, Slote's (1967) intensive analysis of a young Venuzuelan revolutionary – a young man who had not yet been involved in violence. Some violent activists chronicle their ideas and activities in forms that are eventually accessible to behavioural scientists. Active terrorists and their friends and family-members sometimes consent to be interviewed by scholars and jour-nalists, including the dozen Red Brigade members whose views and life experiences are portrayed by Silj (1978). Imprisoned terrorists and revolutionaries can be interviewed, for example Knutson's (1981) in-depth study of a Croatian skyjacker, Morf's (1970) inter-views with imprisoned members of the Canadian FLQ, and Pike's (1966) research on captured members of the Viet Cong. Other terrorists have written memoirs that can be used in secondary analysis: a half-dozen examples are cited in Schmidt (1983) pp. 270–1. One of the most creative studies on this subject is Kellen (1979), who uses interview and written testimony from five terrorists (three German, one Croatian, one Japanese) to generalise about their individual experiences and the characteristics and dynamics of terrorist groups (see also Kellen, 1982). But there is often an element of self-justification in the statements on which such studies are based and they are seldom revealing about day-to-day doubts and decisions. A rare, perhaps unique, exception is Guevara's (1968) diary of his Bolivian campaign.

Research based on interviews and memoirs is also open to criticism because of the small numbers of subjects and the fact that they are probably not representative, either of the range of member-ship within particular organisations or of different types of groups using terrorism. Nonetheless the psychologically-informed analysis of this kind of individual data provides a degree of understanding that is inaccessible by any other research technique. And the results of such analysis are devastating to simplistic theories about the motivations, psychodynamics and personality types of members of terrorist and revolutionary groups (as proposed for example by Kaplan, 1978, and Strentz, 1981).

An alternative approach, which can also be generalised, is the 'profile study' based on the biographies, motivations, and behavioural traits of a particular type of violent activist. One example is the United States Federal Aviation Administration's

(FAA) work in developing a profile of potential skyjackers which specifies thirty-five traits of known skyjackers (Pickrel, 1977; Schultz, 1980, pp. 24–5). Another applied study attempts to assess the criminal and terrorist threat to US nuclear programmes by examining the attributes and motivations of individuals who have been involved in nuclear-related incidents or in analogous non-nuclear crimes (Bass, Jenkins and Kellen, 1982). Both of these studies are prompted by a particular kind of security concern. A broader kind of study is Russell and Miller's (1977) compilation of information on some 350 'known terrorists' from eighteen groups active in different world regions. They use the data to portray the modal demographic characteristics, social background, education, recruitment, end political philosophies of their subjects. Another set of studies is based on information gathered in team research on 250 German terrorists. Their family backgrounds and life histories are analysed by Schmidtchen (1981), who reports that in comparison with their peers more of them had lost parents before adolescence or had had severe social conflicts with parents and others. Groebel and Feger (1982) have used information on the same individuals to analyse the factors which led them to join and remain in terrorist groups.

These last two approaches – in-depth psychological analysis of individual terrorists and biographical/behavioural profiles of large numbers of them – potentially complement one another. What is lacking is agreement on a common conceptual framework that would make it possible to structure and cumulate the information. Such individual-level research should be explicitly designed to provide answers to the kinds of questions raised here and at the group level of analysis: the kinds of social situations from which potential terrorists are recruited, their dispositions to action and how they change over time, the factors which influence their decisions and actions while members of violent organisations. Elements for an empirically-grounded framework of this sort are to be found in the writings of Crenshaw (Chapter 2 of this volume), Groebel (1986), Post (1984), and Kellen (1979, 1982).

The three different kinds of dispositions identified above – reactive, normative, utilatarian – could provide the basis for a composite conceptual framework. Let me propose a specific theoretical argument as an example of its utility. The proposal is that recruitment to terrorist activities proceeds through three stages:

1. At the first stage an existing organisation which advocates political violence attracts potential recruits from young people in groups which already have intense grievances – an ethnic or religious minority; unemployed university graduates. The youth who are most susceptible to recruitment are those who have had serious personal problems and conflicts with parents and others in authority. Their personal and social grievances, combined with the vague expectation that revolutionary action with like-minded others will help to resolve them, provide the primary motivation for joining.

2. During the second stage, new members are socialised to accept the organisation's ideology and goals and receive much encouragement and pressure from new friends to accept the group's control of their lives. Normative dispositions become the major source of continued commitment, and alternatively of decisions to leave the organisation at this stage. Peer pressures are also critical in inducting new members into acts of violence.

3. After the threshold of violence has been passed, however, the utilitarian mode of behaviour becomes increasingly important. That is, members continue to carry out the group's missions both because of their commitment to the group and because they are persuaded, by leaders and by their own estimations, that the acts are instrumental to the group's goals.

All those who are deeply implicated in the group's actions, leaders and followers, are also likely to calculate that the costs of leaving the group are unacceptably high. This rationalistic mode of thought tends to be dominant among leaders and in fact is one of the traits which determines tactical success and promotion of individuals into leadership positions.

This does not imply that the objectives sought by the group are 'rational' from the viewpoint of an external observer. Objectives follow from ideologies whose assumptions may be unrealistic and whose appeal to 'true believers' derives more from their emotional needs and the normative pressures exerted by others in the group than from the content of the ideology. Members are rationalistic to the extent that they make rational calculations about how best to maintain the group and to plan and execute incidents and campaigns. The evidence is that leaders of most terrorist groups tend to be quite rational in the means they use to pursue ends others think are irrational (see Strinkowski, 1985).

This very general mode of motivation and recruitment may prove accurate for some kinds of groups and individuals, not for others. The point is that some model of this sort should be used to structure the collection and interpretation of psychological evidence on violent activists from a variety of sources. It illustrates once again a point made at the beginning of the paper, that questions and theoretical framework should guide the collection and analysis of information.

Research on the psychological consequences of being taken hostage is considerably simpler than research on the motivations of the perpetrators because most hostages survive, most are willing to be interviewed, and many need and seek psychiatric help (see, for example, Ochberg *et al.*, 1982; Miller, 1980; and empirical work by Fields, 1981). Interviews with victims can be instructive about the *process of terrorisation*, i.e. its effects on target audiences. Its only potential utility for aiding our knowledge of *terrorists* is to provide information about how one distinctive type of terrorist acts under stress. I do not know of any published studies which make systematic use of information gathered from hostages to develop profiles or models of hostage-takers' behaviour.

VII CONCLUSIONS: A PRESCRIPTION FOR BETTER RESEARCH

This survey of the empirical literature both amplifies and qualifies my suggestion, at the outset of this paper, that the research questions being asked about the causes and consequences of terrorism are more interesting than most of the evidence brought to bear on them. Although there is a promising cumulation of findings in several research areas, the overall judgement is that there is far too little empirically-grounded research on oppositional terrorism. The principal exceptions are the incident-based analyses of transnational terrorism (mainly the work of Jenkins, Mickolus and their collaborators), in-depth case-studies of a few revolutionary and terrorist movements (to which Bell is the leading contributor), and knowledge about the personal characteristics and life histories of actual and potential terrorists (thanks to such scholars as Kellen,

Knutson, Post, Groebel and Schmidtchen). The paucity of good systematic research on most aspects of terrorism contrasts sharply with the abundant literature on international conflict, political protest, revolution, and *coups* (see the reviews in Gurr, 1980a, and Zimmermann, 1983). One can identify some good theoretical and conceptual essays and also point out a few empirical and case-studies which should be exemplars for future research. But most of the literature consists of naive description, speculative commentary, and prescriptions for 'dealing with terrorism' which would not meet minimum research standards in the more established branches of conflict and policy analysis.

I do not think that the inadequacies of research on oppositional terrorism can be blamed on the lack of researchable questions or appropriate methodologies. Nor should it be attributed to a lack of social scientific talent: some very competent researchers have worked on aspects of the subject. In my view there are two more fundamental problems, one having to do with the ways in which the purpose of research on terrorism has been defined, the other with the lack of sufficient data.

The problem with regard to research purposes is that most research on oppositional terrorism aims principally at *prophylaxis*: how to control and respond to terrorists and terrorism. There is nothing intrinsically wrong with that objective, but in practice it has subtly but persistently distorted the research process. Rather than doing hard and careful research on the *causes* and *dynamics* of terrorism, most researchers – including many of those doing empirical work – devote their attention to examining its trends, its effects (outcomes, victims, media attention), and how best to respond (scenarios of hostage negotiation, analysis of national and international policies). In the language of social scientific analysis, most systematic research on terrorism treats groups and incidents as 'independent variables' rather than 'dependent variables' and focuses on their traits and consequences rather than their causes. Causes – structural, social and individual – should receive as much or more attention. To draw an anology from medicine, another field of applied research, it is as if medical researchers were to concentrate their efforts on the epidemiology and treatment of disease without studying its causes. It is possible through systematic observation of the spread of diseases (or terrorist tactics) and how they respond to different treatments (or government policies) to arrive at some useful generalisations. But prevention and optimally effective 'treatment' both require a reasonably complete and detailed understanding of etiology.

The other problem is the lack of enough reliable data for the analysis of the entire range of questions about terrorism: etiology, processes, and outcomes. It is not coincidental that most of the good empirical research on terrorism cited in this review has come from three groups that have compiled substantial data sets on terrorist phenomena: the Rand Corporation, Edward Mickolus and his associates, and the commission on terrorism established by the West German Ministry of Internal Affairs (see note 8). Repeatedly in this chapter I have referred to important issues that cannot be researched adequately because the necessary kinds of information have not been compiled. In fact there is much data, especially on incidents and groups, which have been compiled by American intelligence and law enforcement agencies and by private research organisations working under contract or for corporate clients (for a survey see Fowler, 1981). The first problem is that most of them are either classified or proprietary, which means that few scholars have had any input into the design of the coding systems and equally few have access to the data sets. The second problem is that most of such data sets are not comprehensive but oriented to the interests of the sponsoring agencies and paying clients. A senior intelligence analyst observed, in response to a public presentation of this argument, that the CIA has 'the best data in the United States on terrorism that the government believes is threatening' but pointed out that much of it cannot be 'shared out', even within the intelligence community, because it comes from foreign intelligence agencies. This illustrates in a nutshell the issues to which I have alluded: the distorting effects of a policy focus on the kinds of data collected, and the inaccessibility of what may or may not be 'the best data' for basic research on terrorism.

Let me highlight the principal omissions in the publicly-available data:

1. There are no comprehensive, current data sets on incidents of domestic terrorism. As a consequence there can be no analyses of their trends, diffusion, or of the relations between transnational and domestic conflicts.[10]
2. There are no data sets which provide systematic information about the identities and characteristics of groups which use

terrorist strategies. As a result we cannot specify with any precision what kinds of groups are most likely to use terror, or the circumstances in which opposition groups shift toward or away from the use of terror, or trace and compare the life-cycles of violent political groups.

3. There are no broadly-based data sets with coded information on the outcomes of terrorist campaigns or on government responses to episodes of domestic terrorism. Therefore it is not possible to anticipate the effects of success or failure on terrorist groups, nor to test the effects of different kinds of government policies toward domestic terrorism.

4. There is no systematic compilation of information from case-studies about ideologies, recruitment practices, organisation, decision-making, or command and control in violent political groups. Therefore the ways in which they operate and how they are likely to respond to changing circumstances and counter-terror policies is largely a matter of speculation.

5. There is no system or common framework for cumulating information on the psychological characteristics, recruitment, and careers of members of terrorist movements. Therefore we have mostly impressionistic evidence about the kinds of people likely to join and lead terrorist organisations, and the kinds of incentives and threats which might induce them to alter their behaviour.

One major recommendation follows directly from this analysis. There is a compelling need to establish procedures for the collection, codification, and analysis of basic information on domestic and transnational terrorism. Such data should be gathered globally, for all countries and world regions. The procedures should be designed with the collaboration of a number of researchers who have done basic and applied research on the subject. The data should relate to four different levels of analysis: individual, incident, group, and national. The data should be gathered and codified as an ongoing activity, with simultaneous (re)coding of the same kinds of information back into the recent past (at least to 1968). The operation should be established in a university research centre or institute, insulated from direct involvement in policy-making or operations. Such an institute should have its own research staff and visiting scholars. And its reports and codified information should be publicly available to all researchers interested in the analysis of terrorism. Herbert

Kelman's comments about foreign policy research, made nearly twenty years ago, are equally appropriate to the contemporary study of terrorism:

> Research that is tied to foreign policy or military operations is, of necessity, conceived within the framework of existing policy. While it may be legitimate in its own right, it does not fulfil the function of providing new frameworks that would not normally emerge out of the policy-making apparatus itself ... For research that is capable of questioning the assumptions of current policy and of introducing new perspectives, it is necessary to turn to independent outside agencies, and particularly to the universities ... To be maximally useful, the research should not only be independent ... but it should also be carried out, as far as possible, within the context of an international community of scholars (Kelman, 1968, pp. 19, 20).

Notes

1. This is a revised version of a paper given to the Symposium on International Terrorism at the Defense Intelligence College, Washington, DC, in December 1985. I am indebted to the editors and to Jeffrey Ross for their comments on the paper and to other conference participants for calling relevant studies to my attention.
2. No purpose is served here by entering into the interminable debate about the esssence of terrorism. Alex Schmid's precise elaboration of Thornton's definition (Schmid, 1983, p. 111) encompasses the subject matter of virtually all the studies cited in this essay. Of course most empirical research focuses on particular sets or aspects of terrorist phenomena, not terror in its definitional entirety.
3. Other surveys which offer general recommendations for research on terrorism are Shaw, Hazlewood, Hayes and Harris (1977), Crelinsten (1978), Mickolus, Heyman and Schlotter (1980), Fowler (1980), and Wardlaw (1982).
4. Two recent surveys of empirical conflict research provide numerous examples of analytic techniques: Gurr (1980) and Zimmermann (1983). For detailed illustrations of the application of quantitative methods to problems of interest to intelligence analysts see Heuer (1978).
5. Bell (1977) contends that, given the inadequacies of hard data on terrorism, case-studies are preferable to quantitative comparative studies. See the discussion of case-studies as a method for analysis of groups, below.

6. In Mickolus's usage terror is transnational 'when, through the nationality or foreign ties of its perpetrators, its location, the nature of its institutional or human victims, or the mechanics of its resolution its ramifications transcend national boundaries' (Mickolus, 1979, p. 148). He reserves the term 'international' for transnational terrorism by groups controlled by sovereign states. Since such control is often unknowable (even to intelligence agencies) this essay uses the term 'transnational' to refer to all political terrorism which involves (in Mickolus's sense) nationals of more than one state. A more narrow and seemingly precise definition is used in the Rand chronology, where international terrorism is defined 'as incidents in which terrorists go abroad to strike their targets ... It excludes violence carried out by terrorists within their own country against their own nationals, and terrorism perpetrated by governments against their own nationals' (Cordes *et al.*, 1984, p. 1). The difference between these two definitions is at least partly responsible for the differences in aggregate numbers of terrorist events and deaths identified in the two sources (see Wardlaw, 1982, pp. 51–2). It is clear from a comparison of the two definitions, and from common sense, that the international dimension or implications of terrorist acts is a variable. Disagreements about precise boundaries distract attention from more fundamental questions: what conditions influence the degree to which terrorism is transnational? And to what extent are domestic and transnational terror (however defined) similar or different in their dynamics? Of course these questions cannot be studied systematically by limiting data collections to incidents defined *a priori* as transnational.

   There are other data sets which include national as well as transnational terror incidents: see the surveys by Fowler (1981) and Schmid (1983, pp. 245–82). Perhaps the most ambitious and comprehensive data collection has recently been initiated by Paul Wilkinson at the University of Aberdeen in cooperation with the Rand group headed by Brian Jenkins.

7. An uncommon exception was the Canadian federal government's use of emergency powers in 1970–1 in response to terrorism by the Quebec Liberation Front (FLQ). The federal government of West Germany, where oppositional terrorism has been far greater than in Canada, has enacted a variety of anti-terrorist measures which according to Wardlaw 'together probably amount to the most repressive anti-terrorist legislation in existence in a liberal democracy' (Wardlaw, 1982, p. 121). A detailed analysis of German legal and institutional responses is Pridham (1981).

8. The Groebel and Feger study is part of a large-scale inquiry into German terrorism commissioned in the late 1970s by the Minister of Internal Affairs of the Federal Republic of Germany. The work of the commission was published in five German-language volumes which appeared between 1981 and 1984, concerned with ideologies and strategy (vol. 1), biographies of terrorists (vol. 2), group processes (vol. 3), power and legitimacy (vol. 4/1), and protest and reaction (vol. 4/2). A critical overview is provided by Zimmerman (1985). Citations from

these studies in the bibliography of this chapter are Fetscher and Rohrmoser (1981), Groebel and Feger (1982) and Schmidtchen (1981, 1983).

9. For critiques of the 'mental instability' approach to explaining the behaviour of assassins and terrorists see Clarke (1982) and Corrado (1981). Representative of the psychodynamic approach is Kaplan (1986), which incorporates a more sophisticated version of the same kind of fallacy: that all people using terror have the same personality traits, including lack of self-esteem and pursuit of absolute ends.

10. Paul Wilkinson has begun a large-scale data collection of this sort at the University of Aberdeen, Scotland (personal communication). It remains to be seen what kinds of coded information will be included and whether the data will be generally available to other scholars.

References

Alexander, Yonah, Carlton, David, and Wilkinson, Paul (eds) (1979) *Terrorism: Theory and Practice* (Boulder, Colorado: Westview Press).

Alexander, Yonah, and Gleason, John M. (eds) (1981) *Behavioral and Quantitative Perspectives on Terrorism* (Oxford: Pergamon).

Barrows, Walter L. (1976) 'Ethnic Diversity and Political Instability in Black Africa', *Comparative Political Studies*, 9, pp. 139–70.

Bass, Gail and Jenkins, Brian M. (1983) *A Review of Recent Trends in International Terrorism and Nuclear Incidents Abroad* (Santa Monica, California: Rand Corporation N-1919-SL).

Bass, Gail, Jenkins, Brian M., and Kellen, Konrad (1982) *The Appeal of Nuclear Crimes to the Spectrum of Potential Adversaries* (Santa Monica, California: Rand Corporation R-2803-SL).

Bell, J. Bowyer (1974) *The Secret Army: The IRA 1916–1974* (Cambridge, Massachusetts: MIT Press).

Bell, J. Bowyer (1977a) *Terror Out of Zion: Irqun Zvai Leumi, LEHI, and the Palestine Underground, 1929–1949* (New York: St Martin's Press).

Bell, J. Bowyer (1977b) 'Trends on Terror: The Analysis of Political Violence', *World Politics* 29 (April) pp. 276–88.

Bell, J. Bowyer (1978) *A Time of Terror: How Democratic Societies Respond to Revolutionary Violence* (New York: Basic Books).

Bell, J. Bowyer (1979) *Assassin! The Theory and Practice of Political Violence* (New York: St Martin's Press).

Bell, J. Bowyer, and Gurr, Ted Robert (1979) 'Terrorism and Revolution in America', in Hugh Davis Graham and Ted Robert Gurr (eds) *Violence in America: Historical and Comparative Perspectives* (Beverly Hills, California: Sage Publications) pp. 329–48.

Box, George E. and George C. Tiao (1973) *Bayesian Inference in Statistical Analysis* (New York: Addison-Wesley).

Bueno de Mesquita, Bruce (1985) 'The War Trap Revisited: A Revised Expected Utility Model', *American Political Science Review*, 79 (March) pp. 156–73.

Clarke, James W. (1982) *American Assassins: The Darker Side of Politics* (Princeton, New Jersey: Princeton University Press).

Cook, Thomas and Donald T. Campbell (1979) *Quasiexperimentation* (New York: Houghton Miflin).

Cordes, Bonnie; Hoffman, Bruce; Jenkins, Brian M.; Kellen, Konrad; Moran, Sue, and Sater, William (1984) *Trends in International Terrorism, 1982 and 1983* (Santa Monica, California: Rand Corporation R-3183-SL).

Cordes, Bonnie, Jenkins, Brian M., and Kellen, Konrad (1985) *A Conceptual Framework for Analyzing Terrorist Groups* (Santa Monica, California: Rand Corporation R-3151).

Corrado, Raymond R. (1981) 'A Critique of the Mental Disorder Perspective of Political Terrorism', *International Journal of Law and Psychiatry*, 4, pp. 1–17.

Crelinsten, Ronald D. (1978) 'International Political Terrorism – A Challenge for Comparative Research', *International Journal of Comparative and Applied Criminal Justice*, 2 (no. 2) pp. 107–26.

Crenshaw, Martha (1981) 'The Causes of Terrorism', *Comparative Politics*, 13 (July 1981) pp. 379–99.

Crenshaw, Martha (ed.) (1983) *Terrorism, Legitimacy, and Power: The Consequences of Political Violence* (Middletown, Connecticut: Wesleyan University Press).

Dahlgren, Harold E. (1978) 'Operationalizing a Theoretical Model: Profiles of Violence in Argentina, Ethiopia, and Thailand', in Heuer (1978) pp. 59–104.

Dror, Yehezkel (1983) 'Terrorism as a Challenge to the Democratic Capacity to Govern', in Crenshaw (1983) pp. 65–90.

Eckstein, Harry (1975) 'Case Study and Theory in Political Science', in Fred I. Greenstein and Nelson W. Polsby (eds) *Handbook of Political Science, Vol. 7, Strategies of Inquiry* (Reading, Massachusetts: Addison-Wesley).

Fattah, Ezzat A. (1981) 'Terrorist Activities and Terrorist Targets: A Tentative Typology', in Alexander and Gleason (1981) pp. 11–33.

Fetscher, Iring, and Rohrmoser, Guenther (1981) *Ideologien und Stratgien: Analysen zum Terrorismus 1* (Opladen, West Germany: Westdeutscher Verlag).

Fields, Rona M. (1981) 'Psychological Sequelae of Terrorization', in Alexander and Gleason (1981) pp. 242–55.

Fowler, William W. (1980) *An Agenda for Quantitative Research on Terrorism* (Santa Monica, California: Rand Corporation P-6591).

Fowler, William W. (1981) *Terrorism Data Bases: A Comparison of Missions, Methods, and Systems* (Santa Monica, California: Rand Corporation N-1503-RC).

Fromkin, David (1975) 'The Strategy of Terrorism', *Foreign Affairs*, 53 (no. 4) pp. 683–98.

Gilboa, Eytan (1981) 'The Use of Simulation in Combatting Terrorism', *Terrorism* 5 (no. 3) pp. 265–79.

Gleason, John M. (1980) 'A Poisson Model of Incidents of International Terrorism in the United States', *Terrorism, An International Journal*, 4 (nos 1–4) pp. 259–76.

Govea, Rodger M. (n.d.) 'Is Terrorism Contagious?' (Cleveland, Ohio: Department of Political Science, Cleveland State University).

Groebel, Jo (1986) 'The Social Motivation of Western Terrorists', paper presented to the 7th Biennial Meeting of the International Society for Research on Aggression, Evanston, Illinois, July.

Groebel, Jo and Feger, Hubert (1982) 'Analyse von Strukturen terroristischer Gruppierungen', in Wanda Baeyer-Katte *et al.*, *Gruppenprozesse: Analysen zum Terrorismus 3* (Opladen, West Germany: Westdeutscher Veriag).

Guevara, Ernesto (1968) *The Diary of Che Guevara, Bolivia: November 7, 1966– October 7, 1967*, edited by Robert Scheer (New York: Bantam Books).

Gurr, Ted Robert (1970) *Why Men Rebel* (Princeton, New Jersey: Princeton University Press).

Gurr, Ted Robert (1979) 'Some Characteristics of Political Terrorism in the 1960s', in Stohl (1979) pp. 23–50.

Gurr, Ted Robert (ed.) (1980a) *Handbook of Political Conflict: Theory and Research* (New York: Free Press).

Gurr, Ted Robert (1980b) 'On the Outcomes of Violent Conflict', in Gurr (1980a) pp. 238–94.

Gurr, Ted Robert, and Lichbach, Mark I. (1979) 'A Forecasting Model for Political Conflict within Nations', in J. David Singer and Michael D. Wallace (eds) *To Augur Well: Early Warning Indicators in World Politics* (Beverly Hills, California: Sage Publications) pp. 153–93.

Hamilton, Lawrence C. (1981) 'Dynamics of Insurgent Violence: Preliminary Findings', in Alexander and Gleason (1981) pp. 229–41.

Heuer, Richards J., Jr. (ed.) (1978) *Quantitative Approaches to Political Intelligence: The CIA Experience* (Boulder, Colorado: Westview Press).

Heyman, Edward S. 'The Diffusion of Transnational Terrorism', in Shultz and Sloan (1980) pp. 190–244.

Heyman, Edward S., and Mickolus, Edward (1981) 'ITERATE: Monitoring Transnational Terrorism', in Alexander and Gleason (1981) pp. 153–74.

Hoffman, Bruce (1982) *Right-Wing Terrorism in Europe* (Santa Monica, California: Rand) N-1856-AF.

Hoffman, Bruce (1985) *Recent Trends in Palestinian Terrorism: II* (Santa Monica, California: Rand) P-7076.

Homer, Frederic D. (1979) 'Terror in the United States: Three Perspectives', in Stohl (1979) pp. 373–405.

Iris, Mark (1983) 'American Urban Riots Revisited', *American Behavioral Scientist*, 25 (January–February) pp. 333–52.

Jenkins, Brian M. (1977) 'Research Note: Rand's Research on Terrorism', *Terrorism* 1 (no. 1) pp. 85–95.

Jenkins, Brian M. (1980) *Embassies Under Siege: A Review of 48 Embassy Takeovers, 1971–1980* (Santa Monica, California: Rand) R-2651-RC.

Jenkins, Brian M. (1981) *The Psychological Implications of Media-Covered Terrorism* (Santa Monica, California: Rand) P-6627.

Jenkins, Brian M. Johnson, Janera, and Ronfeldt, David (1977) *Numbered Lives: Some Statistical Observations from 77 International Hostage Episodes* (Santa Monica, California: Rand) P-5627.

Johnpoll, Bernard K. (1976) 'Perspectives on Political Terrorism in the United States', in Yonah Alexander (ed.) *International Terrorism: National, Regional and Global Perspectives* (New York: Praeger) pp. 30–45.

Jongman, A. J. (1983) 'Appendix II: A World Directory of "Terrorist" Organizations and Other Groups' in Schmid (1983) pp. 284–416.

Kaplan, Abraham (1978) 'The Psychodynamics of Terrorism', *Terrorism, An International Journal*, 1 (nos. 3 and 4) pp. 237–54.

Karber, Phillip A. and Mengel, R. W. (1978) 'A Behavioral Analysis of the Adversary Threat to the Commerical Nuclear Industry – A Conceptual Framework for Realistically Assessing Threats', in Kramer (1978) pp. 7–20.

Kellen, Konrad (1979) *Terrorists – What are they Like? How Some Terrorists Describe their World and Actions* (Santa Monica, California: Rand) N-1300-SL.

Kellen, Konrad (1982) *On Terrorists and Terrorism* (Santa Monica, California: Rand) N-1942-RO.

Kelman, Herbert C. (1968) 'The Use of University Resources in Foreign Policy Research', *International Studies Quarterly*, 12 (March) pp. 16–37.

Knutson, Jeanne N. (1981) 'Social and Psychodynamic Pressures Toward a Negative Identity: The Case of an American Revolutionary Terrorist', in Alexander and Gleason (1981) pp. 105–50.

Kramer, Joel J. (ed.) (1977) *The Role of Behavioral Science in Physical Security: Proceedings of the First Annual Symposium, April 29–30, 1976* (Washington, DC: US Department of Commerce, National Bureau of Standards).

Kramer, Joel J. (ed.) (1978) *The Role of Behavioural Science in Physical Security: Proceedings of the Second Annual Symposium, March 23–24, 1977* (Washington, DC: US Department of Commerce, National Bureau of Standards).

Lewis-Beck, Michael S. (1980) *Applied Regression: An Introduction* (Quantitative Applications in the Social Sciences Series, No. 22. Beverly Hills, California: Sage Publications).

Lewis-Beck, Michael S. (1984) 'Some Economic Effects of Revolution: Models, Measurement, and the Cuban Evidence', *American Journal of Sociology*, 84 (no. 5) pp. 1127–49.

Lopez, George A. (1982) 'Terrorism, Worldviews and Problems of Policy', paper read to the International Studies Association Annual Meeting, Cincinnati, March 1982.

Lopez, George A., and Stohl, Michael (eds) (1986) *Government Violence and Repression: An Agenda for Research* (Westport, Connecticut: Greenwood Press).

Mack, Andrew (1981) 'The Utility of Terrorism', *Australia and New Zealand Journal of Criminology*, 14 (December) pp. 197–224.

Merari, Ariel (1978) 'A Classification of Terrorist Groups', *Terrorism, An International Journal*, 1 (nos 3–4) pp. 331–46.

Mickolus, Edward (1979) 'Transnational Terrorism', in Stohl (1979) pp. 147–90.

Mickolus, Edward, Heyman, Edward S. and Schlotter, James (1980) 'Responding to Terrorism: Basic and Applied Research', in Shultz and Sloan (1980) pp. 174–89.

Midlarsky, Manus I., Crenshaw, Martha, and Yoshida, Fumihiko (1980) 'Why Violence Spreads: The Contagion of International Terrorism', *International Studies Quarterly*, 24 (June) pp. 262–98.

Miller, Abraham H. (1979) 'Hostage Negotiations and the Concept of Transference', in Alexander, Carlton and Wilkinson (1979) pp. 137–58.

Miller, Abraham H. (1980) *Terrorism and Hostage Negotiations* (Boulder, Colorado: Westview Press).

Miller, Reuben (1985) 'Governments' Responses to International Terrorism Denver, Colorado: Graduate School of International Studies, University of Denver.

Miller, Edward N. and Karl-Dieter Opp (1986) 'Rational Choice and Rebellious Collective Action', *American Political Science Review*, vol. 80, no. 2, pp. 471–98.

Morf, Gustav (1970) *Terror in Quebec* (Toronto: Clark, Irwin).

Mullen, Robert K. (1980) 'Subnational Threats to Civil Nuclear Facilities and Safeguards Institutions', in Shultz and Sloan (1980) pp. 134–73.

Muller, Edward N., and Opp, Karl-Dieter (forthcoming) 'Rational Choice and Rebellious Collective Action', *American Political Science Review*, in press.

Ochberg, Frank M., *et al.* (eds) (1982) *The Victim of Terrorism* (Boulder, Colorado: Westview Press).

Pickrel, Evan (1977) 'Federal Aviation Administration's Behavioral Research Program for Defense Against Hijacking', in Kramer (1977) pp. 19–24.

Pike, Douglas (1966) *Viet Cong: The Organization and Techniques of the National Liberation Front of South Vietnam* (Cambridge, Massacusetts: MIT Press).

Pitcher, Brian L., and Hamblin, Robert L. (1982) 'Collective Learning in Ongoing Political Conflicts', *International Political Science Review*, 3 (no. 1) pp. 71–90.

Post, Jerrold M. (1984) 'Notes on a Psychodynamic Theory of Terrorist Behavior', *Terrorism*, 7, pp. 241–56.

Pridham, Geoffrey (1981) 'Terrorism and the State in West Germany During the 1970s: A Threat to Stability or a Case of Political Over-reaction?' in Juliet Lodge (ed.) *Terrorism: A Challenge to the State* (New York: St Martin's Press).

Rebushka, Alvin, and Shepsle, Kenneth A. (1972) *Politics in Plural Societies: A Theory of Democratic Instability* (Columbus, Ohio: Merrill).

Redlick, Amy Sands (1979) 'The Transnational Flow of Information as a Cause of Terrorism', in Alexander, Carlton, and Wilkinson (1979) pp. 73–95.

Russell, Charles A., and Miller, Bowman H. (1977) 'Profile of a Terrorist', *Terrorism*, (no. 1) pp. 17–34.

Sayari, Sabri (1985) *Generational Changes in Terrorist Movements: The Turkish Case* (Santa Monica, California: Rand) P-7124.

Schmid, Alex P., (1983) *Political Terrorism: A Research Guide to Concepts, Theories, Data Bases and Literature* (Amsterdam: North-Holland).

Schmid, Alex P., and de Graaf, Janny (1982) *Violence as Communication: Insurgent Terrorism and the Western News Media* (London and Beverly Hills: Sage Publications).

Schmidtchen, Gerhard (1981) 'Terroristische Karrieren', in Herbert Jaeger *et al., Lebenslaufanalysen: Analysen zum Terrorismus, 2* (Opladen, West Germany: Westdeutscher Verlag).

Schmidtchen, Gerhard (1983) 'Jugend und Staat', in Ulrich Matz and Gerhard Schmidtchen, *Gewalt und Legitimitaet: Analysen zum Terrorismus 4/1* (Opladen, West Germany: Westdeutscher Verlag).

Sears, David O., and McConahay, John B. (1973) *The Politics of Violence: The New Urban Blacks and the Watts Riot* (Boston: Houghton Mifflin).

Shaw, Eric D., Hazlewood, Leo, Hayes, Richard E., and Harris, Don R. (1977) 'Analyzing Threats from Terrorism: A Working Paper', in Kramer (1977) pp. 1–16.

Shultz, Richard H. (1980) 'The State of the Operational Art: A Critical Review of Anti-terrorist Programs', in Shultz and Sloan (1980) pp. 18–58.

Shultz, Richard H., Jr., and Sloan, Stephen (eds) (1980) *Responding to the Terrorist Threat: Security and Crisis Management* (Oxford: Pergamon).

Silj, Alessandro (1978) *Brigate Rosse – Stato Lo scontro spettacolo nella regia della stampa quotidiana* (Florence: Vallecchi).

Sloan, John W. (1979) 'Political Terrorism in Latin America: A Critical Analysis', in Stohl (1979) pp. 301–22.

Sloan, Stephen (1980) 'Simulating Terrorism: An Analysis of Findings Related to Tactical, Behavioral, and Administrative Responses of Participating Police and Military Forces', in Shultz and Sloan (1980) pp. 115–33.

Sloan, Stephen (1981) *Simulating Terrorism* (Norman, Oklahoma: University of Oklahoma Press).

Slote, Walter H. (1967) 'Case Analysis of a Revolutionary', in Frank Bonilla and Jose A. Silva Michelena (eds) *A Strategy for Research on Social Policy* (Cambridge, Massachusetts: MIT Press) pp. 241–311.

Stohl, Michael (ed.) (1979) *The Politics of Terrorism* (New York: Marcel Dekker).

Stohl, Michael, and Lopez, George A. (eds) (1984) *The State as Terrorist: The Dynamics of Governmental Violence and Repression* (Westport, Connecticut: Greenwood Press).

Strentz, Thomas (1981) 'The Terrorist Organizational Profile: A Psychological Role Model', in Alexander and Gleason (1981) pp. 86–104.

Strinkowski, Nicholas (1985) 'The Organizational Behavior of Revolutionary Groups', (Evanston, Illinois: Ph.D. dissertation, Department of Political Science, Northwestern University).

Sundberg, Jacob (1982) 'Operation Leo: Description and Analysis of A European Terrorist Operation', in Brian M. Jenkins (ed.) *Terrorism and Beyond: An International Conference on Terrorism and Low-Level Conflict* (Santa Monica, California: Rand) R-2714.

Targ, Harry R. (1979) 'Societal Structure and Revolutionary Terrorism: A Preliminary Investigation', in Stohl (1979) pp. 119–43.

Thompson, William R., and Rasler, Karen A. (1986) 'The Periodicity of Global Wars: An Empirical Assessment and Validation', paper read to the 1986 Annual Meeting of the International Studies Association, Anaheim, California.

Thornton, Thomas Perry (1964) 'Terror as a Weapon of Political Agitation', in Harry Eckstein (ed.) *Internal War: Problems and Approaches* (New York: Free Press) pp. 71–99.

Tilly, Charles (1978) *From Mobilization to Revolution* (Reading, Massachusetts: Addison-Wesley).

Wardlaw, Grant (1982) *Political Terrorism: Theory, Tactics, and Counter-Measures* (Cambridge: Cambridge University Press).

Wedge, Bryant (1969) 'Students and Political Violence: Brazil, 1964, and the Dominican Republic, 1965', *World Politics*, 21 (January) pp. 183–206.

Weinberg, Leonard (1979) 'Patterns of Neo-Fascist Violence in Italian Politics', *Terrorism*, 2 (nos 3–4) pp. 231–59.

Welfling, Mary B. (1979) 'Terrorism in Sub-Sahara Africa', in Stohl (1979) pp. 259–300.

Wilkinson, Paul (1979) 'Terrorist Movements', in Alexander, Carlton, and Wilkinson (1979) pp. 99–117.

Wolf, John B. (1978) 'Organization and Management Practices of Urban Terrorist Groups', *Terrorism*, 1 (no. 2) pp. 169–86.

Wright, Steve (1981) 'A Multivariate Time-Series Analysis of the Northern Irish Conflict 1969–76', in Alexander and Gleason (1981) pp. 283–328.

Zimmermann, Ekkart (1983) *Political Violence, Crises, and Revolution: Theories and Research* (Cambridge, Massachusetts: Schenkman).

Zimmermann, Ekkart (1985) 'Terrorist Violence in West Germany: Some Reflections on Recent Literature', paper read to the 13th World Congress of the International Political Science Association, Paris, July.

6 States, Terrorism and State Terrorism: The Role of the Superpowers

Michael Stohl

'the standard of justice depends on the equality of power to compel and that in fact the strong do what they have the power to do and the weak accept what they have to accept'

(Thucydides 404 BC)

'There are no rules in [this] game. Hitherto acceptable norms of human conduct do not apply. If the US is to survive, longstanding American concepts of 'fair play' must be reconsidered. We must develop effective espionage and counterespionage services and must learn to subvert, sabotage and destroy our enemies by more clever, more sophisticated, and more effective methods than those used against us. It may become necessary that the American people be made acquainted with, understand and support this fundamentally repugnant philosophy'

(Report of the United States Hoover Commission, 1950).

'Terror is an outstanding mode of conflict in localized primitive wars; and unilateral violence has been used to subdue satellite countries, occupied countries or dissident groups within a dictatorship'

(Thomas Schelling, 1966).

I INTRODUCTION

This chapter explores the context within which we may understand the persistence of state and in particular, superpower, violence and terrorism in domestic and international affairs.[1] The analysis begins with the introduction of an expected utility approach and the

155

assumptions which underlie it in the context of understanding the choice of terrorism as a strategy or tactic by political actors. The relationship between the structure of the state system and the role of violence in politics is then considered. Next, propositions which characterise the post-second-World-War world as they apply to state behaviour in the international system are presented. The fourth section discusses the basic patterns of superpower terrorist behaviour in the international context. There is contained herein no attempt to count events and test predictions of actual patterns. This task is sidestepped because at present there does not exist a comprehensive data set from which to draw such information (see Mitchell *et al.*, 1986, for an analysis of the difficulties of creating such a data source).

Before discussing the conditions under which governments choose to employ strategies and tactices which involve violence and terrorism it is useful to clarify how these concepts will be employed. Violence is defined in accordance with the liberal tradition as an act of physical harm. The US Department of State has employed the following definition of terrorism:

> The threat or use of violence for political purposes by individuals or groups, whether acting for, or in opposition to, established governmental authority, when such actions are intended to influence a target group wider than the immediate victim or victims
>
> (US Department of State, 1983).

That definition is adopted with slight modifications. Terrorism will be considered as:

> The purposeful threat or use of violence for political purposes by individuals or groups, whether acting for, or in opposition to, established governmental authority, when such actions are intended to influence the victim and or a target group wider than the immediate victim or victims.

This definition of terrorism is, on the one hand, slightly wider than that of the US Department of State in that it allows for the possibility that the victim as well as the wider target may be terrorised. At the same time it is also more restrictive in that it assumes intention by its inclusion of the term 'purposive'. It is important to note that both the

Department of State definition and the modified form adopted here allow for the possibility that both the state and individuals or groups may be terrorist actor(s) and that both states and individuals or groups may be potential victims.

An important key to the understanding of how terrorism differs from 'ordinary' political violence is to recognise that in terrorism the act or the threat of the act of violence is but the first step. Terror is purposeful behaviour designed to influence targets beyond the moment of victimisation and/or beyond the direct victims of the violent act. It is a conscious strategy or tactic of influence and not merely violent acts which cause death and destruction. The violence that is terrorism seeks to influence the behaviour of others, not merely to eliminate victims.

The central thesis of this chapter is that the present predominately bipolar structure of the international system (as it will be discussed below) provides the framework within which international behaviours are framed. The two superpowers not only are the strongest military powers, but they also have a considerable influence on the establishment of behaviours which thereafter become norms in the international system. Further, by practising certain forms of behaviour (which I will argue constitute terrorism) and condoning and supporting such behaviour by other states and groups, the superpowers contribute mightily to the overall level of terrorism in the international system. In addition, the argument contends that by virtue of their political and military power as superpowers, they have the greatest capacity and interest in controlling the level of terrorism in the system. They would each prefer their adversaries to refrain from the use of terrorism but they have each continued to employ terrorism in its different forms while decrying its use by others.

Therefore, despite the attention, particularly within the USA, to the problem of state terrorism as it is practised and supported by Syria, Libya and the USSR, it is the USA and the USSR that are the focus of analysis herein because, as is argued below, it is the essence of their position as superpowers that:

1. They have the greatest capacity to use, support, acquiesce, and combat the use of terrorism in the world, in part simply because they have the tools to project their power into more areas of the globe than any other powers, and their actions and inactions are always considered noteworthy;

2. They 'set' the ground rules, the standards by which behaviours are judged, and by their behaviours legitimate behaviours within the international system;
3. We know most about their international behaviours, because more scholarly and media effort is devoted to them, and this is even more the case for the USA;
4. I believe there is more to be learned from an examination of their behaviours, because of their greater capacities than may be learned by studying Libya, Syria and other small states which have employed terrorist strategies in the past decade.

At this point it is useful to state that I have taken seriously the biblical injunction, invoked by the most prominent political realist of our time, Hans Morgenthau, to speak truth to power. In the pages that follow, behaviours of the USA are discussed and evaluated as if these behaviours were performed by 'any' nation and quite often compared with similar behaviours of the USSR. It should be clear that this evaluation does not imply that Soviet terror is thereby more acceptable. The identification of US behaviours as terrorism later in this chapter should in no way be taken to suggest that the adversaries of the USA are favoured or excused or that one nation's terrorism is in any sense acceptable. Further, I do not accept the argument of the 'myth of moral equivalence' school (see Kirkpatrick, 1986; Hook, 1986) that one cannot conduct a comparative analysis of the behaviours of the USA and the USSR. They argue that (i) to do so equates the essence of the two states, but (ii) the two are so obviously different that they exist in a different moral universe and thus cannot be compared. The USA and the USSR are indeed profoundly different societies, with fundamental differences in terms of their long-term domestic structures and international goals. However, it should be first an empirical question, not an axiom of faith, if their behaviours can usefully be analysed using a common framework. Then the question may be asked quite separately if these actions should be judged on the basis of ends and not means. As Justice Robert Jackson eloquently stated more than forty years ago at Nuremberg in reference to another profoundly different nation's behaviour and international standards:

> If certain acts and violations of treaties are crimes, they are crimes whether the United States does them or whether Germany does them. We are not prepared to lay down a rule of criminal conduct against others which we would not be willing to have invoked against us.

Thus, following the insights of Thomas Schelling (1966, 16–17) the position taken throughout this chapter is that whether the terrorism undertaken by governments saves lives or wastes them, American lives or the lives of our adversaries; 'whether punitive coercive violence is uglier than straightforward military force or more civilized'; whether terror is more or less humane than military destruction, we can at least perceive that the actions that are being described are concerned with the manipulation of violence and the threat of pain and the promise of more. As such, I contend it is, quite simply, unacceptable behaviour regardless of the actor.[2]

However, the dominant traditions and beliefs that have guided scholars and policy-makers as to the proper role of states and state authorities that make decisions on their behalf, provide a set of guidelines quite different from my personal evaluation. Whether the analysis commences within the Hegelian or the utilitarian tradition in the modern era, it is quite common for it to end by exempting the state – and derivatively its agents – from moral obligations. Walzer refers to this problem as the problem of 'dirty hands', the concept deriving its label from Sartre's play of that name:

> It means that a particular act of government (in a political party or in the state) may be exactly the right thing to do in utilitarian terms and yet leave the man who does it guilty of a moral wrong
>
> (Walzer, 1974, p. 63).

While the utilitarian perspective on the state discusses the question of moral requirements, the tradition beginning with Hegel concludes that the state has no moral obligation. Cassirer argues:

> Hegel exempted the state from all moral obligations and declared that the rules of morality lose their pretended universality when we proceed from the problems of private life and private conduct to the conduct of states
>
> (Cassirer, 1946, p. 265).

Officials of the state are thereby, both in their own view and in the view of most observers, insulated from the moral requirements their actions might carry if they were acting as private citizens.

> the freedom from all restraints devolves on the central decision-makers from a higher authority, the state, of which he is merely the servant
>
> (Kelman, 1973, p. 45).

These freedoms from restraint are most often invoked on questions of national security. National security is, of course, a familiar, if often abused, concept. Most international relations texts, particularly those in the realist tradition, introduce students to the concept in the first few pages. In these pages students learn that all nations have a common interest in the preservation of core values. These core values usually include protection from invasion and economic security.

This realist vision suggests that states reside within an international system which is akin to the Hobbesian state of nature, with both lacking 'a political authority sufficiently powerful to assure people security and the means to have a felicitous life' (Beitz, 1979, p. 21). Thus states have the right (and the responsibility in the realist tradition) to do what they must to preserve their existence and may expect other states to behave in the same manner. Charles Beitz argues that Hans Morgenthau, the leading realist scholar of the past half century, seems to claim that "a state's pursuit of its own interests justifies disregard for moral standards that would otherwise constrain its action" (Beitz, 1979, p. 21) and indeed, Morgenthau (1978, p. 10) states that the state 'has no right to let its moral disapprobation ... get in the way of successful political action, itself inspired by the moral principle of national survival'. For realists, it would thus appear that there are no limits to actions which may be taken on behalf of the state when it is the national security of the state which is actually at risk.

Thus, since moral considerations are not likely to influence state behaviour in the international arena, we need to consider why and under what conditions states would choose to employ terrorism as a political strategy. To understand why others confront us with this threat it is useful to look at how we and our major adversary employ this tool of the foreign-policy arsenal. While the following is not an examination of tactics and resources, it is a useful reminder as we consider state terrorism that while we recognise that terrorism has become simpler for insurgents because of advances in transport, communication, weaponry, electronic devices and access to the media, the organisational and material resources of the state allow it to make far better use of these developments than can individuals. As Wilkinson (1986, p. 277) points out 'state-sponsored terrorists almost invariably have access to more advanced weaponry and greater firepower than autonomous freelance groups'. Naturally, therefore, direct action by state agents themselves also provides such advantages. In addition, as the following pages make clear, groups whose abilities have been enhanced by the above-mentioned advances are also employed or utilised by the state for the state's purposes.

II EXPECTED UTILITY: A COST-BENEFIT APPROACH TO STATE TERRORISM

An expected utility approach provides useful insights into the process of understanding why a government might choose terrorism as a tactic or strategy in international affairs and also, as (Duvall and Stohl, 1983, p. 202) demonstrate, in domestic affairs. Such an approach calculates the benefit thought possible from the desired outcome, the believed probability with which the action will bring about the desired state of affairs and the believed probable cost of engaging in the action. This approach does not require the analyst to believe that the actor who chooses to employ terrorism is a fanatic, merely that he is a 'rational actor' who has calculated that a terrorist action is to his advantage (for alternative approaches see Crenshaw, Chapter 2, and Schmid, Chapter 3 of this volume).[3]

States (and other terrorist actors) might choose terrorism paradoxically both when they perceive themselves powerless – the sense that other policy-instruments of rule are unavailable or less useful – and when they were in a situation that may be labelled confident strength – when the costs were perceived as low and the probability of success believed high in relation to other means (Duvall and Stohl, 1983). The concept of confident strength may be illustrated by the initiation of the US bombing campaign against Vietnam in 1965:

> Leaders of military powerful countries – like Lyndon Johnson, for example, in his unsuccessful use of air power against Hanoi in 1965 – are tempted to believe that they can, with little risk to themselves, intimidate weaker opponents to give up their gains and objectives. If the opponent refuses to be threatened and, in effect call the bluff of the coercing power, the latter must then decide whether to back off himself or to escalate the use of force
> (Craig and George, 1983, p. 191).

These calculations may, of course, be extended to the state's choice of other violent as well as non-violent strategies as well.

Two further kinds of costs – response costs and productions costs – can be distinguished. *Response costs* are those costs which might be imposed by the target group and/or sympathetic or offended bystanders. The bystanders in the foreign-policy realm may include domestic and foreign audiences, while the target in international as in domestic affairs may be wider than the attacking party may have intended.

Production costs are the costs of taking the action regardless of the reactions of others. In addition to the economic costs – paying the participants, buying the weapons and the like, there is the psychological cost of behaving in a manner which most individuals would, under normal conditions, characterise as unacceptable.

The psychological costs that an actor can expect from perpetrating violence on an incidental, instrumental, victim involve two conjoining factors. The first factor is the extent to which human life is valued (or conversely, the strength of internalised prohibitions against violence in general). The second is the extent to which the victim can be or has been dehumanised in the mind of the violent actor. Where moral/normative prohibitions are weak and especially where victims can be viewed in other than human terms, the self-imposed costs of terrorist actions are apt to be low and hence the choice of terrorist actions more frequent (Duvall and Stohl, 1983, p. 209).

The extent to which victims and potential victims can be dehumanised is affected by two important variables (for an extended discussion of this point see the seminal piece by Herbert Kelman, 1973). The first is the perceived social distance between the government and the victim population. The second is the extent to which action is routinely and bureaucratically authorised, so that personal responsibility is perceived, by all actors in the decisional chain, to be avoided. These production costs for terrorist action are apt to be lower for governments (i) in a conflict situation with those they define as 'inferior' and/or (ii) with a highly bureaucratised coercive machinery.

In the international realm these two important variables are often maximised. When inhibitions are lowered, it is easier for governments to employ terrorist strategies. The two superpowers, operating within a bipolar system, have created an overarching set of assumptions in which other nations and their peoples are defined as less important than the maintenance of the *status quo* itself (see section III below). It is no longer necessary to perceive such peoples as racially or culturally inferior (although of course that is still part of the unspoken equation), rather these considerations are dismissed as less important than the survival of 'The Free World', 'The Socialist Community of Nations', or 'The International System'. It is necessary, therefore, to consider the current international structure to understand the rules of the game which have been developed and how they structure superpower policies with regard to state terrorism in international affairs.

III   ON SYSTEMS AND THE STRUCTURES OF PERSIST-ENCE

A   The Bipolar System

There is a general recognition that the major operational principles of the current international system, from the realist perspective, may be captured in a small set of basic and familiar propositions (see also Cohen, 1981; Keal, 1983; and Waltz, 1979, among many others:

1. 'Two superpowers, each incomparably stronger than any other power or possible combination of other powers, oppose each other' (Morgenthau, 1978: 351).
2. 'In a world in which two states united in their mutual antagonism far overshadow any other, the incentives to a calculated response stand out most clearly, and the sanctions against irresponsible behavior clearly achieve their greatest force' (Waltz, 1979, p. 173).
3. 'The periphery of the balance of power now coincides with the confines of the earth' (Morgenthau, 1978, p. 359).

In short, these propositions argue that there are two military superpowers and that the two understand that it is foolish to resolve their differences by actually facing one another directly in a full-scale war. Nonetheless, the importance of chosen ends forces the two to compete for power and influence on a global scale regardless of the risks such competition automatically entails.

This distribution of power and its consequences are familiar as the core of the concept of a bipolar system. There are recognisable consequential state-interaction patterns within such a system. A first consequence, as noted already, is that the two polar powers tend to define problems *vis-à-vis* one another and these problems are perceived as overshadowing all other aspects of the system. A second consequence is that the rest of the system is defined by the super-powers in terms of what those states which compose the remainder mean to the two polar powers and the continuation of the bipolar system.[4]

Further we recognise that certain additionally restrictive patterns of behaviour result from a bipolar system in which polar states possess nuclear weapons (see Kegley *et al.*, 1987). The two polar states, while seeking advantage over one another, must also seek to avoid direct superpower war. They must therefore, in addition to maintaining or increasing their own military potentials in hope of securing advantages *vis-à-vis* one another, attempt to increase their political power by a combination of the following policies:

(a) increase the number of states that support them;
(b) decrease the number of states that support their opponent;
(c) increase the number of trouble-spots that their opponent will have to confront;
(d) decrease the number of trouble-spots that they themselves will have to contront.

Following these prescriptions does not alter the fundamental structure of the system – at least in the short run – but failure to do so is believed to lead to an alteration in the system in the longer term.

Kenneth Waltz suggests that despite the development of bipolarity and the technological and other changes of the postwar world which were assumed to inhibit the use of the force in the international arena:

> Seldom, if ever, has force been more variously, more persistently, and more widely applied as an instrument of national policy. Since World War II we have seen the political organization and pervasion of power, not the cancellation of force by nuclear stalemate
>
> (Waltz, 1979, p. 188).

Not only has force been widely employed, but also the superpower officials, and quite often scholars examining the record, praise the controlled use of force and the introduction of the new 'rules of the game' which seek to prevent, or at a minimum make more unlikely the direct confrontation of the superpowers.[5] These rules include:

1. The duty to avoid 'surprise' or sudden change in the inter-bloc balance of power relationship;
2. The principle of economy in the use of power;
3. The principle of mutual self-restraint (McWhinney, 1964, cited by Cohen, 1981, p. 57).

and two principles of crisis behaviour:

1. avoid any action that might invite a violent response from the opponent;
2. non-intervention in local disputes by client states (Williams, 1976, cited by Cohen, 1981, p. 58.)

In the areas outside their direct control, the superpowers have sought the advantages the structural conditions would predict. We should note that the label 'superpower' obscures the fact that for many years the USSR simply did not have the capacity to intervene militarily in the Third World and did little more than send statements of encouragement, advisers and small arms and supplies to those engaged in revolutionary struggles. Although this has changed in the past fifteen years (see Porter, 1984), it is still useful to consider the USSR as a junior partner in the superpower condominium (see Jonsson, 1984). Structurally, of far greater importance is the historical domination of the West in the colonial and recently colonial areas which placed the USA in the role of defender of the *status quo* both within states and of the international system as a whole (see Aron, 1974). While the USSR has also developed an interest as a *status quo* power in systemic terms, it is only in the past few years that, with respect to the situation within the sytem of states, the USSR has had more than Eastern Europe to 'defend' and in recent years the USA has both sponsored and encourage groups to challenge Soviet-backed and Soviet-oriented regimes in areas outside Eastern Europe.

The superpowers developed new 'rules of the game' for the use of force after a period of tacit bargaining and accommodation. These rules create expectations of behaviour which make it easier for the two powers to manage the international system by providing clues to the basic acceptable parameters of action. One important set of rules involves the identification of, and behaviour in, spheres of influence.

B Spheres of Influence

In a bipolar world we expect certain patterns of behaviour to develop *vis-à-vis* relations with the poles. In what were traditionally referred to as great-powers' spheres of influence it was assumed that great powers have 'positions of local preponderance' and other great powers 'avoid collisions or friction between them' in these areas (see Bull, 1977, pp. 219-25) The two superpowers have established a tenuous, but noticeable accommodation on behaviour within their own clearly defined spheres of influence. This accommodation did not eliminate the use of violence but rather established rules and justifications to be employed. It is important to stress both the enormous size differential and the generally voluntary/involuntary dimension in the European core of the US and Soviet spheres. The Soviet sphere was limited to Eastern Europe, plus Cuba after 1962, and finally in the 1970s was extended to Afghanistan, Ethiopia, Angola and Mozambique. In this sphere, when Soviet leaders deemed it necessary to maintain control of the parts, the USSR employed military force, as the events in Hungary in 1956, Czechoslovakia in 1968 and Afghanistan since 1979 make abundantly clear.

The USA, as the *status quo* power, in addition to Western Europe and North and South America, seemed quite often to include much of Asia and Africa as falling within its sphere (see Bull, 1977, pp. 223-5; Aron, 1974, pp. 305-10; and Gurtov, 1974.) Fukuyama (1986) argues, echoing Aron, that the US sphere was adapted to the protection of European former colonies in Africa and Asia and Tucker (1981) has argued that the problem of American power in the 1970s was an unwillingness to protect this properly global perspective of the US sphere of influence. As Franck and Weisband (1972) have skilfully demonstrated, by 1968 the Brezhnev Doctrine and the Johnson Doctrine faithfully mirrored one another, and these verbal rationalisations of interventionist behaviour, while drawing ritualised diplomatic opposition, did not bring military responses on the part of the other superpower:

> The analysis of Soviet and American verbal behavior in this study reveals that both we and they have committed ourselves very explicitly to an international system in which two superpowers exercise a kind of eminent domain, each within its own geographical region
>
> (Franck and Wesiband, 1972, p. 9).

Richard Falk (1972, p. 191) has identified this behaviour on the part of the superpowers within their sphere as the 'exercise of supervisory intervention'. While American presidents promised no more Cubas, the Soviet leadership sought to prevent further Yugoslavias. If the superpowers could control the system, there would be no more Castros and no more Titos as symbols of opposition within the core areas of the spheres of influence. However, as Gaddis (1986, p. 110) reminds us, while the superpowers have been remarkably 'tolerant' after the fact of a number of 'breakouts', they have still felt the need to continue to try and exercise such control, and thus mechanisms – short of war – and a rhetoric to match were needed.

The USSR's policy to compete short of war was enunciated in Khrushchev's speech in January 1961 in which he called for support for 'wars of national liberation'. While in China the speech was interpreted as evidence of the 'revisionist' and non-revolutionary character of the Soviet regime, the US assessment was, in Kennedy's words that:

> [W]e are opposed around the world by a monolithic and ruthless conspiracy that relies primarily on covert means for expanding its sphere of influence

(Gaddis, 1982, p. 208).

The conclusion was reached that to oppose such an enemy the USA had to engage in covert activities and to develop the capacity in the words of the military doctrine of the time, of 'flexible response' for any eventuality. In fact, of course, as the opening quotation from the Hoover Commission testifies, the USA had been groping for such a strategy since the end of the Second World War, but the Kennedy years saw the policy become part of declaratory policy as the 'New Frontier' sought to 'rationalise' the American use of force worldwide. In the beginning, the policy was applied in south-east Asia, Latin America and the Congo. Later flexible response was to expand beyond all reasonable conceptions of flexibility to the quagmire of Vietnam. At the end of the 1960s, one of the 'lessons' of the Vietnam experience was translated by Mr Nixon and Mr Kissinger into the Nixon Doctrine. As enunciated by the President on Guam, 25 July 1969, the President suggested that nations in the peripheral world would now have to defend themselves with US material support and encouragement, but primarily with their own troops. Thus, the US sphere of influence would be maintained, but the defenders of the sphere would be local military forces with US dollars and weapons providing the wherewithal for the defence.

Throughout the period, the underlying assumption guiding American policy-makers with respect to instability in the periphery were that difficulties were to be defined as a superpower issue and part of the Soviet threat. While the USA engaged in numerous operations to destabilise foreign governments, these were seen as restorative, not revolutionary. That is, these efforts were defined as attempts to return the system to an earlier *status quo*, to reverse the revolutionary changes that had created regimes that were perceived to threaten the *status quo* in the Third World (e.g. Guatemala, 1954; Iran, 1953; Indonesia, 1958; Cuba, 1961).

In the past decade, the 'successes' of the USSR, limited though they remain, have brought about a situation where they too now have regimes in the Third World (beyond Cuba) that need to be 'protected', e.g. Afghanistan, Angola, Ethiopia, Angola and Mozambique. The Soviet Union is thus, for the first time in the bipolar era, faced with the task of defending regimes outside Eastern Europe and the USA is now openly supporting 'freedom fighters' and 'wars of national liberation' in those states considered to be located within the non-Eastern-European portion of the Soviet sphere of influence. The status of such support has been raised to the level of doctrine and christened the 'Reagan Doctrine' by supporters and opponents alike (see Rosenfeld, 1986, p. 698).

This experience and tacit recognition of the earlier discussed rules has led to a situation therefore where the superpowers have each recognised the supremacy of the other in their respective sphere and have thus restricted their overt interventions in the affairs of the other's client-state to the verbal. At the level of covert operations outside the European core of the two spheres different rules of the game apply and thus both superpowers have therefore developed much greater sophistication in arms supply and overt and covert mechanisms of support and destabilisation.

IV PATTERNS OF INTERNATIONAL STATE TERRORISM

In a previous work (Stohl, 1984a) I identified three broad forms of state terrorist-behaviour in the international sphere. Terrorism as a subset of coercive diplomacy constitutes the first. In *Terrorist Coercive Diplomacy* the aim is to make non-compliance with a particular demand, in the words of Schelling (1966: p. 15) 'terrible beyond endurance'. While the threat is openly communicated by the actions of the state, the threat may be implicit and is quite often non-verbal. Terrorist coercive diplomacy is overt behaviour. The parties to the conflict are fully aware of the nature of the threat.

There are two types of *covert state terrorism* which constitute the second form of state terrorism: 1. *Clandestine state terrorism* is a form of covert action which consists of direct participation by state agents in acts of terrorism. 2. *State sponsored terrorism* is a form of covert action which consists of state or private groups being employed to undertake terrorist actions on behalf of the sponsoring state.

The clandestine services of the national state are generally responsible for initiating, participating in, or coordinating these actions. Government agents operating across national boundaries may choose either national élites or the foreign society itself as the target. In this type of state terrorism, states may thus attempt to intimidate government officials directly through campaigns of bombing, attacks, assassinations and by sponsoring and participating in attempted *coup d'état*. Alternatively, national states participate in the destabilisation of other societies with the purpose of creating chaos and the conditions for the collapse of governments, the weakening of the national state and changes in leadership. The threats to the regime and the society are obvious, but there is an attempt at deniability nonetheless. Both the pattern of such behaviour and the threat of such a pattern being initiated constitute the terroristic aspect of this type of action.

The third broad form of state terrorism involves assistance to another state or insurgent organisation which makes it possible or 'improves' the capability of that actor to practise terrorism either at home or abroad. This form is labelled *surrogate terrorism* as the obvious effect and intent of the assistance provided is the improvement of the assisted actor's ability either to carry out terrorist actions to maintain a regime's rule or to create chaos and/or the eventual overthrow of an identified enemy-state regime.

There are two sub-categories of this form of terrorism. 1. *State supported terrorism* exists when third parties undertake actions on their own which are subsequently supported by the interested state. 2. *State acquiescence* to terrorism occurs when terrorism is undertaken by third parties and while not explicitly supported by the interested state, the actions are not condemned or openly opposed.

In the next section each of these forms of terrorism is briefly examined in relation to the USA and the USSR with the purposes of (i) describing their behaviours; (ii) detecting similarities and differences in the superpower modes of behaviour in each of the three types of terrorism, and (iii) developing an understanding of the difference in possible costs and benefits that the three forms of state terrorist behaviour offer. It is argued that the probabilities of choosing surrogate, covert or overt coercive strategies depend on the difference for each case in the production and response costs. These costs and also the benefits will vary further depending on whether the target state is in the US or Soviet sphere of influence or the periphery and whether they are friends or foes of either of the two superpowers.

A Terrorist Coercive Diplomacy

The defining characteristic of coercive diplomacy as distinct from both diplomacy and traditional military activity is that the force of coercive diplomacy is used:

> in an exemplary, demonstrative manner, in discrete and controlled increments, to induce the opponent to revise his calculations and agree to a mutually acceptable termination of the conflict
>
> (George, 1971, p. 18).

We may speak of terrorism as a subset of coercive diplomacy when violence or its threatened use are present. Not all coercive diplomacy employs violence and thus not all coercive diplomacy is terrorism. For example, one may employ economic sanctions in an allowedly coercive manner, as did the members of the United Nations with respect to South Africa, without employing violent tactics. We will confine our analysis to the violence of coercive diplomacy whose central task has been described as 'how to create in the opponent the expectation of unacceptable costs of sufficient magnitude to erode his motivation to continue what he is doing' (George, 1971, p. 26–27).

The willingness of the superpowers to employ force and to threaten its use in the postwar period provides a context within which to understand their employment of terrorism as a form of the strategy of coercive diplomacy.

We must recognise that by convention – and it must be emphasised *only* by convention – great power use and the threat of the use of force is normally described as coercive diplomacy and not as a form of terrorism. But if we return to the US Department of State definition of terrorism introduced earlier, it is quite clear that certain forms of coercive diplomacy involve the threat and often the use of violence for what would be described as terroristic purposes were it not great powers who were pursuing the very same tactic. Thus Thomas Schelling reminds us:

> The power to hurt is nothing new in warfare, but for the United States modern technology has dramatically enhanced the strategic importance of pure unconstructive, unacquisitive pain and damage, whether used against us or in our own defense. This in turn enhances the importance of war and threats of war as techniques of influence, not of destruction; of coercion and deterrence, not of conquest and defense, of bargaining and intimidation
>
> (Schelling 1966, p. 33).

No less is true for the USSR.

We should also recognise that states, particularly superpowers, find it a much easier task to not only bring force to bear for threats but also to communicate their ability to do so. It is thus less necessary for a state actually to carry out its threat than it is for an insurgent terrorist organisation which has to work much harder to demonstrate the credibility (in both dimensions of capability, i.e. is the actor both willing and able to employ the threat) of their threat to employ force.

Further we must also consider the question of innocents and non-combatants. When coercive diplomacy is in the nature of the traditional gunboat-diplomacy mode, when in principle gunboats face off against gunboats, we have what Schelling (1966, p. 3) described as brute force to overcome strength. However when the 'gunboat' is positioned so as to indicate the ability to strike at the civilian population and not a military target we likewise have what Schelling describes as the threat of pain to structure the opponent's motives. We should recognise that this inclusion of innocent non-combatants should not be considered to be any different in form from that of the insurgent terrorist who threatens to unleash a wave of bombings on city streets. When these innocents are citizens of authoritarian or totalitarian societies who are not considered responsible in any conceivable sense for their government's legitimacy or actions, then coercive power which threatens these citizens to coerce their governments surely involves threats to helpless innocents and must be considered as a form of terrorism.

Blechman and Kaplan (1978) and Kaplan (1981) provide parallel studies of the American and Soviet use of force in the Second World War period. Kaplan's analysis of Soviet behaviour illustrates a number of different purposes and tactics for coercive diplomacy available to strong nations. There were 158 separate incidents in which the use of Soviet armed forces or the threat of armed forces use were employed. Kaplan argues that the USSR pursued coercive diplomacy for expansionary purposes only once after 1951. This occurred when a 'show of force' in 1975 in the form of a missile test in the Barents Sea was intended to influence the Norwegian government.

On the other hand, the use of armed force to maintain fraternal communist regimes remains an important instrument of Soviet diplomacy. The USSR has threatened intervention, placed ground forces in nearby positions, activated units, repositioned military units and participated in the active suppression of outbreaks against Eastern European regimes throughout the past three decades and has intervened with military force in East Germany in 1953, in Hungary in 1956 and in Czechoslovakia in 1968 to protect 'orthodoxy' in Eastern Europe. In the case of Poland in 1980–1, it was clear to all Poles that Soviet troop manoeuvres and other diplomatic consultations with Eastern Europe units were orchestrated to indicate the necessity of limiting threats to orthodoxy in Poland.

The USSR also used coercive diplomacy to 'intimidate neighbours or react to perceived threats presented by neighbours'. This pattern shifted from the early postwar period, when the concern was more clearly the intimidation of neighbours for perceived Soviet security needs, to the more recent past, when the issue has been the manipulation of threats to gain diplomatic advantage or reduce possible threats to the USSR. This use of the threat of armed force within the Eastern European sphere of influence is, of course, a conventional behaviour pattern for a great power. Nonetheless, this 'convention' involves the threat of the use of force for coercive bargaining purposes. It is meant to intimidate not simply the government whose behaviour is being challenged at any one point in time, but also the other fraternal governments and their populations. It should therefore, properly be placed within the terrorist subset of coercive diplomacy even if it represents an economy of force. We should not judge an action as terrorist in nature only if large-scale or hideous violence is employed. Rather, the key element is whether there has been a purposeful intent to manipulate the threat of such violence for coercive purposes, as was the case in the non-military intervention in Poland in 1980–1 as much as in the very real military interventions in Hungary in 1956, and Czechoslovakia in 1968.

Soviet use of coercive diplomacy and terrorist coercive diplomacy in the Third World appears very different from its behaviour within the East European sphere of influence. Kaplan records only one small action in the Third World after the autumn of 1962 in which the USSR threatened military force *against* a regime (Kaplan considers the Soviet invasion of Afghanistan as primarily an act of regime maintenance). This involved the deployment of two warships near the coast of Ghana in February 1969 after unsuccessful diplomatic and non-violent coercive attempts to gain the release of two Soviet trawlers and their crews which had been seized the previous October. The Soviets had taken almost immediate coercive economic steps, threatening to cut technical cooperation and that they would not resume Soviet aid projects. Following this, the USSR discontinued deliveries of fish and oil. When these economic steps had no effect, Soviet President Podgorny warned of possible consequences and the next week two Soviet missile ships approached Ghanaian waters. The Ghanaians, perceiving the connection between the warning and the missile ships, accelerated the legal process and shortly thereafter the ships and their crews were released (see Hall, 1981, pp. 519–69). This is not to say that the USSR has not been otherwise active politically and militarily in the Third World. Rather, it is simply to state that the Soviets appear to place little reliance on the direct and open threat of violence in their diplomacy in the Third World. As we shall now discuss, this represents an approach which is quite different from that of the USA.

The USA has been a frequent employer of the use of force as a political instrument in the post-Second World War era. Blechman and Kaplan (1978) identify 215 incidents in which military units were deployed abroad for political purposes. These involved the use of what Ostrom and Job (1986, pp. 541–2), in a later analysis of the data, described as acts which 'fall between acts of diplomacy and intentional uses of military power such as in Korea and Vietnam'. The USA employed its armed forces as a political instrument to maintain friendly regimes, to provide third-party support in conflicts, to assist allies in conflict, and to encourage parties to terminate their use of force. These US actions, ranging in intensity and danger from threats directed to demonstrate support for the pro-Western governments of Greece and Italy in the early postwar period to the Christmas bombings of North Vietnam in 1972 and the 'Mayaguez' operation in 1975, illustrate the commonplace nature of great powers 'using armed forces to pursue objectives abroad without going to war' (Kaplan, 1981, p. 2). Not all these actions are terrorist in nature, as many are shows of force in support of threatened governments, but as Blechman and Kaplan demonstrate, about half of these incidents involve a clear use of force to compel or deter opponents.

The Christmas bombing of Hanoi in 1972 and the Mayaguez operation against Cambodia in 1975 illustrate a war and on-war use of the terrorist component of coercive diplomacy. The Christmas bombing involved massive saturation runs over Hanoi and the rest of North Vietnam, and were code-named 'Operation Linebacker II'. They were ordered by Nixon after negotiations with the North Vietnamese had stalled because of South Vietnamese objections to the Kissinger–Tho proposed peace treaty. For twelve days American B-52s flew sortie after sortie 'at levels of intensity and sustainment never before achieved in the history of warfare' (Kendrick, 1974, p. 383). Each B-52 carried about two dozen 500 lb. bombs and about 100 B-52s and 500 fighter-bombers flew round-the-clock raids. This was not a military attempt to secure territory or destroy military targets:

> Nixon's logic was that he was bombing for peace. He was trying to bomb Hanoi back to the negotiating table and trying to convince Saigon by this show of force, that he was loyal to his ally. Both parts of Vietnam, Nixon reasoned, would be ready to sign with the United States once the shock treatment was over. By this reasoning, much of Hanoi and Haiphong was reduced to rubble
>
> (Stoessinger, 1976, p. 73).

In May 1975, the merchant freighter Mayaguez was seized by Cambodia. John Gaddis has argued with respect to US intentions that:

eager to make the point that the United States could still act force-
fully despite the Fall of Saigon two weeks earlier, Kissinger persuaded Ford to order air strikes against the port of Kompong Som
and an amphibious assault on the island of Koh Tang
(Caddis, 1982, p. 333).

Further, as James Nathan and James Oliver have written (1981, p.
378), the US did not explore diplomatic alternatives, as had previously been the case when fishing vessels had been seized off
Ecuador, rather 'the entire incident seemed a useful pretext to
demonstrate that the United States would, in Henry Kissinger's
words, maintain its reputation for fierceness'. In other words, lest any
small nation believe that the USA in the post-Vietnam era was not
going to maintain its interests by force and terror, where necessary,
the Mayaguez incident was an opportunity to communicate the Ford
Administration's willingness to uphold American power. The Cam-
bodians were the immediate target of the bombing raid (which took
place, along with the rescue attempt, after the crew had already been
released) but the world was the audience for the actions of this open
coercive terrorist diplomacy.

In terms of terrorist coercive diplomacy the USA has also been far
more active in the Third World than has the Soviet Union. This has
been so, in part because the recognised (if not at times challenged)
US sphere of influence includes a much larger portion of the Third
World (twenty-eight of the US incidents noted by Blechman and
Kaplan occurred in the Western hemisphere, eighteen in the Middle
East, twenty-eight in south-east and east Asia and six in South Asia
and sub-Saharan Africa, thus occurring roughly in proportion to
what areas have been considered important or within the important
areas of the US sphere of influence), but also because the USA, perceiving itself as the *status quo* power, often defined changes in
government in the Third World as threats to the international *status
quo*. The USA thus sought to restore or protect regimes that were
clearly pro-Western and as this has been an area of much change
and instability, the opportunities for intervention have been much
greater. These two studies demonstrate once again that the range of
actions open to a modern state, particularly a superpower with
unlimited geographical range, is extraordinary.

We may see further evidence of this range of activities and also
illustrate the process of terrorist coercive diplomacy and the threat of

violence by briefly examining the two recent major superpower coercive operations – Nicaragua and Poland. Our purpose here is not to provide a definitive analysis of either interaction. Rather at this time we wish merely to report on the instruments and tactics employed as the two superpowers attempted to meet their objectives without recourse to war. In confronting Nicaragua the Reagan Adminstration has had a series of objectives: (i) to end Nicaraguan support to the FDR and FMLN in El Salvador; (ii) to distance the regime from Cuba and the USSR; (iii) to protect capitalist enterprise still existent; and (iv) as time passed, to aid and abet the overthrow of the Sandinista regime itself. Familiar economic instruments of coercive diplomacy were employed against the regime: suspension of aid, blocking of loans in the InterAmerican Development Bank, disruption of export trade and the concentrated diplomatic attack on the Sandinistas in international forums and in public statements emanating from the White House and the Department of State. But an examination of the *New York Times* for the period also reveals the following tactics listed by Blechman and Kaplan (1978) as coercive force options which have been employed: providing a US presence; patrol/reconnaissance/surveillance; movement of a target's military forces or equipment; and interposition. In addition, the administration, also assisted in the mining of Nicaraguan harbours and has also been intimately involved in covert operations against the Sandinistas, as we will discuss below. Nonetheless, the administration thus far has been careful to avoid a direct and open policy of war.

In Poland, the USSR was faced with a situation it found unaccept-able, another challenge to 'orthodoxy' in Eastern Europe. The rise of Solidarity and the apparent inability of the Polish Communist Party and Polish government to manage the situation easily, led to a situation in which the question of protecting the integrity of fraternal com-munist regimes was once again raised by the Kremlin. The Brezhnev Doctrine and the past interventions in East Germany, Poland, Hungary and Czechoslovakia provide the context within which activities relating to the goals of re-establishing clear control and the elimination of challenges to the orthodox *status quo* may best be understood. Soviet behaviour in this instance was clearly linked to the activities of the Polish authorities. While numerous observers speculated on whether or not the USSR would actually invade and if the cost–benefit equation would favour such intervention – given the threat of facing Polish troops on the battlefield defending their homeland – the Soviets employed the traditional instruments for threats of the use of violence and the activation of coercive diplomacy: mobilisation, troop manoeuvres, joint exercises, warnings of Soviet intervention if the situation was not controlled, naval manoeuvres by Warsaw Pact forces, landing operations on the Polish coast, border exercises and alerts.

These instruments were accompanied by the standard non-violent instruments of coercive diplomacy: statements of concern for the internal situation in Poland, assurances that the Polish regime would deal effectively with counter-revolutionary elements, and joint communiqués by Warsaw Pact allies regarding their solidarity. These threats were clearly linked to the willingness of Polish authorities to use their own coercive strategies and instruments. When the military, after its take-over of the government apparatus, demonstrated anew its willingness to use force, the threat of Soviet and Warsaw Pact intervention receded until, with the imposition of martial law, the threats came to an end and were replaced by statements concerning the validity of the Brezhnev Doctrine.

One may argue that the coercive strategies adopted in these two cases illustrate the virtues of such a strategy, 'achieving one's objectives economically, with little bloodshed, for fewer psychological and political costs, and often with much less risk of escalation' (George, 1971, p. 19). Saving lives is indeed a virtue. This virtue, however, does not alter the fact that the strategy is based on terror and the power to destroy if 'proper' responses are not engendered by the threats and/or the relatively low levels of violence employed. Coercive strategies which rely on the threat of violence should therefore be considered state terror policies, regardless of whether or not they save lives or we approve of them (see Schelling, 1966, pp. 16–17). At the same time, it should be clear that US and Soviet policy-makers, confronted in both these cases with situations that they sought (and in the case of Nicaragua still seek) to alter radically, calculated that the costs, both response and production, were too great to justify a more-directly violent approach. While both have the military resources to prevail ultimately, the potential casualty figures – that is the 'production costs', and the 'response costs' which would be imposed by allies and others are simply too high to risk. Coercive terroristic-based diplomacy is clearly a more economical approach, and one that allows for later escalation to the direct employment of brute force to bring about a military solution should the threat of force and its manipulation not bring an acceptable conclusion.

B   Covert State Terrorism

Whereas the terror of coercive diplomacy is obvious to all observers, even if many shrink from labelling the behaviour as such, the terror of the clandestine apparatus of the state in international relations is often quite difficult to discern. Knowledge of these instances of international governmental terrorism is necessarily incomplete and uneven and such knowledge may not become available through investigative reporting, official and unofficial leaks and exposés until quite long after the fact. It is the also the case that we outside the official intelligence apparatus (and, it sometimes appears, those within as well) are not ever comfortable with the accuracy or quality of the revelations of this type of behaviour. This is most often not the type of data that can be subjected to extensive validity studies by those outside the inner circles.

Both the clandestine state terrorism and state-sponsored forms of covert state terrorism in international relations, unlike the coercive diplomacy discussed above, are usually aimed at producing, not compliance, but rather fear and chaos. In addition to the message that the act conveys about vulnerability and the assets (personal and material) that are destroyed, it is hoped that as a result of increased fear and chaos, governments at some later point will be in a weaker bargaining position or will be more willing to make concessions, given the costs that have become apparent. In relative terms, response and production costs are lower than for open coercive diplomacy. The attempt at deniability may create suspicions, but suspicions are generally less costly in the court of public opinion than are open admissions. It is also less expensive to mount most forms of covert operations than it is to 'send the fleet' or mobilise the resources necessary for a fully-open coercive operation. Further, if a covert operation fails the cost is likely to be less than that of the failure of an open coercive operation. Costs increase only as deniability and success become less possible and the various publics involved lessen their support and extract punishment for the failures and embarrassment.

It is the threat of this type of behaviour *in general* that serves to keep elites fearful of outside interference. It also produces public statements by Third World leaders regarding American and Soviet interference which are often dismissed by the American public as the ravings of unstable, paranoid or ideological opponents who merely seek to embarrass or blame their internal difficulties on the

USA or USSR. This was particularly the case before the Pike Committee report was made public in 1976 (see also Halperin *et al.*, 1976). The reaction by the US media and public to the claims of Fidel Castro and Mu'ammar Gaddafi that the CIA had attempted to assassinate them are excellent cases in point. We have, at present, no direct knowledge in the case of Gaddafi (and it is now illegal under US law for employees of the US Government to engage in assassination, although recent leaks suggest continuing attempts to topple his government) but by now the attempts on Castro throughout the 1960s and 1970s are well known (Hinkle and Turner, 1981).

In the past three decades the clandestine services of the USA have had much experience directing and sponsoring covert behaviours which were intended to create fear and chaos in numerous countries around the world. The Central Intelligence Agency is the organisation most often identified as responsible for such behaviour. Marchetti and Marks (1974, p. 108) suggest that 'the crudest and most direct form of covert action is called "special operation" . . . by definition, special operations are violent and brutal'. A partial listing of well-known CIA special operations indicates the range of such activities. In Guatemala (1954), Indonesia (1958), Iran (1953), the Bay of Pigs, Cuba (1961), the USA trained, equipped, and provided tactical assistance to groups attempting to overthrow established governments. Between 1970 and 1973, the USA worked on a number of levels to overthrow the elected government of Salvador Allende in Chile. In addition to non-terroristic strategies such as bribery after the election campaign, the USA embarked on a programme to create economic and political chaos in Chile. The CIA was implicated in the assassination of Rene Schneider, the commander-in-chief of the Chilean Army, who was selected as a target because he refused to sanctions plans to prevent Allende from taking office:

> The United States government attempted to foment a *coup*, it discussed *coup* plans with the Chileans later convicted of Schneider's abduction, it advocated his removal as a step toward overturning the results of a free election, it offered payment of $50 000 for Schneider's kidnapping and it supplied the weapons for this strategy
>
> (Johansen, 1980, p. 210).

After the failure to prevent Allende from taking office, efforts shifted to obtaining his removal. At least $7 m was authorised by the

USA for CIA use in the destabilising of Chilean society. This included financing and assisting opposition groups and right-wing terrorist paramilitary groups such as Patria y Libertad (Fatherland and Liberty). Finally, in September 1973 the Allende government was overthrown in a brutal and violent military *coup* in which the USA was intimately involved. President Ford stated 'I think this was in the best interests of the people of Chile and certainly in our best interests' (Halperin *et al.*, 1976, p. 28). The message for the populations of Latin American nations and particularly the left opposition was clear: the USA would not permit the continuation of a Socialist government in Latin America, even if it came to power in a democratic election and continued to uphold the basic democratic structure of that society. This extension of the Johnson Doctrine was not a logical necessity, but it is certainly not an unexpected development from a realist perspective. The USSR, for its part, went through the normal superpower ritual of condemning the US role, without actually attempting to alter the situation.

In the past few years major US efforts at destabilisation of an increasingly less-than-covert nature have taken place as part of the strategy of destablising and overthrowing the Sandinista regime in Nicaragua. The so-called 'secret-war' attracted so much attention that on 8 December 1982 the House of Representatives voted to halt covert activities by the Central Intelligence Agency abroad, for the purpose of overthrowing the government of Nicaragua or provoking a military exchange between Nicaragua and Honduras. The legislation did not prohibit private organisations from conducting operations (although it did prohibit direct assistance by US agencies to these private organisations). In the summer of 1985, responding to Administration pleas, Congress approved 'humanitarian' assistance to these private groups. Such assistance provides a convenient semantic deniability. Recent testimony by Edgar Chammoro, a former Contra leader, at the World Court (September 1985) makes clear that the lines between public and private, and between US and Nicaraguan Contra as actor in the various covert activities were, at best, always unclear. The fiction of separateness, like many of the other fictions in the case of US actions directed against Nicaragua, is maintained, however, because it is safer in terms of response costs. While everyone now 'knows' that the USA is intimately and directly involved the legal fictions may be maintained and direct responses may be avoided. In this way the utility of clandestine terror is illustrated for even the strongest of nations. It is not necessary for the state (or any actor) to be weak to employ terrorism or terrorist strategies which are normally associated with weakness, it is only necessary for the 'rational' actor to conclude that such strategies are more cost–benefit effective.

But Nicaragua, while the best known current instance, is not the only nation in which US agents have operated in the past few years. Leslie Gelb reports that the CIA is 'secretly' aiding Iranian exiles (*New York Times*, 7 March 1983, p. 1). The *Washington Post* (10 April 1983) reports that the CIA is conducting a covert operation affecting Angola, involving support for Jonas Savimbi and his UNITA forces. It has been charged by the USSR, and administration officials have allowed the impression to be created, that the USA is engaged in assisting the Afghanis against the Soviet occupation (*New York Times*, 10 February 1983; see also the discussion in Peterzell, 1984). It is also the case that the creation of organisational umbrellas such as Citizens for America, and Citizens for Reagan, which actively seek to channel support to anti-Soviet insurgents creates the clear impression that the US government is supportive of private initiatives of Americans cooperating with various insurgent groups that are known to employ terror as an integral component of their military strategy. When such groups are headed by prominent Republicans such as Lewis Lehrman, who not only claims to have the President's blessing but reads to an organising meeting a letter from the President endorsing their purpose, it is clear that the line which separates public and private actions and aims is consciously blurred. The case of Eugene Hasenfus in October 1986, with its complex web of interactions among the CIA, retired Generals Singlaub and Secord, National Security Staff Member Oliver North, Vice President Bush and all the official and unofficial links and winks and nods, illustrates the continuing difficulty of sorting out the private and public roles in the continuing campaign against Nicaragua.

There are differential response and production costs associated with the use of private clandestine agents. It should be noted that both the lines between these agents as state-sponsored versus state-supported terrorists as well as that between the two and clandestine state terrorism, may be easily blurred in the absence of reliable information. However, it should be clear that the distinguishing analytic criteria are temporal – was approval or instigation for an action granted prior to the decision to undertake the act? – and organisational – are the actors members of the state's covert organisation or are they acting on their behalf or being supported before or after the fact? These analytically clear demarcations break down when agents purposefully outline acceptable goals and ambiguous limits to the means with a knowing wink and nod.

It should be the reasonable conclusion of analysts in this field that the USSR has been far less able (although we have nothing but our worst-case suspicions to prevent us from believing that they are simply less willing) to intervene in the Third World on the scale that the USA has achieved in the past few decades. This is apparently the case for both overt and covert interventions. While much is made in the Western media of the strength of the Soviet KGB and the threat that the USSR poses in and for the Third World, in much of the Third World the Soviet presence appears to be relatively benign. They have far less leverage than the USA and far less infrastructure within which to conduct covert operations.

Rubinstein, for example, argues that in Third World policy in general the USSR appears opportunistic and responsive to local initiatives and conditions'; unlike the USA, 'the Soviets have not been well-placed to meddle effectively in leadership quarrels and have wisely concentrated on maintaining good government-to-government relations, reinforcing convergent policy goals and providing such assistance as is necessary to keep a client in power' (Rubinstein, 1981, pp. 214–35; see also Schmid, 1985). This is not to argue that the USSR does not involve itself in 'liberation struggles'. It quite often does, and has assisted groups (e.g. the MPLA in Angola) which they believe will be predisposed to them after achieving power. But assistance to such groups involves the use of a third type of state terror activity, surrogate terrorism, and should be distinguished from covert terror activities of direct intervention, whether they be of the clandestine state terrorist or state-sponsored terrorist variety.

C Surrogate Terrorism

The third form of state terrorism in international affairs, surrogate terrorism, involves assistance to another state or insurgent organisation which makes it possible or 'improves' the capability of that actor to practise terrorism both at home and abroad. There are two forms of this type of terrorism. *State-supported terrorism* occurs when third parties undertake actions on their own which are subsequently supported by the interested state. *State acquiescence* to terrorism is identified when third parties, although not explicitly supported by the interested state, conduct operations which are either quietly approved (because they contribute to state objectives) and/or are not condemned or openly opposed by the interested state. Surrogate terrorism requires even lower response and production costs than the previous forms of state terrorism, but it also provides much less control and by its nature is least likely to lead to benefits that may be calculated in advance. States having few options, or finding themselves in situations where direct actions – even if they have a reasonable chance of deniability – would still be extremely dangerous were they either to fail or be discovered, often find the surrogate choice acceptable if they believe there is a chance, at the very least, to raise the costs of their adversaries.

1 *International Terrorism and Transnational Terrorism-State Supported Terrorism and the Superpowers*

(a) *The Soviet Union.* In his first news conference as President Reagan's newly appointed Secretary of State, Alexander Haig responded to a question (and a follow-up question) concerning strategic interests in Latin America by charging that the USSR was 'involved in conscious policies, in programs if you will, which foster, support, and expand this activity (international terrorism)'. Mr Haig indicated that the Soviet role included training, funding and equipping international terrorists (Haig, 1981, p. 5). Mr Haig was supported in this position by key members of the Reagan Administration such as National Security Adviser Richard Allen and Secretary of Defense Caspar Weinberger (see Miller, 1981, p. 4). Haig's charges focused public attention on an issue which had found increasing attention in the second half of the 1970s, the role of states in the apparently increasing activities of terrorists who operated both within and across state boundaries. Questions had been raised as to how such organisations could operate so capably and suspicions grew that to do so, they needed complex infrastructure and state support. The obvious candidate for the role of state supporter was the USSR. This conclusion was reached because the Soviets would receive the greatest benefits from a 'programme' which encouraged the destabilisation of the west. In place of evidence for suspicions raised, the question *cui bono* (who benefits)? was substituted. If direct Soviet involvement could not be found because of the highly secretive and closed nature of Soviet behaviour, it was argued that one should assume Soviet backing because of the benefits that would accrue to them and focus investigation on surrogates and intermediaries. The assumption was that the tentacles of the plot would lead back to the USSR.

There are two major thrusts in the interconnected argument concerning the role of the USSR in international terrorism. The first concerns the question of cooperation and possibly organisational coordination among terrorists and the second Soviet involvement and possibly organisational control. Despite the assurance with which Sterling (1981a); Haig (1981); Demaris (1977); and others spoke, there has been little publicly available evidence which demonstrates actual Soviet control and/or an actual organisational infrastructure. Few dispute the existence of working relations among some terrorist groups resulting in relatively low-level cooperation regarding safe houses, travel documents, weapons information and the like (see Schmid, Chapter 3, and Wilkinson, Chapter 4 of this volume). However, the cooperative network does not appear any more sophisticated than the 'ordinary' criminal network that exists for the purchase of visas, weapons and silence throughout the world. That groups cooperate at this level should come as no surprise to anyone familiar with organised criminal or insurgent terrorist behaviour (see Wardlaw, 1982).

It is a long leap to assert that this cooperation implies any co-ordinated effort or long-term policy agreement regarding revolutionary upheaval around the world. It is a leap, nonetheless, that in the 1980s American political climate many have willingly made, particularly if they could hope to connect the USSR with the network. Indeed, some, such as US Senator Denton of Alabama, for obvious political purposes, went so far as to suggest that American citizens do not find the link-up with the USSR because the USSR manipulates a gullible American press. It is argued that the USSR has had such success in their 'disinformation' programme to convince Western news readers that they have had no part in international terrorism, that it is now difficult to find Americans willing to believe the Soviet role. Some go much further. Robert Moss, formerly of *The Economist*, is quoted approvingly by Charles Horner for his identification 'of a conspiracy of silence' about the evidence of Soviet involvement in terrorism which operated in order to preserve the appearance of *détente* (cited by Horner, 1980, p. 40). This conspiracy includes the news media and government officials. On the other hand, Claire Sterling, who ardently believes in the connection, simply cannot find anything to explain why the US and Western intelligence agencies do not publicly admit the connection. In despair, she suggests that no single motive could explain the iron restraint shown by Italy, West Germany, and all other threatened Western governments in the face of inexorably accumulating evidence... (Sterling, 1981b, p. 291)

The fact that the intelligence services have not been able to provide the evidence that these analysts all *assume* is there does not seem to provide a simple direct answer. But we should look further into the changes. Sterling, for instance, does not simply suggest, as did Secretary of State Haig, that the Russians are behind it *all*. Rather, she argues that no matter what the original motive and organisation of the terrorist movements in the Western world, the USSR, through the Palestinians with the KGB as agent, has infiltrated and gained a key role in the various terrorist movements in the Western world:

> Direct control of the terrorist groups was never the Soviet intention. All are indigenous to their countries. All began as offshoots of relatively non-violent movements that expressed particular political, economic, religious or ethnic grievances

> (Sterling, 1981b, p. 19).

and

> The heart of the Russians' strategy is to provide the terrorist network with the goods and services necessary to undermine the industrialized democracies of the west

> (Sterling, 1981b, p. 54).

While Ms Sterling argues that: 'The case rests on evidence that everyone can see, long since exposed to the light of day' (Sterling, 1981a, p. 292) 'nobody has yet provided unequivocal evidence that supports a simple-minded Soviet-culprit theory of terrorist control and neither are there any serious analyses of Soviet strategic objectives and the manner in which these ends would be served by support for terrorism (Wardlaw, 1982, p. 56).

Much of this argument against the USSR rests on the assumption that the USSR because it is an anti-*status-quo*-power favours anarchy and disruption within the world system. Thus, the USSR will assist those opposed to the Western states system and particular states, i.e. the *status quo*, because it is to their long-term advantage. Friedlander (1982, citing Edward Marks, coordinator for Anti-terrorist Activities,

US Department of State), refers to this as the 'fishing in troubled waters' thesis. The simple-minded approach to this argument is most clearly presented by Sterling:

> In effect, the Soviet Union had simply laid a loaded gun on the table leaving others to get on with it. Why would the Russians do that? Well, why not?
>
> (Sterling, 1981a, p. 293)

A more sophisticated answer to the question why is given by Edward Luttwak:

> It was only when it became clear that the Soviet Union was ineluctably losing the support of the trade unions and left-wing mass movements of the West that the Soviet leaders began to accept terrorists as useful allies; with the Leninist programme of revolution by the working classes finally exposed as totally unrealistic
>
> (Luttwak, 1983, p. 64).

In other words, Luttwak argues that Soviet leaders reversed the longstanding Leninist antipathy to terrorism, an antipathy based on the belief that mass movements would not be built upon terrorist campaigns (see Terekhov, 1974, pp. 20–2) when these mass movements were also deemed to be failures. While this is not evidence for the position it does at least have the virtue of providing an explanation for the possibilities of doctrinal shift. If we combine Luttwak and Sterling we may extract the basic argument for a state choosing surrogate terrorism as a strategy when it is itself unwilling, because of response and production costs, to carry out the actions it ultimately desires.

In the latest salvo in what has become a mainly polemical battle, Cline and Alexander assert, without seeming to worry if it makes a difference whether the Soviet Union '*benefits*' from or '*directs*' terrorist activity:

> In the 1970s terrorism, whether backed directly or indirectly by the Soviet Union or *independently initiated* [my emphasis added], appeared to have become an indispensable tactical and strategic tool in the Soviet struggles for power and influence within and among nations. In relying on this instrument, Moscow seems to aim in the 1980s at achieving strategic ends in circumstances where the use of conventional armed forces is deemed inappropriate, ineffective, too risky or too difficult
>
> (Cline and Alexander, 1984, p. 6).

Likewise, Cline and Alexander also argue:

> it is obvious from the PLO documents[6] that there exists a carefully developed international terrorist infrastructure that serves Moscow's foreign policy objectives of destabilizing non-communist governments
>
> (Cline and Alexander, 1984, p. 55).

When all the charges and evidence are carefully reviewed, what can we conclude with confidence concerning Soviet involvement with Palestinian and other terrorists? The Soviets have trained, funded and equipped some Palestinians for what they would describe as guerrilla warfare (see Friedlander, 1982). Some Palestinians are Marxists and have developed links with other Marxists and non-Marxist political organisations, governments and also terrorist organisations including most member-states of the United Nations and all the states in the Arab League. Radical Arab states who have purchased arms from the USSR have made some of these arms available to Palestinians (Conservative Arab states who have purchased arms from the USA and other Western states have also made arms available to the Palestinians). We can and should thus make the argument that the USSR, by training Palestinian guerrillas and others in military techniques, weapons use, and tactics at bases within the USSR and the Middle East must bear a share of the responsibility for the practices for which that training is employed. They may certainly be accused of State acquiescence to terrorism and under what we characterise as 'the loaded-gun thesis' of being an 'accessory before the fact'. But this is a very different charge from that of direct responsibility and operational control and hence requires a different response set to try and control than direct involvement. Thus the advice of Robert Friedlander should be heeded:

> Destabilization of democratic societies is in the long range interest of the USSR. But to ascribe to the KGB or the Soviets in general, the responsibility and the credit for worldwide terror is legally unsound and diplomatically unwise. Until hard and fast proof can be presented by competent authorities the so called 'Soviet connection' will remain in the immortal phrase of Sir Winston Churchill 'a riddle inside a mystery wrapped in an enigma'
>
> (Friedlander, 1982; see also Wardlaw, Chapter 7 of this volume).

The response in the case of 'Palestinian' terror is further complicated by the other parties which may also be labelled as accessories before the fact. Many of these parties have very different motives and concommitant anti-Soviet aims:

> Let us be clear about what we do not know. We do not know the extent, if any, to which the Soviets direct any terrorist organization. Moscow seems to have had great influence over the Popular Front for the Liberation of Palestine (PFLP) but less over other factors within the Palestine Liberation Organization (PLO). Most of the money for many terrorist groups probably comes, not from the Soviet Union, but from wealthy Arab nations and from criminal activities
>
> (Wilson, 1981, p. 36).

In the current ideological climate such scepticism and raising of questions regarding Soviet involvement has not been well received:

> *Apologists* [my emphasis] for Soviet foreign policy, on the other hand, are skeptical about direct and indirect Soviet control of terrorist groups. While admitting that Moscow approves of and gives some assistance to what it considers legitimate 'liberation movements', or struggles of people for their independence, proponents of this view argue that the dynamics of modern terrorism are so uncontrollable as to make the Soviet leaders ambivalent about the usefulness of this form of warfare
>
> (Cline and Alexander, 1984, p. 5).

However, it should be recognised that the Palestinian situation is unique in terms of the current international system. There is no question that, as many have argued (see Bishop, 1983; Peleg, 1987; and Wardlaw, 1982, and Chapter 7 of this volume), the PLO as an umbrella organisation of widely disparate political groupings, 'united' only by their original aim of eliminating the state of Israel plays a key facilitating role in any organisational linkages amongst terrorist groups. They, through their now long-term access to money, *matériel*, diplomatic pouches and diplomatic cover, territorial bases and safe territories as well as whole nations, have provided to various European and Asian terrorist groups 'fraternal' assistance and have been able to conduct truly 'transnational' operations. But while many nations may acquiesce to their terrorist operations only a relatively few openly support terrorist operations, after the fact, and still fewer may be placed under suspicion of acting in a manner which raise their activities to that of state-sponsored terrorism (recent revelations concerning Syrian involvement would certainly fall into this category).

(b) *The United States of America.* Within the USA and within the literature of terrorism, there has been far less interest in the US role in 'aiding, abetting, and funding international terrorism' or, in other words, with the USA as a sponsor or acquiescer to terrorism, be it insurgent or state in origin. While, of course, there is a critical literature concerned with the role of the Central Intelligence Agency and its covert operations, that literature is generally concerned with the activities of Americans in clandestine operations and not with the connection among 'terrorist' organisations. In part, this is obviously the result of the current distribution of power within the world. The USA, as the premier *status quo* power simply does not have as many opportunities or choices to make in this area as would the USSR. Since the Second World-War, the US has been in a position to support more regimes and governments, the USSR more opponents and insurgents.

However, we should not conclude that the USA has had no cooperative arrangements with insurgents, wars of national liberation or insurgent terrorists, nor that it has had no involvement in their operations. CIA covert operations in Nicaragua, Angola, Iran, and Afghanistan during the present decade obviously involve the US with insurgents who would be labelled terrorist if they were opposing regimes friendly to the USA (see Wardlaw, Chapter 7 of this volume on the implications for counter-terrorism of not recognising this double standard).

There is an additional group of terrorist organisations (so identified by the FBI) with whom the USA has links. These groups are Cuban and much of the network descends from the ill-fated 1961 Bay of Pigs invasion. According to the FBI, the most dangerous terrorist group operating within the USA during much of the 1970s was OMEGA 7, the clandestine operations arm of the Union City branch of the Cuban Nationalist Movement. In the CIA's ITERATE transnational terrorism data base for 1969–79, Cuban exile groups are given responsibility for eighty-nine separate terrorist incidents within the USA and the Caribbean area. Many of the actions involved attacks on Cuban and Soviet diplomatic personnel in the USA. While the FBI was attempting to prevent acts of terrorism from occurring within the USA, groups which had long-standing connections with the US government were able to continue to cause a domestic law-enforcement problem, even though, of course, their original purpose had been to create such problems for Fidel Castro within Cuba.

One clear international linkage provided by these Cuban organisations concerns their role in the assassination of Orlando Letelier, the exiled former foreign minister of the Allende regime. Agents of the DINA, the Pinochet secret police in Chile, recruited OMEGA 7 members for help in the assassination. While there is no evidence, and I am not suggesting that the CIA was in any way involved in the assassination of Letelier, organisations with which the CIA had been intimately involved certainly were. The linkage but not the responsibility for the particular action is clear. An organisation which the CIA found useful for other purposes had become involved, without CIA help or approval, in the assassination of a former Ambassador a few miles from CIA headquarters. Hinkle and Turner argue:

> Cuban exile terrorism began with assassinations and bombings in the United States, picked up tempo during the 1970s and by the end of the decade had spun a murderous web linking Cuban exiles with elements of the American CIA, the Chilean gestapo known as DINA, the Venezuelan secret police, the Korean CIA and European paramilitary fascist groups
>
> (Hinkle and Turner, 1981, p. 317).

A much more recent connection with Bay of Pigs veterans, the CIA and the Venezuelan secret police has emerged in the story of Eugene Hasenfus and the Nicaraguan Contras. On 22 October 1986, the *New York Times* identified Ramon Medina (the man identified by Hasenfus as a supervisor at the air base from which he took off on his ill-fated flight) as Luis Posada Carriles, a Bay of Pigs veteran imprisoned in Venezuela for his part in the bombing of Cubana Airlines flight 455 on 6 October 1976 which took the lives of all seventy-three on board. Former US Assistant Attorney Eugene Propper (see Branch and Propper, 1982; pp. 99, 101, 604). further identifies Luis Posada Carriles as an official in the Venezuelan Secret Police, DISIP, while Edward Mickolus, who coordinated the CIA's ITERATE file, in his chronology of terrorist events identifies Posada as a 'Cuban who was formerly head of the Venezuelan Secret

Police' (see Mickolus, 1980, p. 653). Four years after the bombing, the Venezuelan War Council announced the unconditional release of Posada and the two Venezuelans who had actually planted the bomb. However, at that time, the prisoners were not actually released as Cuba raised noisy and embarrassing objections. From the October 1986 reporting of events we now learn that Posada mysteriously escaped and eventually, as we now know, found his way to El Salvador to help in the efforts of the Contras.

Further, Hinckle and Turner assert that the CIA financed covert forays against Cuba between 1964 and 1975 through the Castle Bank and Trust Ltd, a CIA bank established in the Bahamas for such purposes. More recently, US links with terrorists in Nicaragua (the Contras) have also involved connections with the Argentinians. Training centres were established by Nicaraguan groups within the USA and a blind eye was turned towards them (*New York Times*, 17 March 1981, p. 14). Camps were also run by Panamanian and Cuban exiles for the purpose of overthrowing their governments (*New York Times*, 24 December 1981, p. 14).

In short, in addition to what Edward Herman (1982) has labelled as the 'Real Terror Network', the organisational linkages and structural conditions which foster cooperative government linkages which promote state terrorism discussed below), the USA does appear to have established links with insurgent terrorist organisations. Both the literature on these links and the network of linkages themselves appear far smaller than those attributed to the USSR. This relative lack of size may result from the reverse of the structural condition that we noted earlier, the USA supports relatively more governments, the USSR relatively more insurgents and 'wars of national liberation'. But the relative size may also be reflective of the history of the 'need' to support insurgents as opposed to governments. It is only six years since the Sandinistas took power and a decade since the MPLA came to power in Angola. While Fidel Castro has now controlled Cuba for twenty-seven years, his original patrons did not include oil-rich nations in addition to those with ideological affinity. While we should expect different levels of superpower involvement in the activities designed to support their respective clients related to the numbers of actual opportunities to become involved, we should also recognise that the so-called Soviet 'Network of Terror' is as important as it is because the USSR is not the only important patron and that a number of quite important international purposes are served by support of the PLO and its many factions by radical and conservative Arab states. No such overlapping interests are served by US support of anti-Sandinista contras.

2   States as Surrogate Terrorists

Within the structures of dominance that exist in the international system, powerful states do not simply exert military force and threats to control all aspects of both the internal and external relations of subordinate states. I have already discussed the intervention of relatively powerful states in the affairs of the less powerful. Powerful states also aid the less-powerful states in their domestic and international affairs and these less-powerful states, in turn, assist the powerful to pursue their objectives. The superpowers sell, grant, and otherwise provide favourable terms by which their coalition partners, allies, client states (and at times neutrals and even adversaries) obtain equipment enabling their regimes to *continue* and/or expand practices of repression and terrorism. I argue that in such cases the superpowers are practising a form of surrogate terrorism which at the very least may be considered as state acquiescence and when the terror serves purposes which have been discussed jointly spills over into state sponsorship. When the superpowers train the personnel that conducts the terror operations, consult with and advise (for 'reasons of state') the security services of 'friendly' states in their use of terrorism, this tool is a form of surrogate terrorism.

(a) *States as Domestic Surrogates.*   The US Army directed a School of the Americas at the Atlantic entrance to the Panama Canal from 1946. The school has had more than 46 000 graduates who have returned to their nation's military forces. The current commandant, bristling at the suggestion that he commands what has been called a 'school for juntas', argues that human rights training was now included in the school 'even if it was just a question of teaching non-commissioned officers that it was more valuable in intelligence to keep prisoners alive than to kill them' (see Ellman, 1983). In 1974 Congress banned US assistance to the police and internal security agencies of foreign governments (under terms of the Anti-terrorism Assistance programme authorised in 1983 such training for specified purposes relating to the control of terrorism is once again authorised). Before the ban more than 7000 high-ranking police, intelligence and internal security officers were trained at the International Peace Academy in Washington, DC. The professionalisation of Latin American police forces was the object of the International Police Academy and the International Police Services Inc., the latter a CIA-sponsored organisation which also had students from Asia and Africa (Langguth, 1978, p. 124). Graduates of the Academy often returned home to practise their trade with exemplary zeal.

While official IPA policy was against torture, etc., many students became proficient at interrogation while enrolled. Knowledge of the establishment of the *Esquadrao da Morte* (Death Squad) in Brazil did not immediately reduce American assistance to Brazilian security efforts. Similar efforts in other nations were accepted for long periods without punishment by the USA. The defeat of communism and instability was considered a greater benefit than the costs of 'due process' violations and state-sponsored and supported terror practices. The US Army and the CIA may not have set out to teach methods of terrorism and repression, but their graduates developed such skills and the USA, making a judgement on the overall merits, acquiesced to such uses by not excluding nationals from certain states nor closing the schools because of the behaviour of its graduates.

In the 1970s, death squads appeared in at least ten Latin American states whose military and police were supported and trained by the USA. In March 1984, the head of El Salvador's Treasury Police, one of the most notorious and brutal of the country's security forces, was accused of being a major figure in the organisation of that nation's death squads and a paid operative of the CIA. While he denied both accusations, the CIA dug the ground out from below him, claiming there was nothing wrong with their paying such foreign nationals because of the useful services they perform for the agency and for the USA (*New York Times*, 23 March 1984, p. 7). It is interesting to note that the 1984 recommendations of the Commission on Central America under the chairmanship of Henry Kissinger included a proposal to lift the ban on US aid to national police forces. The commission argues that the ban 'dates back to a previous period when it was believed that such aid was sometimes helping groups guilty of serious human rights abuses' (cited by Goldberg, 1984). The 'Realpolitik' orientation of the commission's chairman leads back once again to the cost–benefit calculations that led originally to the congressional reaction (from both liberals and conservatives) against Mr Kissinger's dismissal of what were believed to be tradition US human rights concerns during his tenure as National Security Advisor and Secretary of State (see Stohl *et al.*, 1984).

States are also quite willing to help provide other states the tools of the terror trade. Wright (1978), and Klare and Arnson (1981) make clear that the new technologies of repression are widely available and widely distributed. The USA has been an active provider of the instruments of terrorism and repression to Third World client-states to employ on their populations and also in quite a number of cases to train the security services of these societies in the proper employment of these instruments. It is also a lucrative trade and the US government assists corporations in the marketing of their wares. Other Western governments have similarly assisted their national corporations in this regard and the USSR and Czechoslovakia, while exercising some control on the basis of ideological requirements, have sought needed hard currency by supplying small (and large) arms to willing purchasers.

When in November 1979 the Carter Administration informed the Shah of Iran that his administration would continue to back the Peacock Throne and sent tear-gas, police batons, protective vests and other riot-control equipment, it was clear that even a President reviled by his conservative critics for being 'soft' and placing human rights above security was not going to deny the instruments of repression (which were used for terror purposes as well) to an ally in need. This followed, of course, upon the heels of Carter's post Black Friday (8 September 1979) telephone call to the Shah in which he reiterated US support and hopes for continued liberalisation following the imposition of martial law and the gunning down of somewhere between 700 and 2000 people (Rubin, 1981, p. 214). In the end, the Shah's use of terror fell short. Once the population, *en masse*, had indicated they were not afraid to continue to die in order to rid themselves of the Shah, the threat of death which the security forces could present was no longer politically meaningful.

On the other hand, the reaction of many American policy-makers (particularly those of the current administration) to developments in Iran is important in this regard. The presumption appears to be that the Shah's regime fell in the end because the Carter Administration was unwilling to provide *enough* military hardware and possibly the actual employment of American troops to prevent the overthrow. The US reliance on the Shah's use of terror thus apparently also fell short of providing the 'proper ending'. In short, one may argue that the Reagan Administration's analysis of the failure of the Carter Administration's policy suggests that the failure was not connected with Carter's unwillingness to see the Shah use terrorism and supply him with the needed equipment, rather it was its choice of surrogate terrorism in preference to direct and forceful military intervention on the side of the Shah. The Carter people held too long to the indirect support that their sponsorship and acquiescence provided. The US policy of surrogate terror was a failure because the Shah was incompetent and lost the support of key elements in society. Unwilling to pay the response and production costs of shifting from a policy of surrogate terrorism to direct military intervention, the USA paid the cost of losing the continued benefits of the Pahlavi dynasty.

Successive US administrations had assisted the Shah as well as the governments of El Salvador, Guatemala, Nicaragua under Somoza and numerous other repressive client-states because they concluded it was easier and less costly to do so than to 'do the job themselves'. In other words, these governments provided a mechanism by which the USA believed its national interest would be served.

Likewise the USSR has, and continues to train and support, its own surrogates in Afghanistan (where its original surrogate government was not up to the task), in Ethiopia, and of course in Eastern Europe, where many of the current regimes have consistently challenged the bounds of their surrogate status.

(b) *States As International Surrogates.* In a bipolar world within which the polar powers have nuclear weapons, it has become obvious to most observers (including, after more than six years in office, the current occupants of the White House and Department of Defense) that it is impractical and undesirable to become involved in major wars, that the infinite cost of a nuclear holocaust outweighs the possible benefits of eliminating the opposing superpowers. In the post-Hiroshima world, to engage in war is truly to risk *all*. A conventional war may not easily slide into a nuclear holocaust if both sides have access to nuclear weapons, but much of American military strategy since the McNamara era has certainly maintained this to be the case.

The US experience in Vietnam, the Soviet's experience in Afghanistan, and the recent ongoing Iranian-Iraqi war (reflect on the possible consequences had not Israel destroyed the reactor at Osiraq) should also have demonstrated that protracted 'low-level' war may be equally unattractive as an instrument of national policy.

Some military experts (ignoring much of the reality of the existence of what has already been discussed have therefore recently argued that terrorism *may* become accepted as part of a nation's military strategy. As long ago as 1975 Brian Jenkins (1975; see also Jenkins, Chapter 8 of this volume) worried that nations might employ groups as surrogates for engaging in warfare with other nations. These surrogates (both state and non-state actors), he argued, might be employed:

1. to provoke international incidents;
2. to create alarm in an adversary;
3. to destroy morale;
4. to cause the diversion of an enemy's resources into security budgets;
5. to effect specific forms of sabotage;
6. to provoke repressive and reactive strategies and the revolutionary overthrow of targeted regimes (what we may designate the Marighela strategy as applied by state rather than insurgent actors, see Marighela, 1971).

We recognise that terrorism has become simpler for insurgents because of advances in transport, communications, weapons, technology and access to the media. We should also recognise that the vast resources of the state allow it to make far greater use of these developments than many individuals and insurgent groups.

Beginning with the Nixon Doctrine and extending into the Carter Administration there was much discussion of the development and employment of the forces of regional power centres to avoid direct US military action in the Third World. During the Reagan Administration, the USA has appeared to be building up the Honduran army to serve a surrogate role in the Central American region. The USSR likewise, it may be argued, appears to employ state surrogates, particularly in Africa. While the reasons for Cuban involvement in Africa may be directly related to the policy prescriptions of Fidel Castro rather than Soviet leaders (see Robbins, 1983, for an excellent analysis) there does appear to have developed a system whereby the USSR and East Germany provide most of the technicians and advisers and the Cubans most of the foreign troops. These activities have been located entirely within nations friendly to these powers and so far they have not participated in overt military activities against other regimes. Their disposition combined with US support for insurgents and regimes rather than direct participation in Africa reduces the likelihood that clashes in Angola, for example, would escalate so as to involve the superpowers in a direct confrontation. We should expect more rather than less of this pattern in the future.

Here as elsewhere in the consideration of terrorism as a strategy, the cost–benefit analysis leads superpowers to choose a terror strategy rather than a straightforward traditional policy or direct military force.

V CONCLUSION

The preceding pages argue that strategies and tactics of terrorism have become important foreign-policy instruments of the super-powers. As in the domestic realm, the practice of terror, when identified as such, brings almost universal condemnation. But as in the domestic realm, when it is the state that is the perpetrator of the terrorist act, few even pause to label the action as such. A recent example of this refusal may be seen in the attempts of both Margaret Thatcher and Jeane Kirkpatrick to identify the actions of the French secret service in Auckland Harbour when they blew up the Green-peace ship, *Rainbow Warrior*, as something other than an act of State terrorism. This despite the fact that the French government did in fact take responsibility (see King, 1986, p. 194). There has been a remarkably complete silence on the part of the US government on the matter. States and proponents of their actions shrink from labelling what they themselves or those they support do as 'terror', preferring more 'neutral' designations such as 'coercive diplomacy', 'assistance' to a friendly state in its pursuit of internal security or 'aid' to freedom fighters or wars of national liberation.

The differences in the behavioural patterns of the superpowers may be seen as resulting from the structural constraints and oppor-tunities presented to them as the defenders of the current inter-national system. While both require the survival of the system, and by implication the survival of their major adversary, they have both continued to seek advantages within that system. The current system finds the USA with more governments to protect, aid and abet than has the USSR, while the USSR continues to have greater involve-ment with a greater number of insurgent organisations and 'wars of national liberation'. The behavioural patterns may thus be dis-similar but this does not translate to a necessary difference in motivations or scruples. The superpowers, like other international actors, appear to employ terrorism when they calculate that response and production costs are lower than probable benefits.

Why then does it appear from the preceding remarks that the USA has made greater use of the various methods of state terrorism in the international system than has the USSR? If we turn first to an examination of the use of open coercive threats there are four distinguishing features which arise from both international structural conditions and the differences in domestic structure that should prove fruitful arenas for further research:

1. The USSR has traditionally adopted a much more conservative style in its foreign policy based on a much higher level of secrecy. Threats may give too much away of what one is considering and thus the manipulation of threat may simply go too much against the grain;

2. The USSR has not always had the full panoply of tools to play a flexible threat game and has never had the military and infrastructural capabilities of the USA. As the USSR increases the size of its blue-water navy and its ability to base air- and land-forces at sites quite distant from Moscow perhaps this increasing capability may well be translated into increased attempts at coercive behaviour. Alternatively, of course, the USSR may simply not believe as much in the utility of open threats in foreign policy;

3. The different effectiveness of open threats within ones own sphere of influence as opposed to that outside finds the USSR with far fewer opportunities to influence behaviour in this manner. Certainly the USSR has not been reluctant to use such a policy within the Eastern European sphere, but that after all applies to only six states. The sheer size differential of the third world sphere of influence between the USA and the USSR must be a starting-point for an accounting of the difference in the willingness to use threats.

4. In open societies, threats may play a domestic role in rallying publics behind the President. The leaders in the Kremlin, with their greater ability to control the flow of foreign news do not need to move as quickly or as openly to confront or redress possible threats, nor do they have to worry about the next election and charges of weakness (Stoll, 1984, finds that the Presidential use of force identified by Blechman and Kaplan increases during Presidential election campaigns.

When we turn to the question of the differences in Soviet and American clandestine and surrogate behaviour it should also be clear that much of the difference in our analysis may be traced to the question of secrecy and the closed versus open nature of Soviet and American society. It is quite clearly much easier to learn of American involvement in such actions. In addition to the work of American and other Western journalists, American public officials and former CIA operatives have simply been far more open about their behaviours. The use of private groups and multinational corporations has also extended the size of the possible network while also increasing the number of persons 'in the know'. In that sense the CIA's involvement in Chile during the Allende years and the resultant political furore and increased scrutiny of the agency by Congressional oversight and investigative committees may be the single most important cause of what we have learned about US behaviour. We simply cannot expect the same wealth of information to be made available if some future KGB dissidents decide to inform the West of Soviet behaviour in some past or future enterprise.

If the theoretical framework employed to guide this analysis is useful, the management of the problem of states and terrorism will come in increasing the response and production costs of terrorism as a possible strategy within the foreign-policy repertoire of states. The first step in such a process is the delegitimation of the option. It is necessary to tear away at the protective clothing that allows agents of the state and the public to ignore the human consequences that state terrorist behaviour generates. If we may delegitimise such behaviour, we increase the psychic production costs for state decision-makers. By challenging the behaviour and raising public awareness both at home and abroad we increase the possibilities of bystanders of the terrorism challenging the behaviour. This will contribute to an increase in the response costs that policy-makers will have to add to their decision calculus.

At one level, it is clear that the current administration recognises the utility of this suggestion. Speaking to the American Bar Association on 8 July 1985, President Reagan identified five states – Iran, Libya, North Korea, Cuba and Nicaragua – as 'terrorist' states and as states which sponsor terrorism. The President, in his speech, identified a number of 'illegitimate' activities by these states – state-approved assassination, backing terrorist groups, using agents or surrogates, secret arms agreements with terrorist groups and governments, harbouring terrorists and the creation of a confederation of terrorist states – 'a new international version of "Murder Incorporated"'.

While the President was primarily interested in generating

domestic support for tougher approaches to the problem of international terrorism and in scoring a few propaganda points, the
utility of raising the problem should not be lightly dismissed.
However, the President's position is undermined by the selective
manner in which he designated 'terrorist' states and by the
unwillingness to provide direct evidence for his charges. The raising
of the issue will obviously be more effective in pluralistic Western
societies than elsewhere in the international system. While these
states are less likely to employ terrorist strategies within their own
states, their acceptance of the international rules of the game has
allowed them actively to pursue terrorist strategies abroad and also
to ignore, except in political selected cases, terrorism by states and
insurgents of which they approve. The administration's confusion
over the proper response to the 1985 Israeli bombing raid on PLO
headquarters in Tunis is a case in point. Was this an effective and
acceptable counter-terrorism reprisal or was it an unacceptable
attack on the territorial integrity of a friendly state? Did it properly
serve notice to states that would harbour terrorists or did it go
beyond the bounds of acceptable international behaviour (see the
Introduction to this volume)?

This chapter has identified five forms of state terrorist behaviours.
There is no magic formula by which to eliminate the problems posed
by each of these forms. However, it should be recognised at the start
of designing effective counter-policies that each of the five forms
requires a different level of information and response (see the
excellent discussion by Wardlaw, Chapter 7 of this volume). Not all
state-terrorist behaviours can be managed or countered in the same
way and while all states can operate at levels equivalent to
insurgents, it is quite often the case that the costs of doing so are
larger than the expected benefits and thus they choose not to do so. It
is our task to find useful procedures to increase the costs of terrorist
operations across the board.

Notes

1. This chapter is part of a continuing research project which seeks to
   examine the role of terrorism as an instrument of state policy (see Stohl,
   1983, 1984a, 1984b; Duvall and Stohl, 1983; and Mitchell, Stohl, Carleton
   and Lopez, 1986.

2. Mrs Kirkpatrick suggested that there is an importance difference between international terrorism and the sabotage of the Greenpeace ship Rainbow Warrior by agents of the DGSE (the French Secret Service): 'I'd like to say that the French clearly did not intend to attack civilians and bystanders and maim, torture and kill.' This statement came after the French government had accepted responsibility, and the Defence Minister and the head of the Secret Service had been forced to resign because of their part in the affair (AP and UPI wire service reports, 25 September 1985). For its part, the US government has been conspicuously silent on the matter.

3. This may be expressed as

$$U_i = P_i (B - C_i)$$

where U_i is the expected utility from engaging in action i; B is the benefit received from the desired state of affairs, P_i is the believed probability with which action i will bring about the desired state of affairs and C_i is the believed probable cost of engaging in action i. (Duvall and Stohl, 1983, p. 202).

4. While realist analysis may move beyond these core propositions, I would argue that these propositions provide the fundamental framework from within which realists discuss strategic 'realities'.

5. On the 'rules' perspective in general see Raymond Cohen (1981). On the rules and the superpowers and the stability of the US–USSR Relationship see Gilpin (1981, pp. 231–44), Waltz (1979, pp. 202–9), Gaddis (1986) and Keal (1983).

6. Captured in Beirut, Lebanon, by the Israelis in 1982, a selection is translated and reproduced in Cline and Alexander (1984).

References

Aron, Raymond (1974) *The Imperial Republic* (Cambridge, Massachusetts: Winthrop).

Beitz, Charles (1979) *Political Theory and International Relations* (Princeton, New Jersey: Princeton University Press).

Beres, L. R. (1980) *Apocalypse* (Chicago: University of Chicago Press).

Bishop, Vaughn (1983) 'The Role of Political Terrorism in the Palestinian Resistance Movement June 1967–October 1973', in M. Stohl (ed.) *The Politics of Terrorism* (New York: Marcel Dekker) 2nd ed.

Blechman, Barry, and Kaplan, Stephen (1978) *Force Without War* (Washington: Brookings Institute).

Branch, Taylor, and Propper, Eugene (1982) *Labyrinth* (New York: Viking).

Bull, Hedley (1977) *The Anarchical Society* (New York: Columbia).

Carleton, D. and Stohl, M. (1985) 'The Foreign Policy of Human Rights: Rhetoric and Reality from Jimmy Carter to Ronald Reagan', *Human Rights Quarterly*, vol. 7, no. 2, May, pp. 205–29.

Cassirer, Ernst (1946) *The Myth of The State* (New Haven: Yale University Press).

Chomsky, Noam, and Herman, Edward (1979) *The Political Economy of Human Rights*: Volume 1, *The Washington Connection and Third World Fascism*; Volume 2, *After the Cataclysm: Postwar Indochina and the Reconstruction of Imperial Ideology* (Boston: South End Press).

Cline, Ray and Alexander, Yonah (1984) *Terrorism: The Soviet Connection* (New York: Crane & Russak).

Cohen, Raymond (1981) *International Politics: The Rules of the Game* (New York: Longman).

Craig, Gordon A. and George, Alexander (1983) *Force and Statecraft* (New York: Oxford University Press).

Demaris, Ovid (1977) *Brothers in Blood* (New York: Charles Scribner's Sons).

Duvall, R. D. and Stohl, M. (1983) 'Governance by Terror', in M. Stohl (ed.) *The Politics of Terrorism* (New York: Marcel Dekker) pp. 179–219.

Ellman, Paul (1983) 'Training Democrats and Dictators', *Guardian*.

Falk, Richard (1972) 'Zone II as a World Order Construct', in J. Rosenau, V. Davis and M. East, *The Analysis of International Politics* (New York: Free Press).

Fein, Helen (1979) *Accounting for Genocide* (New York: Free Press).

Franck, T. and Weisband, W. (1972) *Word Politics* (New York: Oxford University Press).

Friedlander, Robert A. (1982) 'A Riddle Inside a Mystery Wrapped in An Enigma: Terrorism and the "Soviet Connection"', *Clandestine Tactics and Technology*, vol. VIII, Issue #11, International Association of Chiefs of Police.

Fukuyama, Francis (1986) 'Military Aspects of US–Soviet Competition in the Third World', in Marshall Shulman (ed.) *East–West Tensions in the Third World* (New York: Norton).

Gaddis, John Lewis (1982) *Strategies of Containment* (New York: Oxford).

Gaddis, John Lewis (1986) 'The Long Peace', *International Security*, vol. 10, no. 4, Spring, pp. 99–142.

Gelb, Leslie (1981) 'Soviet Terror Ties Called Outdated', *New York Times*, 18 October.

George, Alexander (1971) 'The Development of Doctrine and Strategy', in A. George, D. Hall and W. R. Simons, *The Limits of Coercive Diplomacy* (Boston: Little, Brown) pp. 1–35.

Gilpin, Robert (1981) *War and Change in World Politics* (Cambridge: Cambridge University Press).

Goldberg, Nicholas (1984) 'Don't Aid Central American Police', *New York Times*, 23 February.

Gurtov, Melvin (1974) *The United States Against the Third World* (New York: Praeger).

Haig, Alexander (1981) News Conference, 28 January, *Current Policy*, no. 258, Department of State, p. 5.

Hall, David K. (1981) 'Naval Diplomacy in West African Waters', in Kaplan (1981) pp. 519–69.

Halperin, Morton; Berman, Jerry, Borosage, Robert, and Marwich, Christine (1976) *The Lawless State* (New York: Penguin).

Herman, Edward (1982) *The Real Terror Network* (Boston: South End Press).

Hinkle, Warren and Turner, William (1981) *The Fish is Red* (New York: Harper & Row).

Hook, Sidney (1986) 'Between Democracy and Despotism', *Imprimis* vol. 15, no. 2, February.

Horner, Charles (1980) *The Facts About Terrorism*, Commentary, vol. 69, no. 6 (June) pp. 40–5.

Jenkins, Brian (1975) 'International Terrorism: A New Mode of Conflict', California Seminar on Arms Control and Foreign Policy Research Paper no. 48, Santa Monica, California.

Johansen, Robert C. (1980) *The National Interest and the Human Interest* Princeton: Princeton University Press).

Johansen, Christen (1984) *Superpower: Comparing American and Soviet Foreign Policy* (New York: St Martin's Press).

Kaplan, Stephen (1981) *The Diplomacy of Power* (Washington: Brookings Institute).

Keal, Paul (1983) *Unspoken Rules and Superpower Dominance* (New York: St Martin's Press).

Kegley, Charles, Sturgeon, T., Vance and Wittkopf, Eugene (1987) 'Structural Terrorism: The Systemic Sources of State-Sponsored Terrorism', in M. Stohl and G. Lopez (eds) *Terrible Beyond Endurance? The Foreign Policy of Terrorism* (Westport CT: Greenwood Press).

Kelman, Herbert (1973) 'Violence Without Moral Restraint: Reflection on the Dehumanization of Victims and Victimizers', *Journal of Social Issues*, 29, 4, pp. 25–61.

Kendrick, Alexander (1974) *The Wound Within* (Boston: Little, Brown).

King, Michael (1986) *Death of the Rainbow Warrior* (Auckland: Penguin).

Kirkpatrick, Jeane (1986) 'The Myth of Moral Equivalence', *Imprimis*, vol. 15, no. 1, January.

Klare, Michael T. and Cynthia Aronson (1981) *Supplying Repression: US Support for Authoritarian Regimes Abroad* (Washington DC: International Foreign Policy Studies).

Langguth, A. J. (1978) *Hidden Terrors* (New York: Pantheon).

Luttwak, Edward (1983) *The Grand Strategy of the Soviet Union* (New York: St Martin's Press).

McWhinney, Edward (1964) *Peaceful Coexistence and Soviet–Western International Law* (Leyden: A. W. Sythoff).

Marchetti, Victor and Marks, John (1974) *The CIA and the Cult of Intelligence* (New York: Dell).

Marighela, Carlos (1971) *Minimanual of the Urban Guerrilla* (Harmondsworth: Penguin).

Mickolus, Edward (1980) *Transnational Terrorism: A Chronology Of Events 1968–1979* (Westport, Connecticut: Greenwood Press).

Miller, Judith (1981) 'Soviet Aid Disputed in Terrorism Study', *New York Times*, 29 March.

Mitchell, C., Stohl, Michael, Carleton, David, and Lopez, George, (1986). 'State Terrorism: Issues of Concept and Measurement', in M. Stohl and G. Lopez (eds) *Government Violence and Repression: An Agenda for Research* (Westport, Connecticut: Greenwood Press).

Morgenthau, Hans (1978) *Politics Among Nations* (New York: Alfred A. Knopf) 5th revised edn.

Nathan, James and Oliver, James (1981) *United States Foreign Policies and World Order* (Boston: Little, Brown) 2nd edn.

Ostrom, Charles W. and Job, Brian (1986) 'The President and the Political Use of Force', *American Political Science Review*, vol. 80, no. 2, June 1986, pp. 541–66.

Pear, Robert (1981) 'FBI Chief Sees No Evidence Soviet Aids Terrorism in US', *New York Times*, 27 April.

Peleg, Ilan (1987) 'Terrorism in the Middle East: The Case of the Arab-Israel Conflict', in M. Stohl (ed.) *The Politics of Terrorism*, (New York: Marcel Dekker) 3rd edn.

Peterzell, Jay (1984) *Reagan's Secret Wars* (Washington: Center for National Security).

Pike, Otis (1976) 'The Select Committee's Investigation Report', *The Village Voice*, 16 February.

Porter, Bruce (1984) *The USSR in Third World Conflicts* (Cambridge: Cambridge University Press).

Quester, George (1987) 'Some Explanations for State-Supported Terrorism in the Middle East,' in M. Stohl and G. Lopez (eds), *The Foreign Policy of State Terrorism* (Westport, Connecticut: Greenwood Press).

Quester, George (1987) 'Some Explanations for State-Supported Terrorism in the Middle East,' in M. Stohl and G. Lopez (eds), *Terrible Beyond Endurance? The Foreign Policy of State Terrorism* (Westport, Connecticut: Greenwood Press).

Robbins, Carla Anne (1983) *The Cuban Threat* (New York: McGraw-Hill).

Rosenfeld, Stephen S. (1986) 'The Guns of July', *Foreign Affairs*, vol. 64, no. 4, Spring, pp. 698–714.

Rubin, Barry (1981) *Paved With Good Intentions* (New York: Penguin).

Rubinstein, A. (1981) *Soviet Foreign Policy Since World War II* (Cambridge, Massachusetts: Winthrop).

Schelling, Thomas (1966) *Arms and Influence* (New Haven: Yale University Press).

Schelling, Thomas (1982) 'Thinking About Nuclear Terrorism', *International Security*, vol. 6, pp. 61–77.

Schmid, A. P. (1985) *Soviet Military Interventions Since 1945* (Leyden: COMT).

Schurman, Franz (1974) *The Logic of World Power* (New York: Pantheon).

Sterling, Claire (1981a) *The Terror Network* (New York: Holt, Rinehart & Winston) 357 pp.

Sterling, Claire (1981b) 'Terrorism: Tracing the International Network', *New York Times Magazine*, 1 March, p. 16.

Stoessinger, John (1976) *Henry Kissinger: The Anguish of Power* (New York: Norton).

Stohl, Michael (ed.) (1983) *The Politics of Terrorism* (New York: Marcel Dekker) 2nd edn.

Stohl, Michael (1984a) 'International Dimensions of State Terrorism', in M. Stohl and G. Lopez (eds) *The State as Terrorist* (Westport, Connecticut: Greenwood) pp. 43–58.

Stohl, Michael (1984b) 'National Interests and State Terrorism', *Political Science*, vol. 36, no. 1, July, pp. 37–52.

Stohl, M., Carleton, D. and Johnson, S. (1984) 'Human Rights and US Foreign Assistance from Nixon to Carter', *Journal of Peace Research*, vol. 21, no. 3, pp. 215–26.

Stoll, Richard (1984) 'The Guns of November', *Journal of Conflict Resolution*, vol. 28, pp. 231–46.

Terekhov, F. (1974) 'International Terrorism and the Struggle Against It', *Novoye Vremya*, 15 March, pp. 20–2.

Tucker, Robert W. (1981) *The Purposes of American Power* (New York: Praeger).

Ulam, Adam (1974) *Expansion and Coexistence* (New York: Praeger).

US Department of State (1983) *Patterns of International Terrorism 1982* (Washington: US Department of State).

Waltz, Kenneth (1979) *Theory of International Politics* (Boston, Massachusetts: Addison-Wesley).

Walzer, Michael (1974) 'Political Action: The Problem of Dirty Hands', in M. Cohen, T. Nagel and T. Scanlon, *War and Moral Responsibility*, pp. 62–82.

Wardlaw, Grant (1982) *Political Terrorism* (New York: Cambridge University Press).

Wicker, Tom (1981) 'The Great Terrorist Hunt', *New York Times*, 28 April.

Wilkinson, Paul (1986) *Terrorism and the Liberal State* (New York: New York University Press) 2nd edn.

Williams, Phil (1976) *Crisis Management* (Oxford: Martin Robertson).

Wilson, James Q. (1981) 'Thinking About Terrorism', *Commentary*, vol. 72, no. 1, 8 July, pp. 34–9.

Wright, Steve (1978) 'New Police Technologies', *Journal of Peace Research*, vol. XV, no. 4, pp. 305–22.

7 State Response to International Terrorism: Some Cautionary Comments
Grant Wardlaw

INTRODUCTION

Terrorism is a phenomenon that is increasingly coming to dominate our lives. It influences the way governments conduct their foreign policy and corporations transact their business. It causes changes to the structure and role of our security forces and necessitates huge expenditures on measures to protect public figures, vital installations, citizens and, perhaps in the final analysis, our system of government. It affects the way we travel, the places we visit and the manner in which we live our daily lives. Our newspapers, radios and televisions saturate our every waking moment with the lurid details of the latest terrorist spectacular.

Democratic governments seem peculiarly vulnerable to what many believe to be a novel contemporary form of political violence.[1] Small groups with little or no direct political power seem to be able, by employing terrorist tactics, to achieve effects on a target community which are entirely disproportionate to their numerical or political importance. But just how great a threat does terrorism pose? And if it is a threat, what exactly does it threaten? After all, although terrorism is bloody and getting bloodier (Cordes, Hoffmann, Jenkins, Kellen, Moran and Sater 1984), its track record as a cause of death and injury pales into insignificance beside such other causes of death as motor vehicle accidents, which cause untold annual carnage but seem somehow to be 'accepted' as a lamentable, but inevitable, consequence of modern life.

Contemporary political terrorism came of age in the 1960s and 1970s. A wave of spectacular aircraft hijackings and embassy takeovers, together with an almost routine fare of bombings, assassinations and kidnappings, ensured that terrorism was given constant media exposure. Public apprehension was heightened, minor tactical gains were made by the terrorists, and governments responded with increased security and a growing resolve not to accede to terrorist demands. But terrorists did not succeed in translating tactical successes into concrete political gains. No governments fell because of terrorist action. No significant national or international policy changes were forced as a concession to terrorist threats. No terrorist strategy has yet shown that terrorist violence is directly related to the acquisition of positive political power (Jenkins, 1984a).

In the late 1970s and early 1980s the security authorities in a number of countries notched up major victories in counter-terrorist operations, prompting some commentators to claim that the 'war on terrorism' was being won. The hardening resolve of the authorities was demonstrated by such successes as Entebbe, Mogadishu, and Princes Gate. It was pointed out that the pressure exerted on democracies by groups such as the Palestine Liberation Organisation, the Red Brigades, and the Baader–Meinhof gang had been substantially reduced. In the Middle East, the Israeli invasion of Lebanon and the subsequent dispersal of the PLO, together with its own internal problems, were seen by some as limiting the scope of Palestinian terrorism for the immediate future. In Europe, the capture and imprisonment of large numbers of the Italian Red Brigades and the mopping up of the remnants of the Baader–Meinhof gang in Germany were predicted to bring a substantial reduction in terrorism on the Continent.

But that optimism has lately given way to a grim realisation that terrorism is indeed here to stay and is set to exert increasing influence on the world political scene. Since the early 1980s the number of international terrorist incidents has again been on the rise. In addition, the number of groups involved in terrorism continues to grow. In 1982, the State Department reported that 117 groups representing seventy-one nationalities claimed responsibility for terrorist incidents, the second-largest total since 1968. In Europe and the Middle East there has been a resurgence of terrorism by groups thought largely to have been neutralised (Bolton, 1984; Hoffman, 1984; Horchem, 1985; Kellen, 1985; O'Ballance, 1985). Terrorism is far from defeated.

Not only is terrorism now increasing in incidence, it is also resulting in higher casualties. Since 1977, the number of international terrorist incidents resulting in fatalities has increased each year (Cordes *et al.,* 1984). In 1984, the total number of incidents which were lethal or clearly intended to be lethal increased at least proportionally to the total number of incidents (Oakley, 1985). Ironically, the increasing number of casualties associated with terrorism is partially a result of successes in developing anti-terrorist methods. Established, major terrorist groups have largely abandoned the embassy takeovers and airplane hijackings of the 1960s and 1970s because of the successful response of governments to these methods. Increased security, refined hostage negotiation procedures, and an increased willingness on the part of governments to refuse to make major concessions and to use force if necessary to terminate terrorist sieges have made skyjackings and hostage-taking much less attractive options for terrorists. For many, resort to such methods now involves too many risks and too few rewards.

Paradoxically, however, we are also seeing the emergence of a new breed of fanatical terrorists willing to martyr themselves for their cause. The result is a return to the time-honoured methods of the bomb and the bullet. The use of bombings and assassinations has meant that security forces have had less successful contacts with terrorists and that casualties have been higher. While relatively few hostages died in sieges or hijackings, the much more indiscriminate and destructive nature of bombings results in large numbers of deaths and injuries. Bombings such as those of the US Marine headquarters in Beirut in 1983, with death-tolls in the hundreds, are still relatively unusual, but they are increasing and could well become standard terrorist practice.

In spite of the attention devoted to terrorism carried out by revolutionary or insurgent groups, however, it is not this brand of violence which poses the most serious threat to either internal stability or international affairs. That role is reserved for state-sponsored terrorism. The threat lies not in the terrorist act itself. The importance of such events as the murder of WPC Fletcher outside the Libyan People's Bureau in London or even the bombing of the US Marines in Beirut, lies not so much in the horrendous nature of the acts themselves (which are rightly condemned) but in their implications for international relations. If such acts become too frequent and too effective, when state-sponsored terrorism turns into a real threat to national interests, the conflict will almost certainly escalate into something more dangerous than mere terrorism. The great danger is that terrorism may come to be seen generally as part of the armoury of states. If this occurs we face the spectre of a spiral of terrorism, preemptive action, punishment raids and reprisal terrorism conducted and financed by states with their vast resources. The potential consequences for international peace and stability are easy to imagine.

In addition to examining terrorism as a phenomenon of international relations, attention is increasingly being focused on the possibility of terrorism providing an alternative means to dominating situations that are normally influenced by conventional military forces. Many analysts see an emerging role for terrorism as a means of 'surrogate warfare' employed by states against other nations (Jenkins, 1984a; Kupperman, Alexander, van Opstal and Williamson, 1984; Motley, 1984; Wright, 1984).

There is evidence of a trend towards the development of low-level conflict as an important part of the world strategic mosaic. Early predictions that low-level conflict would replace costly conventional wars (Halle, 1973) seem to have been somewhat overstated in that major conventional engagements still occur (e.g. the Arab–Israeli wars, the current Iran-Iraq struggle) and show little sign of becoming obsolete. But modes of conflict such as guerrilla warfare and terrorism continue to increase. What is more important is that they are being used not only by insurgents, but by states as well.

Possibly the increased use of low-level conflict is related to the diffusion of power in the world today (Sloan, 1982). Ethnicity and nationality compete as the basis for legitimate political authority. At present, the United Nations is growing by approximately three new nations a year. If this trend continues, we will have 200 independent nations by 1990 and even more by the turn of the century. A good many of these nations will be 'ministates' which are economically dependent and vulnerable to external pressure. Others may not be classed as ministates, but still feel unable to exert sufficient influence over their own affairs or those of their region because of the influence of larger powers. Resort to the tactics of terrorism, or the formation of alliances with terrorist groups, provides an option which allows such nations, which would otherwise be unable to mount challenges using conventional force, to carry out surrogate warfare against their opponents. Some analysts go further and suggest that even large nations may resort more readily to forms of low-level warfare, including terrorism, in the face of the massively escalating costs of conventional warfare. Once again, predictions of this nature over-emphasise the likelihood or the extent of this development. Nevertheless the evidence is there of a trend in this direction and we should certainly be devoting more resources to the study of terrorism as an element of military strategy and to the development of appropriate military (as opposed to police) doctrine and countermeasures. Indeed, Jenkins (1984a) has pointed out how important the interaction of conventional war, guerrilla warfare and international terrorism is likely to be in the future.

If one wants evidence of the usefulness of the new strategy of terrorism one has only to consider recent events in the Middle East. Instead of (or as well as) using terrorism as a tactic to overthrow incumbent regimes, terrorists now seek to use it as an instrument to change the foreign policy of nation-states. Look, for example, at the case of the hijacking of TWA flight 847 in June this year. What did the terrorists want? The call for the release of the 766 Lebanese, mostly Shi'ites, held by Israel was merely a pretext for an act with wider implications. Israel had already announced that it would soon free the prisoners and it is doubtful that their perceived plight was ever the terrorists' primary concern. Instead, what was desired was the humiliation of the USA. Whether or not it appears that way to us, the message conveyed to the Middle East was that the USA was a blustering giant, full of rhetoric, invective and brave statements of intention, but incapable of – or lacking the political will to take – any real, effective action. The government that insisted it would not negotiate with terrorists was made to appear as if it had (and may, in fact, have) done just that. The President who had spoken so loudly about how he would never find himself in the situation of Jimmy Carter over the seizure of the US Embassy in Tehran found himself in exactly that situation – and faced the same realities limiting effective action. The subsequent posturing of administration officials (for example, National Security Adviser Robert McFarlane's threat to bomb the 'nerve centres' of terrorism) and statements by President Reagan (for example, asserting after viewing the film 'Rambo' that he would 'know what to do next time') only served to underline further the emptiness of American threats.

As with most other terrorist spectaculars, the incident was cleverly choreographed to ensure maximum media coverage and maximum exposure of their propaganda world-wide. Indeed the novel and complex scenario which unfolded as the original terrorists were superseded first by Nabih Berri's Shi'ite Amal militia, and eventually by President Assad of Syria stands to date as the cleverest example of terrorist manipulation of the free world's news media. The result was an astonishingly successful propaganda *coup*, complete with statements of solidarity and sympathy both from some of the hostages themselves and from many journalists and commentators who while 'disagreeing with the terrorists' methods' found them 'understandable' and condemned Israeli actions and US involvement in the region.

As an editorial in the magazine, *New Republic*, pointed out, there were also two major political impacts of the affair. First, the incident and its handling at least temporarily disrupted the relationship between the USA and Israel. Second, and perhaps the major aim of the exercise, the hijackers influenced the political atmosphere in the Middle East to disrupt the emerging peace process. The tentative moves being made by Jordan's King Hussein (with US encouragement) to bring Israel and the PLO into some kind of dialogue were brought to a halt by first the hijacking and destruction of a Jordanian airliner and then the hijacking of TWA 847. As *New Republic* put it:

> Talk of a settlement was all but silenced. The so-called moderate Arabs had been gaining stature. Now they are weakened, and the irreconcilable foes of Israel are strengthened. Consider who gained the most in the hostage crisis – Hafez al-Assad of Syria. He is the new force to be reckoned with. And his game is not to forge peace between Israel and its neighbours, but to make certain that peace does not break out (29 July 1985).[2]

Subsequent events in the Middle East illustrate how complex a matter it is to take the firm action which is generally advocated as the antidote for terrorism and to ensure at the same time that the treatment has the desired effect. For all its moral virtues and for all its high appeal to domestic opinion in the USA, the forcing-down by US fighter planes of the aircraft carrying the Achille Lauro hijackers is still an action of uncertain benefits. Yes, it sent a message that the USA will not stand by and do nothing in the face of terrorism. But it also carried important costs. The mosts obvious, of course, were the fall (even if only for a short time) of the Italian Government and the souring of relations with Egypt. But it also, in my mind, set an unfortunate precedent in showing a willingness to engage in actions which were either of doubtful legitimacy or were simply illegitimate under international lawe (depending on whose advice one accepts) in order to achieve a morally legitimate end. Particularly in view of the fact that it is entirely uncertain what effect, if any, the action will have on the incidence of international terrorism, the precedent could be an unfortunate one which could serve to undermine other US initiatives to seek to find at least partial solutions within the framework of international law.

It seems, then, that we are entering a new era of terrorism with different aims. Terrorism as part of civil wars, of separatist struggles, or attempts to overthrow incumbent regimes will continue to form the backdrop. If handled properly, such terrorism is not likely to be the major component in any strategic successes gained by dissidents and certainly does not fundamentally threaten healthy liberal democracies. But state-sponsored international terrorism poses a different type of threat. Its aims are more precise, more restricted, and more achievable than those of terrorism conducted in a national context (which either aims at all-embracing ends, such as overthrowing a regime, or at achieving what in reality are impossible or highly improbable results, such as the establishment of an Armenian homeland). It is increasingly obvious that international terrorism particularly of the state-sponsored variety, *can* influence the foreign policy of nations, *can* disrupt and perhaps destroy political processes which are of importance to the international community, and *does* present a real threat to international order and stability. The challenge for the international system is to construct a flexible and imaginative counter-terrorist mechanism which can deal with this emerging threat and can mesh with the counter-terrorist machiney which individual states have established to combat terrorism aimed at their own national integrity. In order to meet this challenge we need first to assess the nature of the threat posed by international terrorism.

THE NATURE OF THE THREAT

In assessing the threat posed by terrorism, can we separate the media image from the reality – indeed are they the same or different? Certainly we seem to receive images of terrorism in a highly selective manner. Terrorism currently seems endemic in a number of regions of the world as a seemingly inevitable part of violent domestic conflicts. But little continuing attention and, certainly, few headlines are devoted to many of these instances of terrorism. If an IRA bomb explodes in London killing some innocent victim we are inundated with news flashes, extensive news coverage, and interminable back-ground analyses. A steady diet of bombings and assassinations in, say the Lebanon, El Salvador or Iran goes virtually unreported, however, unless a hapless Westerner is one of the victims. The moral tone of reporting is similarly distorted. The bombing of a hotel in Brighton is reported in tones of moral outrage, whereas a bombing in South Africa is covered generally in value-neutral or even positive terms (we 'understand' the act as an inevitable response to 'intoler-able' provocation' or an 'evil system of repression'). Spokespersons for various governments make distinctions between 'terrorists' and 'freedom fighters', whilst being unable to accept that similar dis-tinctions with the opposite value-connotations are made by governments from other political traditions or systems. As the leader in the campaign against international terrorism, the USA is par-ticularly vulnerable to charges of such inconsistency. Obviously, the US-sponsored covert operations in such places as Nicaragua, Angola and Afghanistan involve the USA with forces who would be labelled terrorist if they were opposing regimes friendly to the USA. The rapidity with which Syria was dropped from the official US list of terrorist states following the involvement of President Assad in negotiating the release of American hostages in the recent TWA hijacking drama in the Lebanon is ample proof of how subjective and ideologically loaded a term 'terrorist' is. I must emphasise that to point out the inconsistency here is not to condemn support for some groups. But we must be clear that such support *is* support for terrorism in some cases. In order to gather widespread support for forms of terrorism that are largely condemned by the community of nations, however, leading states should avoid the resounding moral language which to many can only smack of hypocrisy. While it may appeal to domestic audiences to denounce terrorists as 'animals', as 'roving bands of criminals' and as 'sick', such language does little to advance our understanding of terrorists or terrorism. There are many forms of violence, including those utilised by nations, which are equally reprehensible, yet which draw no such extreme condem-nation. For many acts of terrorism, the motives are clear and specific. We may despise the morality of the acts, but the perpetrators are not irrational. The use of moralistic hyperbole provides too convenient an excuse for some nations to opt out of international cooperation and generates yet more sources of discontent and inflammatory rhetoric among those who would maim and kill for any cause.

Leaving aside the superfluous morality and concentrating on a common response to a shared threat will produce more tangible results and lead into fewer irrelevant sidetracks.

Taking a more detached view of terrorism may help also to provide realistic assessments of the threat posed by different types of terrorism. We need a much more complex and sophisticated approach to terrorism which differentiates between different types, assigns varying degrees of threat, and produces individualised recommendations for countermeasures. The idea of a general policy against terrorism is inherently faulty – terrorism has to be countered in a discriminating, case-by-case way.

While there is a pressing need for sophisticated, well-exercised and capably-led counter-terrorist *machinery*, our counter-terrorist *policy* must necessarily remain at a general level if we are to have the flexibility which is necessary in order to deal imaginatively with the literally infinite range of possible terrorist scenarios. There is certainly an argument for enunciating a small range of policies such as 'no concessions' policies, or stating that options such as reprisals or military rescue operations will not be excluded from the counter-terrorist armamentarium. Such enunciation will serve some effect, but even here there may eventually be costs to be borne for stating these principles too loudly or in too strident terms. Clearly, there will be occasions upon which the political realities of a particular incident will make, for example, a 'no concessions' or a 'no negotiations' policy impossible to sustain and in such circumstances decision-makers should have the latitude to change direction in a timely fashion rather than have to capitulate in an embarrassing scene of public humiliation.

The issue of how strictly a state should delineate its counter-terrorist policy is intimately bound up with the issue of the language with which terrorism is discussed, particularly the moral tone of the language used. It is especially important for the credibility of a nation's counter-terrorist posture that there is a close match between words and deeds. Rhetoric may be a useful debating tool and may be an inevitable part of political discourse, but great care must be taken to ensure that the rhetoric is not shown to be devoid of real meaning. In my judgement, the credibility of the USA has been damaged severely by the stream of overstatement, empty threats, distracting and partial characterisations, and careless asides on terrorism which has glowed from Administration spokespersons. President Reagan's comparison of Libya, Iran, North Korea, Cuba and Nicaragua as an international terrorist network comparable to Murder Incorporated and his famous quip that Americans would not tolerate 'these attacks from outlaw states run by the strangest collection misfits, looney tunes and squalid criminals since the advent of the Third Reich'[3] may have been great theatre, but it was not great statesmanship. Other statements by US officials have stressed the essentially anti-American nature of much modern terrorism – a view which naturally tends to create a siege mentality and an understandable tendency to hit back to defend honour and perceived vital interests. But this characterisation too is, in most cases, an oversimplification. While there are important anti-American elements to some terrorism, most is *not* an anti-American crusade and it should not be portrayed as such. Because of her status as a superpower, because of her global reach, and because of her dominant position in the world economy, the USA provides many of the most obvious and convenient targets for terrorist attack. As such, the USA suffers disproportionately as the target of international terrorism. But much of the anti-Americanism is symbolic rather than seriously threatening. This is no consolation whatsoever to the growing list of American victims of terrorism, but it is an important factor which should temper the official response. Clearly, the USA is the leader of the global effort to counter international terrorism and carries the burden of an extra responsibility to set the appropriate tone and suggest the appropriate balance of the response to the foul crimes which are committed in the name of growing numbers of ideologies and issues. In my view, it is these issues of balance and tone which the Western democracies have yet to resolve.

Balance applies both to the balanced judgement as to the nature and level of threat posed by international terrorism to the vital interests or proper functioning of democratic states and to the balanced response to the assessed threat. The first issue is that of threat assessment. Just how much of a threat is international terrorism? Is the threat inherent in the terrorist acts themselves or is the threat partially, equally, or more particularly created by some of the possible reactions to terrorism. The well-known intentions of terrorist theoreticians such as Carlos Marighela (Marighela, 1974) to provoke the authorities into heavy-handed over-reaction to domestic terrorism translate easily to the international scene. There is no doubt that the provocation of an ill-considered and emotionally-based over-reaction to international terrorism would equally serve the purposes of terrorist groups or their state sponsors. At the same time, the failure to act resolutely will surely do considerable damage. At the extremes, irresolute responses to international terrorism may result in a small, ruthless and unrepresentative group dictating the policies and actions of states. At the least, public confidence in the ability of legitimate governments to provide for the security of its citizens will be undermined, with the very real possibility of the development of private initiatives to punish the offenders and the consequent further destabilisation of the international system (Crenshaw, 1983a; Nathan, 1981). The first balance we need to seek, then, is that between prudence and paranoia, between action and inaction, and most importantly, between paying too much attention to international terrorism and paying too little attention to it.

An essential element in discovering this balance is the ability *and the willingness* to distinguish between different types of terrorist threat. To date, states have been too ready to perceive international terrorism as a monolithic entity posing an immediate and real threat to vital state interests or to the survival of states or the international system. Even where it has been clear that some incidents pose less of a real threat than others, most states have, at least in their public utterances, been unwilling to distinguish between them. It is my contention that this failure has grossly exaggerated the real threat posed by terrorism and has inflamed public reaction to incidents to the point at which politicians now find their options severely constrained if not, in some cases, virtually predetermined. Once again the parallels between domestic and international terrorism are apparent. While many governments address domestic terrorism in terms of a battle for the very existence of democracy, a very cogent argument can be mounted to support the proposition that 'terrorist groups are, by their very nature, and that of the strategies they pursue, incapable of posing *any* threat to democratic states (Mack, 1981, p. 199, emphasis in original). Mack argues convincingly that while revolutionary terrorism can be effective under certain circumstances, the necessary conditions do not exist in democratic societies. As I have argued elsewhere (Wardlaw, 1986), it is largely the exploitation of the terrorist image by the media and perceptions which flow from sensationalist coverage of terrorist spectaculars which are responsible for the widespread belief that terrorism poses a significant challenge to the survival of democracies. In many ways our perceptions of domestic terrorism and reactions to it fall within the category of a 'moral panic' in which often there is a major discrepancy between the perceived threat and the reality. The great difficulty, of course, is to be able to divorce oneself sufficiently from the human tragedy and the barbarism of terrorism to be able to assess just what damage is done away from the scene of the horror.

The disjunction between the perception of and the reality of much terrorism serves to elevate terrorism to undeserved prominence on policy agendas and grossly to inflate the importance of terrorist groups. Indeed, as Cerny observes:

> The potential power of these groups seems to lie not in their threat to overthrow society by force of arms *per se*, but in their ability to symbolise the fragility and vulnerability of the social order and to force that order to subvert itself by eroding the liberal and democratic values upon which its own legitimacy is based
>
> (Cerny, 1981, p. 92).

In the case of international terrorism, governments have often been the willing accomplices of the news media in generating and maintaining the hysteria which surrounds terrorism and have thus themselves been guilty of subverting the process of accurate threat assessment. The result has been that the issue of international terrorism has assumed monumental proportions. Let me be quite clear that I consider international terrorism to be a serious problem which deserves the attention of all nations. However, I believe much of the debate about methods of responding to terrorism has become unfocused because of our failure to distinguish one sort of threat from another and to articulate to the public why certain tactics used in certain circumstances may seriously impair a state's ability to conduct its necessary affairs, why and which vital national interests are in jeopardy, and how the functioning of the international system may be threatened. By failing to make these distinctions and to argue through their consequences, we are consigned to viewing international terrorism as a much more potent force than it is in many cases. We underestimate the resilience both of democratic states and of the international system and thereby elevate terrorism to a position from which it is able to determine a state's foreign policy. In short, our crisis of confidence hands the terrorists or, more importantly, their sponsors, an unnecessary victory. Walter Laqueur summed up the need for the sense of perspective which I am advocating when he wrote of the importance of pointing out:

the wide discrepancy between the facts about terrorism, which almost always fails, and the mistaken perceptions of an all-powerful, omnipresent monster... Historically terrorism has been no more than a minor nuisance – tragic as far as its victims are concerned, but on the whole ineffective. To regard it as one of the gravest challenges to US interests is not just a mistake. It is dangerous, for it focuses attention on a sideshow in a sideshow – some cut-throats from West Beirut or other such places, who may or may not be manipulated from afar; wretched figures of little consequence, the wrong enemy in the wrong place.[4]

Thus my argument is that any policy for counter-terrorism, at any level, must make fundamental distinctions between types of terrorism. Any policy which assumes all terrorists to be fundamentally similar or to pose essentially similar threats will miss opportunities to intervene in some cases and will intervene inappropriately in others. What is needed is a more sophisticated analysis which allows us to respond differentially to terrorism and which recognises that terrorism is not the only nor the greatest danger facing us. 'We need not an unconditional, single-minded commitment but intelligent wariness, a capacity to sort out contending priorities and a readiness to determine what resources it is prudent to bring to bear and what costs it is necessary to pay.'[5] Such a perspective may assist states to avoid making policy changes in response to international terrorism, which must assist in reducing the pay-off for this tactic. Indeed, one of the greatest dangers posed by international terrorism is that it can succeed in forcing policy changes by states. Accordingly, one of the main ways of deterring terrorism is to demonstrate that terrorism *does not* change state policy. To be in the position of strength necessary to withstand the onslaught, however, states must carefully reappraise the justification for some present policies so that those likely to be the target of terrorist demands are those to which the state is highly committed. The withdrawal of US Marines from Lebanon following the bombing of the Marine component of the Multi-National Peacekeeping Force was viewed by many in the Middle East as a victory for terrorism, vindicating the use of such tactics. But the decision to withdraw, although occasioned by the attack, was of course, a result of a complex of factors including domestic dissent over the appropriateness of the commitment, lack of clear definition of the force's mission, and absence of a cogent and well-articulated policy on the Lebanon which would have heightened the political will to maintain the force in place. For all practical purposes, foreign policy succumbed to terrorism. The appearance of vacillation and weakness flowing from the decision to withdraw subsequent to the bombing serves only to underscore my contention that states must be committed to the policy which is the real target of a terrorist attack if they are to provide any true deterrent to future international terrorism. Of course, what undermines even this degree of commitment is that it is unlikely in reality to be uniform across states. Although the community of nations is coming to the realisation that no state is now immune from terrorism, it still remains true that it impacts less severely on some than on others. Further, despite general condemnation of terrorism many states have ambiguous policies with regard to particular groups or situations. Thus, as Jenkins notes:

> The relationship between governments and terrorists is not a simple conflict between terrorists and the state. Governments have variously – sometimes simultaneously – tolerated, combated, fomented, supplied, and exploited terrorist groups. Beneath the rhetoric of moral outrage is a labyrinth of secret wars, deals, direct action, and deliberate inaction
>
> (Jenkins, 1984a, p.24).

While we all wish that cohesive international action against terrorism were possible and while all states of good will should continue to work towards this end, we must remain cognisant of the realities of individual state interests. The failure of the international community to act in concert (particularly of Western democratic nations which we presume to be more motivated to fight what their rhetoric says is a 'common enemy'), and the instances of backsliding when confronted with actual incidents of terrorism (due to economic considerations, fear, or sympathy with the cause, if not the methods, of some groups) all serve to ensure that terrorism will continue, even in the face of a hardline approach by some states. Nevertheless, there are signs of an emerging consensus which may lead to more unified international action in at least some circumstances. The recent refusal of a number of states in the Mediterranean area to accept the entry into their ports of the hijacked liner *Achille Lauro* or the landing of the aircraft spiriting the hijackers out of Egypt (the plane subsequently being forced by US Navy fighter planes to land at a NATO base in Italy) was an encouraging sign that even states which have stridently supported Palestinian terrorism can now see circumstances in which it is in their own interests, and that of the international community, to condemn some acts of terrorism and to take steps to counter them. Indeed this was but the latest in a growing list of instances in which states have had to resolve value conflicts over support for elements of the international system versus support for particular ideologies. Crenshaw believes that:

> the problem of terrorism emphasises the value to all states of fundamental norms that guarantee the safety of diplomatic and commercial exchanges. As terrorism comes more and more to involve attacks on diplomats, travellers and business executives, it provokes a clash between two competing sets of values, and it poses the question of whether the pursuit of anti-colonialism is worth abandoning traditional standards of state behaviour, such as diplomatic inviolability and the responsibility of host governments for the safety of foreigners. The consensus among states has moved gradually toward rejection of those forms of political expression which violate such basic trust
>
> (Crenshaw, 1983b, p. 28).

Even the USSR which has been loudly condemned for its sponsorship of international terrorism, [6] has felt constrained to support some restricted initiatives when its own interests have been threatened (Goren, 1984). The recent kidnapping in the Lebanon of four Soviet diplomats and the subsequent murder of one of them may at least serve to alert the Soviets to the fact that they are increasingly likely to reap the whirlwind they helped to sow and may impel them to participate in a meaningful way in international initiatives against terrorism.

Although there are many cases which negate the positive impact of the instances I have cited, the undoubted fact of an increasing realisation of the potentially destabilising impact of terrorism on international relations and the tendency towards cooperation against terrorism, particularly on a bilateral or regional basis, are encouraging signs that some sort of cohesive response is possible. Our vision for the future of international cooperation can, therefore be one of moderate hope. This middle course may not be very exciting, but it is realistic. Prescriptions for countermeasures must avoid the extremes of either the pessimism of many current commentators who see international terrorism as the leading threat to world peace or the visionary optimism of those who dream of an international legal order capable of resolving all the issues of definition, state sovereignty and appropriateness of response which so bedevil current proposals for international cooperation. In reality, neither extremely negative not extremely positive outcomes are the most likely. Perhaps one could characterise the most likely outcomes as extremely pedestrian. This view is expressed well by Carlton in his warning about the difficulties of predicting the future of terrorism:

> those who examine subjects such as war and violence may be consciously or subconsciously fascinated by apocalyptic possibilities and hence may tend greatly to underrate the evidence or trends that could lend themselves to unexciting conclusions. For example, the least diverting prediciton for the future of terrorism would be one that foresaw neither uncontrolled escalation nor deescalation after a dramatic reassertion of authority by sovereign states, but rather one that forsaw a continuing untidy pattern of incidents largely unrelated to one another and each of only transient significance to an increasingly unconcerned world
>
> (Carlton, 1979, p.202).

Even so, the problem of international terrorism is serious enough, and there always remains the possibility of escalation to new forms of mass-destruction or mass-casualty terrorism as groups become more extreme, extensive media coverage becomes harder to ensure (because audiences become hardened to the consequences of lesser events), and states become more intransigent in their dealings with terrorists (Wardlaw, 1982). Further, terrorism will occupy more of the attention of governments and military planners as an important part of the emerging pattern of imprecise, multi-faceted forms of warfare which may well characterise the future (Jenkins, 1984a).

As we contemplate the future of terrorism, a number of rather contradictory facts emerge. It is clear that there *are* some objective causes of terrorism and that some groups will not eschew the tactics of terror entirely while the underlying problems remain unresolved. This will be true however harsh the response to terrorism. In extreme desperation, extreme tactics will be used (and what is considered 'extreme' may not be objectively true nor may the response conform to our conception of a morally justifiable tactic of change). However, much international terrorism is not of this nature and will be less so, proportionately, as states make calculated decisions to engage in, sponsor or give support to international terrorism in furtherance of foreign policy objectives. This increase in state-backed international terrorism implies that the states involved have made some sort of cost–benefit analysis which has indicated that employing terrorism is cost-effective. This being so, it is clear that raising the costs of participation will change the equation and, eventually, the decision to become involved. The case of desperate or totally extremist regimes sponsoring terrorism without regard to the costs is highly unlikely. Even regimes such as those in power in Libya and Iran which are routinely described as 'insane' or 'out of control' are forced to participate to some extent in the international system and unless they are willing to provoke an all-out military confrontation are thereby restrained to some extent in their support or use of terrorism. Certainly there is much extremist language emanating from Tripoli and Tehran but the resultant terrorism, although producing individual murders or more shocking mass casualties from vehicle-bomb attacks, has not achieved the scale or scope promised by the speechmakers. In large part, this may be because even these regimes realise there is a point beyond which it is not worth them going. Thus we see the paradoxical situation in which it is claimed that the international system is too weak to fight international terrorism, yet the essential features of this system have themselves produced the restraints which have thus far prevented terrorism from assuming the monumental proportions which the media are so fond of reporting. This observation leads one to suppose that we ought to be more imaginative in trying to find ways to exploit the reliance of states on international connections so that these might be threatened by the community of nations if one of its members is implicated in an act of international terrorism. Instead of turning hastily to talk of military reprisals perhaps we should put much more of our resources into making the international system work for its members. This may be emotionally less satisfying than some spectacular reprisal, but may be much more productive in the long term.

In discussing how we might use the system of international relations to fight terrorism we return inevitably to the questions of definitions, standards, and style of language. Let me reiterate that I believe that those who aim to lead the fight against international terrorism must first ensure that they set their own house in order. It is difficult for some states, for example, to accept criticism from the USA about lack of a willingness to extradite terrorists or failure to take action to prevent the training of terrorists on their soil when US courts have denied the extradition to Britain of four men wanted for terrorist crimes in Northern Ireland, and Sikh terrorists and others are trained in insurgency warfare techniques in schools operating openly and legally in America.

The second point is that we must be careful and, above all, consistent in our use of the term 'terrorist'. This word is used promiscuously by governments of all persuasions to embrace many things (guerrilla warfare, civil violence, ordinary crimes,) which are not by accepted definitions 'terrorist'. There is a corresponding lack of willingness to label a clearly terrorist act as such if it is committed by one's friends. In practical terms, for such purposes as reaching international agreements on terrorist crimes, it is sensible to avoid using the word terrorist at all and instead concentrate on specific acts (such as taking diplomatic hostages or hijacking aircraft) which most states can agree should be proceeded against whatever the motive for them. But in political and everyday discourse the term terrorism will not be abandoned and it therefore behoves responsible states to encourage its rational and even-handed use. In particular this implies that an act committed by a friendly nation which fits the definition of terrorism should be condemned. We can expect no better from those we criticise about their response if we remain silent about some cases of terrorism, yet violently condemn others. This even-handedness need not degenerate into the morass which has become the debate on moral equivalence presided over by the ex-US Ambassador to the United Nations, Jeane Kirkpatrick (Kirkpatrick, 1984, 1985). Crenshaw, for example, argues that 'we can develop a neutral definition of terrorism while retaining the ability to make moral judgements about its use in different political circumstances. Labeling an action 'terrorist' is not in itself a moral claim' (Crenshaw, 1983, p. 5). One *can* therefore, make moral distinctions about both the means and ends of terrorism. Further, it is simply not valid to assert that condemnation of behaviour which a neutral definition would label as terrorist, perpetrated by groups sponsored, for example, by both the USA and the USSR, is to say that there is a moral equivalence between the two societies or their ideologies. Let me say quite categorically that democratic values are morally superior to totalitarian ones. That fact, however, does not lead me into blind acceptance of all the *methods* used or supported by democracies or their proxies. As Nye reminds us 'a democracy can be good and do evil – sometimes even when it is trying to do good' (Nye, 1985, p. 17). To condemn terrorism used by a group of whose cause we approve does not imply condemnation of either the cause or the group's right to struggle. But we must be consistent and condemn *similar acts* regardless of their source. Certainly, *all* terrorist acts involving innocent civilian bystanders *must* be condemned on *all* occasions.

Part of the difficulty experienced by democratic states in taking the consistent approach which I am advocating is that they feel that there may indeed be circumstances in which terrorism is justified or in which even democratic states must employ 'dirty' methods in order to combat effectively an enemy who refused to 'play by the rules'. In extreme circumstances this may be true, but to adopt this mode of thinking is itself dangerous. Again we return to the issue of defining the seriousness of the threat. My contention is that we have reached nowhere near the level of threat from international terrorism which would justify employing similar tactics as terrorists in order to defeat them. Indeed, I consider that even if such a situation existed there would be little hope that resorting to such tactics would in fact eliminate the threat. It seems entirely likely that the situation would instead degenerate into one of international anarchy. In most conceivable circumstances the superiority of democratic states lies precisely in their adherence to higher standards. If the West is to claim that it is morally superior then it must be held to higher standards. This indeed creates some asymmetries, some difficulties and possibly some dangers for us. But these are the costs we pay for what we hold dear. If we abandon our principles and our commitment to justice in panic and turn to the ugly and unprincipled tactics being used by extremists the world over, we have surely completed for them the job they began. It needs to be stressed, though, that adherence to democratic values does not imply weakness. It need not rule out the use of force, which *can* be justified and *can* be used in a principled manner. But we underestimate, I believe, the impact of calm resoluteness on other nations. We underestimate the psychological dimension in international relations. Sometimes a clear adherence to our own espoused standards will add to our stature. As Robert Hunter observed:

> The United States is expected to behave by civilized standards – the Bulgarians, Soviets, and Libyans are not – and our meeting that test can be a strength of American foreign policy.[7]

It is my contention, then, that we can erect a principled and effective defence against the worst consequences of international terrorism. To do so, however, requires a realistic appraisal of the threat and a restrained approach to its discussion. We must avoid the notion of the simple fix. International terrorism is a complex, dynamic phenomenon and must be matched by a similarly structured response. We must be realistic in the choice of aims for our counter-terrorist policies. For example, it is not realistic to expect that terrorism can be eliminated. There is no cure for terrorism. We must realise that no particular mode of response will provide the answer. Occasionally something works in a specific situation, but there is no guarantee that it will work next time or even if it works as an operation that its consequences in the long-term will be similar. In discussing terrorism, states, particularly those taking the lead in the international campaign against terrorism, will need to focus on rather narrow aspects of it if they are to attract widespread international cooperation. As Jenkins pointed out:

> if the United States treats terrorism as a component of its global contest with the Soviet Union, or of its involvement in regional conflicts in the Middle East or Central America, it risks alienating allies who might be willing to cooperate in combating terrorism but who differ with US policy and methods for dealing with Marxist guerrillas, or who, for political or economic reasons, are reluctant to participate in America's battles
>
> (Jenkins, 1984b, p. 4).

In short, definitions used by states in their public discussion of terrorism should not appear to be aimed at sectional political interests and must be constant over time. There is a real danger in naming sponsor-states unless action against them is possible and contemplated. The sheer number of states now explicitly or implicitly identified by the USA as sponsors of international terrorism makes the impact of such identification rather diffuse, particularly when some are friends of the USA and there is no chance of sanctioning them. The dropping of Syria from the official list of terrorist sponsor-states, the confusion over the US position on the bombing by Israel of the PLO headquarters in Tunis, and the reluctance to comment on the bombing of the Greenpeace ship *Rainbow Warrior* in New Zealand by French agents are all equivocations which detract from the effort to gain international agreement to counter *all* forms of terrorism. Jenkins rightly claims that to single out some sponsors of international terrorism whilst remaining silent on other cases:

would be to expose the entire effort to the suspicion of being purely politically motivated and hypocritical. Thus to be effective, we must formulate a more restricted definition of a state that aids international terrorism, and carefully marshall evidence to support any US actions against those who we feel should have sanctions imposed on them

(Jenkins, 1981, p. 4).

Tempering the way states discuss the involvement of other states in terrorism is most certainly not to imply that they should not reveal such sponsorship when they have evidence for it. Rather it is to counsel that the facts be revealed without the rhetorical or moralistic elaboration which has tended to debase much of the discussion by states on this topic. As Oseth has warned in discussing US counter-terrorist policy 'The line between an information program and politicized propaganda can be a fine one, but it must be respected if the US policy stance is to gain credibility internationally' (Oseth, 1985, p. 73). Further, credibility will be undermined if strong statements are made (usually at different times) about who are the sponsor-states and how sponsors should be punished. In the international context deterrence, if one believes in it, should be aimed primarily at the sponsor, not the sponsored. But is anybody really going to do anything about Soviet sponsorship? Unless we are *really* prepared to bomb Tehran, Damascus, Tripoli, or Moscow, talk about bombing the nerve centres of terrorism does much to demonstrate the futility of the threat, and little to deter terrorism. Of course, if we were prepared to carry out such an act we would have committed two further grave errors, We would have elevated terrorism to a position that would totally dominate international affairs and we would have fallen into the trap of believing that the 'centres' are the cause of international terrorism – which they are not.

COUNTER-TERRORIST OPTIONS

In order to be confident of having an effective counter-terrorist system, individual states need to enunciate a set of principles based on an analysis of successful tactics used in the past, contained within the bounds of some basic assumptions about the sorts of actions acceptable in a democratic society, and capable of absorbing change as a result of research, intelligence and new data flowing from contemporary operational experience. Most states have now established a set of principles which determine the core elements in their response capabilities. In general, the elements of a successful counter-terrorist plan include good intelligence (including intelligence-exchange arrangements with other states); adequate laws which give specific necessary powers to the authorities in declared emergencies; a closely-reasoned set of governmental responses to particular terrorist threats; a well-equipped and frequently tested counter-terrorist crisis-management organisation; adequately trained and equipped police and military units; adequate protective security arrangements for vital points and individuals; and well-planned and negotiated arrangements with the news media for coverage of terrorist incidents.

These features describe the basis of an adequate domestic counter-terrorist system. But what of the response to state-sponsored international terrorism? Here a whole new range of complex relationships and issues are involved. Any really effective system for countering state-sponsored international terrorism would require an unparalleled degree of international cooperation. A campaign to isolate a sponsor state, for example, inevitably runs into problems of the economic interests of boycotting states, its effects on other regional or international political issues, and the personal safety of the citizens of boycotting states against whom there may be retaliations or who may be used as hostage pawns. Such difficulties militate against the maintenance of a solid international front in dealing with any specific incident. While like-minded states may issue tough-talking declarations after summit meetings, it is surprising (or maybe not surprising) how many of them will feel that there are 'special circumstances' which make it 'inappropriate' for *them* to become involved in stern action on *this* occasion!

The recent TWA hijacking illustrated both the types of responses favoured by states and the practical difficulties of implementing them. There seem to be two types of knee-jerk reactions to major acts of terrorism. The first is to complain about lack of security and to call for vast increases in physical protection at airports or embassies or wherever the latest outrage has taken place. The second is to think in terms of retaliation or retribution. Like all knee-jerk reactions, these contain valid elements but miss the point if thinking does not proceed beyond them.

Let us take security first. It is certainly the case that improved security at vital points or for individuals or groups who are potential targets can contribute to lower levels of some forms of terrorism. At the very least, governments owe their citizens a satisfactory level of security. Thus, it is desirable to maintain a high level of security screening at airports and it is necessary to improve the physical and procedural security at embassies. But we cannot place too much emphasis or too much reliance on physical protection. It is both limited and eventually, self-defeating. We simply cannot defend all potential targets against terrorist attacks. Even with specific cases security faces the law of diminishing returns. Take airports, for example. We now have a very high level of screening and protection for aircraft and at and beyond the customs barrier in most countries. This has deterred many attacks, but one response has been merely to target the relatively less-protected baggage and ticketing areas. The immediate response to the bombing of these areas at Frankfurt airport recently was to call for the same level of security there as applies at the customs barrier. But clearly the terrorist response to such a move would be simply to explode a device outside the airport at, say, the point where passengers are dropped off by taxi or car. Even if airports could be adequately protected in total, it would just mean a shift of targets to, say, bus or train stations. Although it is an extremely difficult judgement to make, we must determine the point at which increased security is simply not effective.

As well as being ineffective in the long run, extremes of security can also be counter-productive. Although protecting a military base against terrorist attack should be assigned a high priority (especially in areas of high terrorist threat) there comes a point beyond which the diversion of manpower into security functions may seriously interfere with the primary mission of the organisation. A similar problem faces proposals to increase security at diplomatic premises. Clearly there is a need for a high level of security. But turning an embassy into a fortress and restricting both access to diplomats and the freedom of those diplomats to move about the host-nation can, in the extreme, severely damage the institution of diplomacy and the effectiveness of its mission. Anyway, as with any other target, making diplomatic premises more difficult to attack may result only in more sophisticated and dangerous attacks or to a change of target to diplomats themselves or to some other target altogether. Again, then, we are faced with the incredibly difficult problem of deciding on the balance between security and other interests. In fact we are left, I believe, with the realisation that there is no adequately defence against terrorism and that we must accept that some casualties are the price we have to pay for the system of modern life whose fruits we enjoy. The problem is to keep those casualties as few as possible.

Apart from increased security, the most frequently voiced suggestions for reducing the incidence of international terrorism involve various military responses to incidents in an effort to deter future attacks. Such options are clearly high on the US agenda at the moment, but decisions made in actual cases recently illustrate the limited application of military measures. Jenkins (1984c) has listed four major types of military response to terrorism. These are:

1. preemptive operations – those actions, ranging from evacuation in a hostile environment to invasion, based on credible and accurate intelligence which could preempt a planned terrorist operation;
2. search and recovery operations – the use of one country's armed forces to recover from a hostile country, for example, a stolen nuclear weapon or nuclear material which might fall into terrorist hands,
3. rescue operations – the use of specially-trained units to extract hostages taken by terrorists where the local government cannot or will not carry out the assault, or where it invites the target nation to do so on its behalf;
4. retaliatory or punitive raids – where military forces either attack terrorist bases or targets upon the territory of sponsor states as punishment for a terrorist incident and as an example that such behaviour will not be tolerated.

Jenkins's analysis of these options shows that the number of circumstances in which any of them could be employed appropriately is low, the chances of success are often low and there are often other factors (such as public opinion or relations with other nations) which effectively rule out their use even if they could succeed in their tactical goals.

Jenkin's analysis of the limitations on the use of military options should temper the enthusiasm of those who have rushed to embrace them as a panacea for terrorist ills. In addition to the purely technical problems raised by options such as preemptive or retaliatory raids there are also, of course, a host of moral, legal and political issues raised. First there is the question of effectiveness. Is it possible, as Secretary of State Shultz suggests to use violent retaliatory tactics without creating 'a cycle of excalating violence beyond our control' (Schultz, 1984, p. 17)? It seems entirely uncertain what the effects of such retaliation might be, but it is at least as likely that retaliation would almost inevitably provoke counter-retaliation, not only in the region which is the focus of the terrorism, but in the territory of the retaliating state itself. Certainly with respect to some forms of terrorism in the Middle East there is a high risk that a retaliatory raid by the USA against a terrorist group or its sponsor would hasten the arrival of international terrorism to the continental USA.

Many policy-makers, including Secretary Shultz, have turned to the Israeli experience as evidence that retaliatory policies would be effective. In his address at the Park Avenue Synagogue on 25 October 1984, the Secretary praised Israeli counter-terrorist policies claiming that 'no nation has made a greater contribution to our understanding of the problem and the best ways to confront it' (Shultz, 1984, p. 15). To say the least, however, there is far from unanimous agreement on the efficacy of Israeli retaliatory tactics. Doubts have been expressed by those who have served in the Israeli military forces (Alon, 1980) and analysts known for their hard-line attitude to terrorism (Livingstone, 1982). Evidence from an analysis of retribution raids by Israel against Palestinian targets also indicates that such techniques may not be as successful a deterrent as many seem to believe when measured in terms of changes in the level of terrorist activity (Hoffman, 1985). Finally, the pro-Palestinian literature is replete with anecdotal evidence of the extremism and hatred generated amongst the Palestinians who become the objects of the Israeli reprisal raids (see, for example, Frangi, 1983).

While the Israeli model has much to recommend it psychologically (it serves a vital function in demonstrating to a population under siege that they are not just helpless targets and to the terrorists that Israel cannot be attacked with impunity) and morally (Israel has certainly been the target of vicious and unprincipled attacks which entitle her to seek redress), there remains considerable doubt about the results. In both moral and practical terms the policy has had mixed outcomes. I believe that some of the reprisals have been unprincipled themselves, in that they have been disproportionate to the original act and have caused innocent deaths and injuries which could and should have been avoided. But the greatest shortcoming of the policy is that it has tended to become an end in itself. The satisfaction engendered by having struck back at the terrorists has stunted the motivation to strive for longer-term solutions. Schlomo Gazit, former head of Israeli military intelligence, has argued frequently that there is no technical military solution to the problem of terrorism. The solutions are political ones. General Gazit believes reprisals to be a useful tool for the political leadership because 'once the terrorist realises that he cannot impose his will on you, he will be much more prepared to deal'.[8] However, he contends that Israel has not exploited this advantage and has not come up with the political solutions necessary to make serious inroads into the use of terror.

Given that there are serious doubts about the effectiveness of the Israeli retaliatory policy (Blechman, 1978), the moral and political costs must weigh more heavily, especially when a nation such as the USA contemplates embracing such a policy. Secretary Shultz was right to warn that 'we cannot allow ourselves to become the Hamlet of nations, worrying endlessly over whether and how to respond' (Shultz, 1984). The international community, and especially targeted countries, must take resolute action against terrorism. But as an editorial in the Milwaukee Journal also reminds us, it is equally important to devise methods of dealing with terrorism which avoid us becoming the Claudius of nations.[9] That is, we must resolve the question, can a state fight villainy without becoming a villain? We must avoid letting a thirst for vengeance be quenched by turning to tactics which caused terror themselves, unless we can be sure that they are precisely targeted on the offenders and unless we can be sure (or as sure as humanly possible) that the act *will* have a deterrent effect and will not serve only to ensure further terrorism. I submit that the number of occasions on which these criteria can be met will be very small indeed and it is misleading and counter-productive to suggest to the public that military methods in general and reprisals in particular will ever feature very largely in the fight against international terrorism. Anger and disgust are the legitimate reactions to acts of terrorism but they are no sound basis for foreign policy. Just as we do not allow the rape victim to determine the punishment for the rapist, so the international community must strive to temper the reactions of states which are victims of international terrorism. But as with the criminal justice system, the international system must support the victim and must take action against the offender lest frustration lead to the development of lynch law.

In addition to moral considerations, proponents of retaliation raids must also take into account some of the practical difficulties and political costs of the policy. The first problem is that retaliation, as well as serving to satisfy the desire to 'get even', is aimed primarily at deterrence. But at whom is this deterrence aimed? The raid subsequent to a suicide-bombing clearly will not deter other bombers, for they are prepared to die anyway. It may be aimed at the sponsors, but then the retaliator has the problem of deciding what will make an appropriate target. Will it be the terrorist base or will it be an unrelated facility in the sponsor country? How can the terrorists be identified and their bases targeted without causing innocent civilians to suffer? Whence can the strike be launched? How can the launch-site be protected from counter-attack? What happens if members of the retaliatory team are captured? A policy of retaliation may also mean that future options are cut off. For example, the Syria that might have been targeted after the Beirut bombings is the same Syria that was called upon by the USA to help to secure the release of the hostages from the TWA hijacking and has a role to play in stabilising the situation in the Lebanon. A policy of retaliation may merely serve to radicalise opposition and make it more dangerous and more fanatical. As well as encouraging counter-terror and increasing regional tensions, retaliation may also drive some sponsor states into, or further into, the arms of the USSR, further destabilising the region and going against another, more vital, goal of limiting Soviet influence. The political costs may spread diffusely as even friendly governments fail to support the retaliatory action because their own interests in the region may be jeopardised by such endorsement. Retaliation must also bear in mind that some sponsor states can bear punishment more readily than we could and might well be able to exploit their suffering for propaganda purposes. For example, in the current context of the Iran–Iraq war and the degree of religious radicalism in Iran, what kind of retaliatory action would a nation have to mount in order to have a deterrent effect on Iranian-sponsored international terrorism?

Nations contemplating retaliation in the aftermath of a terrorist attack find themselves in an extremely difficult psychological situation (Jenkins, 1984b). First, the opportunity to respond decisively diminishes as time passes – the level of emotional reaction decreases, the public pressure to act becomes less vociferous and there is a correspondingly increased necessity for accurate intelligence allowing very precise targeting with no innocent loss of life. Second, the frustration of being unable to respond rapidly, decisively, and successfully engenders a growing fear that the state will look (and be) impotent, with the increasing danger that ill-considered action will be taken just to avoid humiliation. To be politically viable, any retaliatory action needs to be immediate,[10] thus degrading the likelihood that available intelligence will be of sufficient quality and precision to be absolutely certain who exactly was responsible. The danger lies in the possibility that we will cross some ill-defined 'threshold of tolerance' and launch a retaliatory raid merely because that threshold has been breached. Such a raid could well be counter-productive. Reacting in haste increases the dangers of any intervention. The costs of contested or failed interventions (Scalapino, 1983) may well exceed the potential benefits. The aborted mission to rescue the US Embassy personnel held in Tehran, although not conceived in haste, illustrates well the costs of failure. It seems to me that this is one of the most cogent arguments against states making loud and frequent threats, without subsequent action. Continued hard-line rhetoric which minimises the real problems of effective and morally justifiable forms of retaliation may serve to inflame public opinion to such an extent that official options are heavily circumscribed so that retaliation becomes inevitable, even if it may be inappropriate or its costs may eventually outweigh its benefits.

The problem of rhetorical oversell does not mean that threats are not useful. The declaration of National Security Directive 138 in 1984 should have had value in that it served notice that hard options would be considered. Its impact, however, has been considerably lessened by the wasteful use of threats since then, without the execution of those threats. If threats are to be made, they must be meaningful – they must be backed up by the political will, the authority and the ability to carry them out – and if some defined threshold is crossed, they must be carried out.[11] Although it is, of course, hard to gauge, it appears that most threats are (or become) public and may thus serve domestic ends more than external ones. However, states should not forget the value of private threats – warnings made on a confidential basis, government to government, or through intermediaries. Indeed private threats may sometimes have more effect because of the avoidance of the loss of face which might accompany seeming to cave in to threats. Measures which allow sponsor states to change their policies without loss of 'prestige' or 'face' (Gilpin, 1981; Schelling, 1966) need therefore to be considered. Indeed diplomatic initiatives should also look for opportunities to 'coopt' sponsor states, as has happened with conservative

Arab regimes (which supported terrorism until it began to threaten their own interests) and even more radical states such as Syria (the TWA hijacking) and Somalia (which was 'sweetened' with the promise of West German aid into allowing the GSG-9 assault on the Lufthansa aircraft at Mogadishu in 1977). Isolating some sponsor states by threatening them vociferously before the world may sometimes be counter-productive because it distances these states from the traditional norms and values and reduces their value conflict over adherence to these norms versus support for terrorist tactics (Crenshaw, 1983b). Perhaps, instead, we should do more in a comprehensive way to 'define the limits' of state sponsorship in an effort to prevent opportunities from arising in the first place. Such a policy would encompass 'the entire spectrum of ... diplomacy, including economic aid, bilateral and multilateral negotiations, and conflict resolution' (Taylor and Townsend, 1984, p. 218).

This analysis points to the conclusion that retaliation by military means is both difficult to justify morally (because of the problems of accurate targeting and avoiding unconnected casualties) and difficult to implement practically (because of the logistic and planning difficulties or because of its negative side effects). Even so, there are bound to occur a small number of circumstances in which retaliation is both possible and appropriate or is simply judged to be necessary. We certainly need to have available both the doctrine and the forces capable of meeting this mission, as well as being able to mount less controversial hostage rescue operations and to counter terrorism which may be employed in war or in situations short of war to degrade the military's ability to deploy forces or weapons (Jenkins, 1983). Even though there will be very few instances in which military tactics will be appropriate and able to be employed, the importance of exploiting those instances and the devastating costs of failure mean that we should devote considerable thought and resources to the need for the military to develop high-quality counter-terrorist doctrine and capabilities (Kupperman, Alexander, van Opstal and Williamson, 1984). The general trend towards the employment of various forms of 'low-intensity conflict' make this a priority task for military planners and should include the development of doctrine, increased security and intelligence capabilities, expanded anti-terrorist training, upgraded planning, command, control and communications, and response capabilities. As well as the development of specialist units, a particular emphasis should be placed on training 'line' units in counter-terrorist tactics. In this context we need also to address the question of moral justification as a frame of reference for decisions about some of the more controversial and unconventional alternatives available. The conference on this topic convened by USN Chief of Naval Operations, Admiral James D. Watkins, at the US Naval War College in 1984 provided a useful starting-point for this discussion (Watkins, 1984). Conference participants agreed that in the area of *jus ad bellum* (the right to respond to an act of terrorism) several conditions must be met before a nation may morally take action to prevent or respond to an act of terrorism by military means. These conditions are:

(i) there must be a *just cause* – self defence against an unjust aggressor or protection of legitimate state interests;
(ii) the decision to use force must be made by a *competent authority*;
(iii) military force must only be used as a *last resort*;[12]
(iv) the operation must have a *reasonable likelihood of success*;
(v) *more good than evil* must be seen as coming from the proposed response.

In terms of *jus in bello* considerations, the conference agreed that the response, to be justified, must be *proportionate* to the threat and must be highly *discriminate* in its application.

The myriad difficulties associated with the use of military options such as retaliation may encourage those who favour 'hard' measures to turn to policies of covert action, working through proxies, or pre-emptive operations as possible attractive alternatives. However, the difficulties associated with these options present, if anything, greater obstacles to implementation than do retaliatory raids. Brian Jenkins argues that:

> while covert operations may be necessary under extraordinary cirumstances, if we are obliged to use force in response to terrorism we ought to do so with the legitimately constituted armed forces of this country – openly, and with an unambiguous message as to who is responsible and why we are doing it.[13]

With covert operations involving violence there is always a chance that the agency involved will begin to make official policy itself. It is vital that governments maintain effective control over the response to terrorism, and do not delegate authority to autonomous security bureaucracies (Crenshaw, 1983a) or let authority slip into their *de facto* control. There *are* good arguments for a properly-controlled unconventional warfare capability, but extreme caution must be exercised to ensure that it remains a 'tool of foreign policy, not a substitute for it' (Bair, Barrows, Goldman, Kinsman, McKay, Strong and Walsh, 1983, p. 80).

Working through proxies to conduct counter-terrorist operations is even more complex and dangerous. There are obvious problems of lack of control, possible unreliability, unpredictability, and the working to private or non-sponsor agendas. The dangers were illustrated graphically by the furore caused in 1985 by the alleged CIA backing for the Lebanese counter-terrorist unit which was responsible for the killing of about eighty people as a result of the car-bombing aimed (unsuccessfully) at Mohammed Hussein Fadlallah, leader of the Shi'ite Party of God (*Hezballah*), who had been implicated in earlier bombings of American facilities in the Lebanon. Regardless of later inquiries which cleared the CIA of involvement, the incident demonstrated the extreme damage which could be done by the media exposure of covert links which is almost certain to follow a counter-terrorist failure. As Maynes puts it, 'preemptive covert actions that cross a certain moral threshold not only are wrong but also unwise because of the risk of exposure and popular repudiation' (Maynes, 1985, p. 17). The message is clear – if counter-terrorist operations are legitimate they should be carried out under clear national control and responsibility. If they are illegitimate they should have no place in our counter-terrorist policies.

Preemptive raids carry excessive costs except in extreme circumstances. Many of the same considerations of accuracy of intelligence, choice of target, trial of alternative methods, proportionality of the operation, and so forth as apply to retaliation raids apply also to preemptive ones. In addition, in many cases preemptive raids will be likely to be viewed by much of the world community as intervention in the affairs of a sovereign state, and will, therefore, be judged to be either illegal under international law or illegitimate, or both. To the extent that world opinion is important to an attacking state, this may be a major cost of a preemptive operation. Nevertheless, as with all military options, preemption cannot be excluded altogether as a legitimate response to international terrorism. But preemptive raids can only be used where there is a clear and serious threat to a state's vital interests, where the intelligence is precise enough and accurate enough to allow a strike with surgical precision, and where the costs and risks of escalation are deemed necessary (Taylor and Townsend, 1984). Preemption, as with other methods, must never be contemplated to serve the propping up of some 'Ramboesque' image. As I have emphasised on a number of occasions in this chapter, restraint within the bounds of law and morality may limit our action as democratic states, but it is the rule of law and morality that distinguish us from the terrorists. As Oseth says, these self-imposed restraints:

> inevitably limit the US capability to take pro-active measures. But this is a circumstance our society lives with constantly and knowingly even in domestic law and order matters. American citizens pay a price for valuing freedom, running risks that our major competitors refuse to endure. That is what distinguishes us from them, and it is a distinction that makes a difference. We believe that it is what civilizes our behaviour, disciplining our actions by elevating to highest priority the preservation of human dignity. Repressive societies do not have much of a terrorism problem. But they are repressive societies
>
> (Oseth, 1985, p. 74).

If military operations against terrorism are either illegitimate, illegal, or able to be mounted in only a very few situations, then surely measures such as economic sanctions offer an alternative? Perhaps so, but here too the evidence is that sanctions are often of dubious practical value (Ayubi, Bissell, Korsah and Lerner, 1982; Doxey, 1980; Schreiber 1973). Bienen and Gilpin (1980) discuss a number of sanctions which might be employed against international terrorism, including trade embargoes, curtailment of investment, blocking borrowing through international agencies, denial of most-favoured-nation treatment, and slow-down of technlogy transfer. They conclude that there are dangers attaching to the use of any of these options. They are ineffective if applied unilaterally, they may be counter-productive and they are very costly to the sanctioning states. However, they may be more effective if there is prior agreement to multilateral action in the event of a specific terrorist action, for example, at the Bonn Economic Summit in 1978, the major Western nations declared a willingness to suspend commercial airline services between themselves and any country harbouring hijackers.

Flores (1981) examined specific US attempts to apply economic sanctions to terrorism. Many attempts so far have focused on cutting off aid to countries sponsoring or supporting terrorism. The difficulties here are that most terrorist states do not receive massive financial assistance from the US and that using foreign aid as a lever of coercion has, in the past, inflamed passions and increased the resolve of the targeted government. Exceptions to much of the legislation have, anyway, undercut its potential force. For example, the International Security Assistance Act of 1977 (US) required termination of sales, credits and guarantees under the Act to sponsors of terrorism, but a national security exception undermines it. Similar exceptions exist in the Omnibus Multilateral Development Institutions Act of 1977 and the 1978 amendment to the Export–Import Bank Act. Examining the problems with use of provisions in the Export Administration Act of 1979, Flores concludes that:

> the control of exports to … terrorist-supporting countries is a symbolic act, not an instrument of coercion. In terms of costs and benefits, export controls seemingly make no sense as instruments to control international terrorism
>
> (Flores, 1981, p. 589).

Ayubi *et al.'s* (1982) review of economic sanctions in US foreign policy is similarly pessimistic about their efficacy. They believe there exists a striking consensus that economic sanctions have not necessarily altered the positions of the targets in the long run, have been ineffective in the fulfilment of their objectives, and have often failed to achieve their avowed political purposes. The major impediments to success are the problems of coordinating sanctions between countries, ensuring enforcement, the development of self-reliance by the target state, and the fact that peripheral effects of the imposition of the sanctions may distort their original intention. Nevertheless, Ayubi *et al.* claim that sanctions may have some positive effects. They provide a demonstration effect by indicating to the target state the seriousness with which the sanctioning state views their behaviour. They may also play a major part in mobilising other forms of opposition to the target state. One might also add that there are some situations in which non-application of sanctions may be more costly in terms of lack of credibility than the costs imposed by applying sanctions. In some cases of state-sponsored terrorism where the link is undeniable, the victim may simply not be allowed by public opinion to avoid taking some sort of sanction action – even if, economically, it hurts the sanctioning state.

The difficulties of gaining international cooperation on economic sanctions against sponsor states is illustrated by attempts to include terrorism on the agenda of the London Economic Summit held in June 1984. At that meeting, France was reportedly totally against including a discussion of terrorism and opposed any measures against terrorism which would damage French economic interests in countries likely to be the subject of sanctions (Wilkinson, 1984). Largely at the insistence of the British Prime Minster, terrorism was eventually discussed and the final communiqué did call for a number of measures against terrorism. However, the meeting failed 'to issue any binding resolution on collective sanctions against states engaging in international terrorism' (Wilkinson, 1984, p. 297). It seems, then, that economic sanctions will only work in most unusual circumstances in which widespread international commitment to the decision would make them effective. Such circumstances will rarely occur and states will have to consider very carefully the advisability of embarking on sanctions unilaterally.

CONCLUSION

This chapter has argued strongly that many of the 'hard' options for countering international terrorism are either escalatory or counter-productive in effect or may be used legitimately and practically on so few occasions as to make it foolhardy for nations to look to these methods as the major ways towards control of terrorism. It has been argued that many of our problems with counter-terrorist policies stem from a lack of conceptual clarity and an unwillingness to make necessary moral, political, and strategic distinctions between different forms and acts of international terrorism. This lack of discrimination is particularly apparent in many official speeches on terrorism, which encourage exaggerated perceptions of threat, have often raised the issue of terrorism too high on foreign policy agendas, and have led to a focus on aggressive responses which has taken the impetus out of support for more mundane, but probably more effective, policy options. Analyses such as the present one will be seen by some as pessimistic and weak, if not inviting the escalation of terrorism. I believe, however, that we have been making significant progress through the less glamorous alternatives and that it is essential that we throw our major effort into those, especially as they are consistent with democratic values and the rule of law. Clearly, the first line of defence is intelligence, and more resources need to be devoted to this area (Gazit and Handel, 1980; Ofri, 1984), particularly to HUMINT. We should continue to negotiate international agreements against specific terrorist tactics, rather than waste time on futile attempts to outlaw terrorism. Regional agreements (such as the European Convention on the Suppression of Terrorism) which attempt a reasonably comprehensive coverage of counter-terrorist measures are more likely to be reached, but here, too, problems such as those relating to the so-called 'political offence exception' make their operation very dependent on the individual circumstances surrounding any particular terrorist incident. The best hope of effective action is probably to be found in bilateral agreements and in less formal exchanges between the free nations' police, intelligence and military agencies. I believe much more needs to be done to seek imaginative diplomatic and political ways to place pressure on sponsor states, as well as to enforce existing provisions on such matters as abuse of diplomatic privileges. The whole area of psychological operations (PSYOPS) and the role it could play in disrupting the motivation of terrorist-group members, undermining internal cohesion and the credibility of terrorist leaders, and driving a wedge between terrorist groups and their sponsors or the civilian infrastructure has been largely overlooked and should be accorded a much higher priority for development. As far as terrorists themselves are concerned, we should make every effort to bring them to justice. This will involve negotiation of extradition treaties and intensified international legal cooperation but should also include resources being devoted to more novel suggestions such as the establishment of an organisation to track known terrorists, to disrupt their activities and to arrange for their arrest when the circumstances are appropriate. These and similar suggestions consistent with maintaining democratic values (see, for example, Wilkinson, 1981; Waugh, 1982; Maechling, 1984) need to be pursued with vigour and, above all, consistency. In addition, we must improve our doctrine and military capabilities to be able to respond appropriately with aggressive methods where their use is justifiable and will have beneficial outcomes (Cline and Alexander, 1985; Jenkins, 1985). Above all we must remember not only whom we are fighting, but also for what we are fighting. As Ambassador Anthony Quainton has noted, a central problem for a government fighting terrorism is that of how to maintain and strengthen its own authority while diminishing the legitimacy of the terrorists. A government faced with terrorism must, therefore, be concerned with both the effectiveness *and* the legitimacy of its policies. I believe George Ball's warning should stand as the touchstone for those who must decide on counter-terrorist policy. He admonished that we should:

> take care that we are not led, through panic and anger, to embrace counter-terror and international lynch law and thus reduce our nation's conduct to the squalid level of the terrorists ... For we would be tragically wrong to abandon those cherished principles of law and humanity that have given our country its special standing among nations.[14]

Notes

1. For arguments about the nature of the terrorist threat to democratic societies see Bell (1978); Crenshaw (1983a); Dror (1983); Horowitz (1983); Mack (1981); Wardlaw (1982, 1986); Wilkinson (1977).
2. 'Unfinished Business', *The New Republic*, 29 July 1985.
3. 'Reagan Steps Up the War of Words', *Sydney Morning Herald*, 10 July 1985.
4. Walter Laqueur, 'Terrorists and Spies', *The New Republic*, 29 July 1985, pp. 20 and 21.
5. Stephen S. Rosenfeld 'Terrorism Over-simplified', *Washington Post*, 29 June 1984, p. 19.
6. Numerous books and articles in recent years have attempted, with varying degrees of success, to document the case for Soviet sponsorship of terrorism. See, for example, Alexander (1982); Cline and Alexander (1984); Francis (1981); Goren (1984); Halperin (1982); Sterling (1981). For trenchant criticism of some of these views, especially those of Claire Sterling, see Herman (1982) and Stohl (1983).
7. Robert E. Hunter, 'Terrorism: Fighting Fire With Fire. Poorly Justified Actions Can Only Weaken US Case', *Los Angeles Times*, 14 May 1985, Part II, p. 5.
8. Quoted in Thomas L. Friedman, 'Israel Turns Terror Back on the Terrorists, But Finds No Political Solution', *New York Times*, 4 December 1984, p. 12.
9. 'Peril in Striking Terrorists', *Milwaukee Journal*, 29 October 1984.
10. To retain the Shakespearian idiom: 'If it were done when 'tis done, then 'twere well it were done quickly' (Macbeth).
11. For similar arguments in the context of Soviet proxy warfare, see Taylor and Townsend (1984).
12. Admiral Watkins argues that other options must be *exhausted* before the military one may be tried. I would weaken this requirement to mandate

242 *State Response to International Terrorism*

that the alternatives do not have to be actually tried, but merely carefully evaluated. There seems little to be gained morally by trying a method which is bound to fail in the circumstances and in some cases such experimentation may produce a situation which then excludes the possible effective use of the military option.

13. Brian Michael Jenkins, 'We Needn't Rule Out the Use of Force Against Terrorists', *Los Angeles Times*, 2 May 1985, Part II, p. 5.
14. George Ball, 'Shultz is Wrong on Terrorism', *New York Times*, 16 December 1984, p. E21.

References

Alexander, Y. (1982) 'Some Perspectives on Terrorism and the Soviet Union', *International Security Review,* C7, 1, pp. 35–45.

Alon, H. (1980) *Countering Palestinian Terrorism in Israel: Toward a Policy Analysis of Countermeasures* (Santa Monica, California: Rand).

Ayubi, S., Bissell, R. E., Korsah, N. A-B and Lerner, L. A. (1982) *Economic Sanctions in US Foreign Policy* (Philadelphia: Foreign Policy Research Institute).

Bair, A. H. Jr, Barrows, W. L., Goldman, D. J., Kinsman, N. R., McKay, G. L., Strong, B. W., and Walsh, J. J. (1983) 'Unconventional Warfare: A Legitimate Tool of Foreign Policy', *Conflict*, 4, 1, pp. 59–81.

Bell, J. B. (1978) *A Time of Terror: How Democratic Societies Respond to Revolutionary Violence* (New York: Basic Books).

Bienen, H. and Gilpin, R. (1980) 'Economic Sanctions as a Response to Terrorism', *Journal of Strategic Studies*, 3, 1, pp. 89–98.

Blechman, B. M. (1978) *The Consequences of the Israeli Reprisals: An Assessment*, Ph.D. dissertation, Georgetown Unversity Ann Arbor, Michigan: (University Microfilms) 71–28, 052.

Bolton, C. (1984) 'Italian Terrrorism: Dead or Dormant? *Journal of Defense and Diplomacy*, November, pp. 39–42.

Carlton, D. (1979) 'The Future of Political Substate Violence', in Y. Alexander, D. Carlton and P. Wilkinson (eds) *Terrorism: Theory and Practice* (Boulder, Colorado: Westview Press). pp. 201–30.

Cerny, P. G. (1981) 'France: Non-terrorism and the Politics of Repressive Tolerance', in J. Lodge (ed.) *Terrorism: A Challenge to the State* (Oxford: Martin Robertson) pp. 91–118.

Chine, R. and Alexander, Y. (1984) *Terrorism: The Soviet Connection* (New York: Crane Russak).

Cline, R. and Alexander, Y. (1985) *State-Sponsored Terrorism*, Report prepared for the Subcommittee on Security and Terrorism for the use of the Committee on the Judiciary, US (Washington DC: USGPO).

Cordes, B., Hoffman, B., Jenkins, B. M., Kellen, K., Moran, S. and Sater, W. (1984) *Trends in Internaional Terrorism, 1982 and 1983* (Santa Monica, California: Rand).

Crenshaw, M. (1983a) 'Introduction: Reflections on the Effects of Terrorism', in M. Crenshaw (ed.) *Terrorism, Legitimacy, and Power: The Consequences of Political Violence* (Middletown, Connecticut: Wesleyan University Press) pp. 1–37.

Crenshaw, M. (1983b) 'The International Consequences of Terrorism', paper presented at the 1983 Annual Meeting of the American Political Science Association, Chicago, 1–4 September.

Doxey, M. (1980) *Economic Sanctions and International Enforcement* (New York: Oxford University Press).

Dror, Y. (1983) 'Terrorism as a Challenge to the Democratic Capacity to Govern', in Martha Crenshaw (ed.) *Terrorism, Legitimacy, and Power: The Consequences of Political Violence* (Middletown, Connecticut: Wesleyan University Press).

Flores, D. A. (1981) 'Note: Export Controls and the US Effort to Combat International Terrorism', *Law and Policy in International Business*, 13, 2, pp. 521–90.

Francis, S. T. (1981) *The Soviet Strategy of Terror* (Washington, DC: The Heritage Foundation).

Frangi, A. (1983) *The PLO and Palestine* (London: Zed Books).

Gazit, S. and Handel, M. (1980) 'Insurgency, Terrorism, and Intelligence', in Roy Godson (ed.) *Intelligence Requirements for the 1980s: Counter Intelligence* (Washington, DC: National Strategy Information Center) pp. 125–47.

Gilpin, Robert (1981) *War and Change in World Politics* (New York: Cambridge University Press).

Goren, R. (1984) *The Soviet Union and Terrorism* (London: Allen & Unwin).

Halle, L. J. (1973) 'Does War have a Future?', *Foreign Affairs*, 52, pp. 20–34.

Halperin, E. (1982) 'Terrorism: Moscow's Motive', *International Security Review*, 7, 1, pp. 69–78.

Herman, E. (1982) *The Real Terror Network* Boston: South End Press.

Hoffman, B. (1984) *Recent Trends in Palestinian Terrorism* (Santa Monica, California: Rand).

Hoffman, B. (1985) 'The Plight of the Phoenix: The PLO since Lebanon', *Conflict*, Q. 5, 2, pp. 5–17.

Horchem, H. (1985) 'The Development of West German Terrorism after 1979: An Overview', *TVI J.* 5, 4, pp. 10–16.

Horowitz, I. L. (1983) 'The Routinization of Terrorism and its Unanticipated consequences', in M. Crenshaw (ed.) *Terrorism, Legitimacy, and Power: The Consequences of Political Violence* (Middletown, Connecticut: Wesleyan University Press) pp. 38–51.

Jenkins, B. M. (1981) *Combatting Terrorism: Some Policy Implications* (Santa Monica, California: Rand).

Jenkins, B. M. (1983) *New Modes of Conflict* (Santa Monica, California: Rand).

Jenkins, B. M. (1984a) 'New Modes of Conflict', *Orbis*, 28, 1, pp. 5–27.

Jenkins, B. M. (1984b) *Combatting Terrorism Becomes a War* (Santa Monica, California: Rand).

Jenkins, B. M. (1984c) *The Lessons of Beirut: Testimony Before the Long Commission* (Santa Monica, California: Rand).

Jenkins, B. M. (1985) 'The US Response to Terrorism: A Policy Dilemma', *TVI J.* 5, 4, pp. 31–6.

Kellen, K. (1985) 'The New Challenge: Euroterrorism against NATO', *TVI J.* 5, 4, pp. 3–6.

Kirkpatrick, J. J. (1985) 'Moral Equivalence and Political Aims', *Society* (March/April) pp. 1–8.

Kirkpatrick, J. J. (1984) 'The Unauthorized Violence of Terrorism', *Journal of Defense and Diplomacy* (November) pp. 6–8.

Kupperman, R. H., Alexander, Y., van Opstal, D. and Williamson, D., Jr (1984) 'Terrorism: the Challenge to the Military in the 1990s', in R. H. Kupperman and W. J. Taylor, Jr (eds) *Strategic Requirements for the Army to the Year 2000* (Lexington Massachusetts: Lexington Books). pp. 187–207.

Livingstone, N. C. (1982) *The War Against Terrorism* (Lexington: Lexington Books).

Mack, A. (1981) 'The Utility of Terrorism', *Australian and New Zealand Journal of Criminology*, 14, pp. 197–224.

Maechling, C., Jr (1984) 'Containing Terrorism', *Foreign Service Journal* (July/August) pp. 33–7.

Marighela, C. (1974) *Urban Guerrilla Minimanual* (Vancouver: Pulp Press).

Maynes, C. W. (1985) 'Logic, Bribes, and Threats', *Foreign Policy* (Fall) pp. 11–19.

Motley, J. B. (1984) 'If Terrorism Hits Home, will the Army be Ready?', *Army* (April) pp. 18–21, 25–6.

Nathan, J. A. (1981) 'The New Feudalism', *Foreign Policy*, 42 (Spring) pp. 156–66).

Nye, J. S., Jr (1985) 'Motives, Means and Consequences', *Society* (March/April) pp. 17–20.

Oakley, R. B. (1985) *Combating International Terrorism* (Washington, DC: Bureau of Public Affairs, US Department of State) 5 March (Current Policy no. 667).

O'Ballance, E. (1985) 'NATO and the Enemy Within', *RUSI*, 130, 2, pp. 45–9.

Ofri, A. (1984) 'Intelligence and Counter-terrorism', *Orbis*, 28, 1, pp. 41–52.

Oseth, J. M. (1985) 'Combating Terrorism: The Dilemmas of a Decent Nation', *Parameters*, 15, 1, pp. 65–76.

Quainton, A. C. E. (1983) 'Terrorism and Political Violence: A Permanent Challenge to Governments,' in M. Crenshaw (ed.) *Terrorism, Legitimacy, and Power: The Consequences of Political Violence* (Middletown, Connecticut: Wesleyan University Press) pp. 52–64.

Scalapino, R. A. (1983) 'The Political–Strategic Outlook for International Violence,' in T. Adeniran and Y. Alexander (eds) *International Violence* (New York: Praeger) pp. 165–81.

Schelling, Thomas C. (1966) *Arms and Influence* (New Haven, Connecticut: Yale University Press).

Schreiber, A. (1973) 'Economic Coercion as an Instrument of Foreign Policy: US Economic Measures against Cuba and the Dominican Republic', *World Politics* (April) pp. 387–412.

Schultz, G. (1984) 'Terrorism and the Modern World', *Department of State Bulletin* (December) pp. 12–17.

Sloan, S. (1982) 'International Terrorism: Conceptual Problems and Implications', *Journal of Thought*, 17, 2, pp. 19–29.

Sterling, C. (1981) *The Terror Network* (New York: Holt, Rinehart & Winston).

Stohl, M. (1983) 'Review Essay: The International Network of Terrorism', *Journal of Peace Research*, 20, 1, pp. 87–94.

Taylor, W. J., Jr, and Townsend, J. J. (1984) 'Soviet Proxy Warfare', in R. H. Kupperman and W. J. Taylor, Jr (eds) *Strategic Requirements for the Army to the Year 2000* (Lexington: Lexington Books). pp. 209–26.

Wardlaw, G. (1982) *Political Terrorism: Theory, Tactics, and Countermeasures* (Cambridge: Cambridge University Press).

Wardlaw, G. (1986) 'Terrorism, Counter-terrorism and the Democratic Society,' in G. A. Lopez and M. Stohl (eds) *Government Violence and Repression* (Westport, Connecticut: Greenwood Press).

Watkins, J. D. (1984) 'Countering Terrorism: A New Challenge to our National Conscience', *Sea Power* (November) pp. 35–7.

Waugh, W. L., Jr (1982) *International Terrorism: How Nations Respond to Terrorists* (Salisbury, North Carolina: Documentary Publications).

Wilkinson, P. (1981) 'Proposals for Government and International Responses to Terrorism,' in P. Wilkinson (ed.) *British Perspectives on Terrorism* (London: Allen & Unwin) pp. 161–93.

Wilkinson, P. (1984) 'State-sponsored International Terrorism: The Problems of Response', *The World Today* (July) pp. 292–8.

Wilkinson, P. (1986) *Terrorism and the Liberal State* (London: Macmillan).

Wright, J. W. (1984) 'Terrorism: A Mode of Warfare', *Military Review*, (October) pp. 35–45.

8 Future Trends in International Terrorism

Brian Jenkins

When will it stop? Where will it all end? Will terrorism, having reached its peak in the mid-1980s, now diminish as a world-wide problem? Will we see simply more of the same? Will terrorists escalate their violence without changing their basic tactics? Or will terrorists, in the future, employ chemical, biological, or even nuclear weapons, perhaps to hold cities hostage? These questions reflect our growing frustration, our deepening fears. We want an end to terrorism, once and for all. We fear that if it continues, terrorists will enter the domain of mass destruction. Our answers, though necessarily speculative, are nonetheless important, for they define our attitudes and shape our responses.

WILL TERRORISM PERSIST?

Several factors might lead one to think that terrorism will decline in the coming years. Previous waves of terrorism at the beginning of the twentieth century and again in the 1920s surged, then declined. At least some of the political issues that led to the rise of contemporary international terrorism in the late 1960s have been removed or resolved in other ways. The USA ended its participation in the Vietnam War more than a decade ago, thereby incidentally removing what had been a catalyst for political protest and some terrorist activity in North America, Western Europe, and Japan. The urban guerrilla groups responsible for the rise of international terrorism in South America in the late 1960s and early 1970s were suppressed by local authorities, sometimes brutally. Those countries have since cautiously returned to democracy. Operating under greater constraints, authorities in Western Europe nonetheless substantially reduced domestic terrorist violence, although some of the groups survive. Of the original causes that led to terrorism in the late

1960s, the Palestinian issue remains a major source of international political violence in the mid-1980s.

Seen from that perspective, terrorism may be expected to diminish gradually. But it seems more likely to continue. After all, political violence in one form or another has existed for centuries. The waves of terrorist violence at the beginning of this century, when anarchists stalked heads of state, and again in the 1920s and 1930s were eclipsed only by the far greater violence of two world wars. Terrorism seems to flourish during periods of 'world peace'. When the Second World War ended, terrorist activity reemerged. It accompanied postwar decolonisation struggles in places like Palestine, Kenya, Cyprus, and Algeria, some of which continued throughout the 1960s. The terrorist campaigns that were a part of colonial liberation movements like the Jewish underground in Palestine and the FLN in Algeria provided inspiration and models for contemporary terrorist groups.

Modern theories of guerrilla war – which, of course, is not synonymous with terrorism but did contribute doctrinally to the use of terrorist tactics – developed during this same period, from the late 1940s to the early 1960s. Since the second World War, which represented the culmination of state-organised violence, there has been a long-range trend toward the 'privatisation' of violence.

All these facts argue for the continuation of some kind of political violence outside conventional warfare. But will international terrorism persist in its present form? Probably it will, for a number of reasons. International terrorism, as we know it today, not only grew out of the unique political circumstances that prevailed at the end of the 1960s, but also reflects recent technological developments which have enhanced the use of terrorist tactics.

Modern air travel provides world-wide mobility of people, ideas, *and conflict*. Instantaneous access to a world-wide audience through the modern news media, particularly television, is another factor. This technology is still only in its infancy, and may become uncontrollable in its appetite for news and its ability to broadcast events live from where they happen.

The proliferation of inexpensive minicameras and remote satellite broadcasting capabilities will enable the electronic medium of television to cover the world as they now cover a football game. With so many images pouring in from all over the world, editorial selectivity in television may be reduced to split-second decisions regarding which picture, which angle, to screen next. Television news may resemble the play-by-play coverage of sporting events, forcing political leaders, even more than now, to make instant decisions in public. Television is the battlefield of the future, and one where terrorists have the advantages of terrain.

The increasing availability of arms to anybody with the money to buy them is another irreversible change. We are not talking about major weapons systems – ballistic missiles, intercontinental bombers, nuclear submarines, battle tanks – but about increasingly powerful and increasingly accurate weapons that can be carried by a man. Terrorist use of automatic weapons has grown in the past ten years, and even ordinary street crimes are being committed with the newest sub-machine-guns that boast enormous firepower. The number of machine-guns in the USA alone is estimated to be in excess of 500 000. Right-wing extremists recently arrested in the mid-western United States had at their hideout automatic weapons and rocket-propelled grenades; they had protected their redoubt with land-mines, and were building their own tank at the time of their arrest. Police dealing with such terrorists, drug traffickers, criminal gangs, and barricaded suspects have been compelled to create specialised tactical response units equipped with armoured vehicles, rapid-fire and heavy-calibre weapons, and specialised explosives for breaching barriers and stunning defenders. Tactical operations are of necessity increasingly militarised.

The apparent inability of the world to limit or regulate arms traffic will impose greater demands on physical security or, alternatively, on regulating the people that might use those arms. The landscape of political violence has been permanently altered.

Over the years, a semi-permanent infrastructure of terrorism has emerged. Individual terrorists can be arrested, terrorist groups can be 'defeated', but governments find it extremely difficult to identify and destroy the resilient web of political fronts, personal relationships, clandestine contacts, foreign connections, alliances with other groups, support structure, resources and suppliers of material and services that sustain the terrorist underground. There are also economic incentives to use terrorist tactics. Kidnapping and extortion based upon threats of violence have become routine means of financing revolutionary movements. Many groups realise a substantial cash flow from their criminal activities.

All these reasons suggest that terrorism as we know it now is likely to persist as a mode of political expression as well as an instrument of diplomacy or as a means of warfare among states.

Growing sponsorship is another reason terrorism will persist. To a certain extent, international terrorism has become institutionalised. State sponsors provide terrorists with resources and a sanctuary where they can retreat, recuperate, rest, and rearm. State sponsorship also means that an office or agency is designated to be in charge of relations with the terrorists. Like any bureaucracy, that agency competes for influence and budget, promises results, and resists dismantling. Having learned to use the new tool of terrorism, the agencies responsible for terrorist activity will have their own vested interest in continuing to use it.

WHAT WILL BE THE FUTURE SOURCES OF TERRORISM?

There will be no shortage of potential causes for terrorism: rising population; increased poverty and scarcity; racial tension; inflation and unemployment; increased tension between the have and have-not nations; waves of refugees shoved about by wars and repression; immigrants moving from poorer states to wealthier ones, often bringing with them the conflicts of their home country, sometimes causing resentment among native citizens; rapid urbanisation the disintegration of traditional authority structures; the emergence of single-issue groups; the rise of aggressive fundamentalist religious groups or religious cults.

However, one must be cautious here. Research has not been able to demonstrate a connection between poverty, scarcity, inflation or any other socio-economic indicator and terrorism .Indeed, countries experiencing the highest levels of terrorism are often among the economically and socially most advanced nations in their region or in the world, and often the least authoritarian. Contemporary terrorism seems to come with modern society.

As for the collapse of traditional authority structures, they are collapsing all the time. They collapsed during the French revolution, during the industrial revolution, after the abolition of slavery, after the First World War, after the Second World War, with the fall of the colonial empires, with the advent of transistor radios. And to be sure, all these developments have been associated with a measure of violence.

Ideology and ethnic nationalism have been the two major engines of modern terrorism. Ideology drove the urban guerrillas in Latin America and their terrorist imitators in Western Europe and the

USA. Most of these groups adhered to some variation of Marxism. A few, like the anti-Castro Cuban *émigrés* came from the right. Dreams of an independent homeland inspired groups like the Irish Republican Army, the Basque separatists, the Croatians, the Palestinians, and the Armenians. More recently religious fanaticism, although directed toward secular ends and secret wars waged by states have accounted for a growing share of the world's terrorist violence.

Responding in a 1985 poll, authorities on terrorism identified state-sponsorship, ethnic conflict and religious fanaticism as the most likely sources of future terrorist violence. Ideological conflict came in fourth. Several factors may explain why the experts think ideology will decline as a future source of terrorist violence. Ideology was never a major factor in the USA. Although they expressed themselves in Marxist rhetoric, America's bombers of the late 1960s and early 1970s were motivated primarily by a single issue rather than an ideology: opposition to the Vietnam War. When the USA ended the draft and withdrew from Vietnam, the tiny terrorist cells were deprived of any potential constituents and dried up. US military intervention in some Third World context, such as in Central America or the Middle East, could spark a new wave of political protest and violence.

Ideological conflict was always a more serious business in Europe where in the 1960s many adults could still recall the great ideological contests of the first half of the century. But after a few years of terrorism, the public grew tired of the violence which until then had been fashionable at least in some circles. Discredited by their actions, groups on the far left lost ground as the political centre of gravity moved right on both sides of the Atlantic in the late 1970s. This fundamental shift narrowed the recruiting space of groups like Italy's Red Brigades and Germany's Red Army Faction, while authorities reduced their operational capabilities. The resurgence of so-called 'Euroterrorism' in 1984 and 1985 demonstrated that the left-wing extremists did not abandon the field. They did, however, abandon their millenialist visions of revolution and instead concentrated on more concrete issues that offered them a potential constituency: disarmament, opposition to NATO and the deployment of further nuclear weapons. Meanwhile the shift to the right seems to have brought with it an increase in right-wing violence in the 1980s.

Ideology may remain a more powerful force in the Third World where left-wing guerrillas battle against governments in Latin America, Africa, and the Philippines, while anti-Marxist guerrillas wage war on Marxist governments in Central America, Africa, Afghanistan, and Indo-China. All these guerrilla groups, left and right, have their terrorist branches to intimidate foes, enforce obedience, extort funds or gain publicity. This traditional use of terrorism will no doubt continue. The use of terrorism by insurgent groups could increase as some of the movements are defeated or stalemated.

It is also possible that some of the Third World groups will find common cause and launch terrorist campaigns directed against targets in the developed world on behalf of Third World causes. Terrorist groups have obliged corporations to pay them revolutionary 'taxes', provide free food and medical supplies to the poor or finance philanthropic enterprises. One can imagine a consortium of terrorist groups carrying out campaigns of violence aimed at coercing the world into a new international economic order or to extort concessions to relieve the Third World's massive debt burden. Terrorists have retaliated against corporate managers for chemical spills and industrial accidents that harmed workers. It is then, perhaps, not inconceivable that Third World terrorists might retaliate for pollution or industrial disasters in the Third World. On the other hand, terrorist groups have not had much success in making common cause in the past so we must consign all these scenarios to the category of intriguing but far-fetched.

WILL TERRORISM INCREASE?

Will terrorism increase? Despite the successes of some governments in combating terrorist elements, the total volume of international terrorism, measured by the number of incidents, has increased. It traces an irregular line with peaks and valleys, but the trajectory is clearly upward.

Overall, the volume of terrorist activity has grown at an annual rate of about 12–15 per cent. If the rate of increase continues, we could see a doubling of terrorism by the end of the decade – not an inconceivable prospect. Several factors suggest the likelihood of continued growth.

The increase in the volume of terrorist activity has been matched by the geographic spread of terrorism – a slow, long-term trend. Although a handful of nations have been the favourite targets of terrorists the number of nations targeted by terrorists has also increased. The number of countries experiencing some sort of terrorist activity has increased each year. In the late 1960s, international terrorist incidents occurred in an average of twenty-nine countries each year. This average climbed to thirty-nine countries in the early 1970s and forty-three in the late 1970s. For the first three years of the 1980s, the average number of countries experiencing international terrorist incidents was fifty-one, and for the period 1983 to 1985, the average was sixty-five.

And though it is difficult to monitor with any precision the appearance and disappearance of the many hundreds of groups that claim credit for terrorist actions – some of them are only fictitious banners – the level of international terrorist activity no longer appears to depend on just a few groups as it did in the early 1970s. Despite the virtual destruction of some terrorist groups and the decline in operations by others, the total volume of terrorist activity grows (see Figure 8.1).

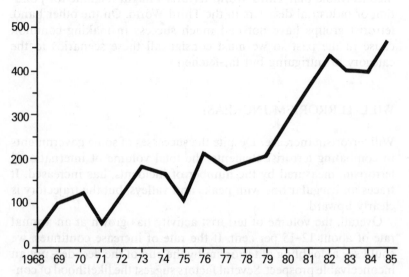

Figure 8.1   Number of international terrorist incidents

WILL TERRORISM ESCALATE?

Will terrorism escalate? Simply killing a lot of people has seldom been a terrorist objective. Terrorists want a lot of people *watching*, not a lot of people *dead*. Most terrorists operate on the principle of the minimum force necessary. Generally they do not attempt to kill many, as long as killing a few suffices for their purpose.

Statistics bear this out. Only 15–20 per cent of all terrorist incidents involve fatalities; and of those, two-thirds involve only one death. Less than 1 per cent of the thousands of terrorist incidents that have occurred in the last two decades involve ten or more fatalities; incidents of mass murder are truly rare.

Arbitrarily taking 100 deaths as the criterion, only a handful of incidents of this scale have occurred since the beginning of the century. Lowering the criterion to fifty deaths produces a dozen or more additional incidents. This in itself suggests that it is either very difficult to kill large numbers of persons, or it is very rarely tried.

Unfortunately, as we have seen in recent years, things are changing. Terrorist activity over the past twenty years has escalated in volume *and* in bloodshed. At the beginning of the 1970s, terrorists concentrated their attacks on property. In the 1980s, terrorists increasingly directed their attacks against people – the soft target. The number of incidents with fatalities, and multiple fatalities, has increased. A more alarming trend in the 1980s has been the growing number of incidents of large-scale indiscriminate violence: huge car-bombs detonated on city street, bombs planted aboard trains and airliners, in airline terminals, railroad stations, and hotel lobbies, all calculated to kill in quantity. Figure 8.2 shows numbers of deaths from major incidents of sabotage and terrorism.

Why are they killing more? Like soldiers in a war, terrorists who have been in the field for many years have been brutalised by the long struggle; killing becomes easier.

As terrorism has become more commonplace, the public has also become, to a degree, desensitised. Terrorists can no longer obtain the same amount of publicity with the tactics they used ten years ago. They have to escalate their violence in order to keep public attention.

Terrorists have become technically more proficient, enabling them to operate on a higher level of violence.

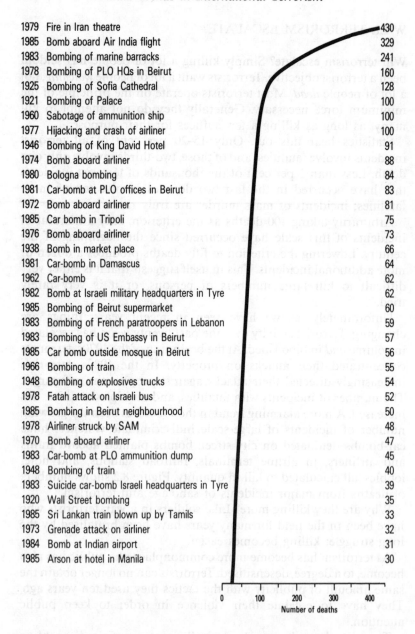

1979 Fire in Iran theatre	430
1985 Bomb aboard Air India flight	329
1983 Bombing of marine barracks	241
1978 Bombing of PLO HQs in Beirut	160
1925 Bombing of Sofia Cathedral	128
1921 Bombing of Palace	100
1960 Sabotage of ammunition ship	100
1977 Hijacking and crash of airliner	100
1946 Bombing of King David Hotel	91
1974 Bomb aboard airliner	88
1980 Bologna bombing	84
1981 Car-bomb at PLO offices in Beirut	83
1972 Bomb aboard airliner	81
1985 Car bomb in Tripoli	75
1976 Bomb aboard airliner	73
1938 Bomb in market place	66
1981 Car-bomb in Damascus	64
1962 Car-bomb	62
1982 Bomb at Israeli military headquarters in Tyre	62
1985 Bombing of Beirut supermarket	60
1983 Bombing of French paratroopers in Lebanon	59
1983 Bombing of US Embassy in Beirut	57
1985 Car bomb outside mosque in Beirut	56
1966 Bombing of train	55
1948 Bombing of explosives trucks	54
1978 Fatah attack on Israeli bus	52
1985 Bombing in Beirut neighbourhood	50
1978 Airliner struck by SAM	48
1970 Bomb aboard airliner	47
1983 Car-bomb at PLO ammunition dump	45
1948 Bombing of train	40
1983 Suicide car-bomb Israeli headquarters in Tyre	39
1920 Wall Street bombing	35
1985 Sri Lankan train blown up by Tamils	33
1973 Grenade attack on airliner	32
1984 Bomb at Indian airport	31
1985 Arson at hotel in Manila	30

Number of deaths

Figure 8.2   Deaths from major incidents of sabotage and terrorism

The composition of some terrorist groups has changed as the faint-hearted who have no stomach for indiscriminate killing drop out or are shoved aside by more ruthless elements.

The religious aspect of current conflicts in the Middle East allows the participants to slaughter one another without conscience. Moslems have no monopoly on martyrdom or mass murder. As we have seen throughout history, the presumed approval of God for the killing of pagans, heathens, or infidels permits acts of great destruction and self-destruction.

And finally, governments themselves have provided terrorists with the resources and technical know-how to operate at a higher, more lethal level of violence.

At the same time, however, several factors work against escalation. Security is one limiting factor. Protective measures taken in the wake of the huge car- and truck-bombings in the Middle East will reduce the vulnerability of the most obvious targets to this type of attack. If there are more bombings like that which probably caused the crash of the Air India jumbo jet in 1985, more stringent airport security measures will be applied on a permanent basis to prevent their repetition. Of course, terrorists can obviate security measures by shifting their sights to other, still vulnerable targets, but this forces them to become even less discriminate. There are also technical ceilings. Unless they resort to more exotic weapons, terrorists are approaching limits to their violence. As shown in Figure 8.3, the numbers of deaths in the deadliest terrorist incidents roughly equal those in the worst accidental disasters. Death on a larger scale is seen only in the slaughter of great battles or in natural disasters like earthquakes and floods. The most plausible scenarios involving chemical or biological weapons in a contained environment – a hotel, a convention, a banquet – would produce deaths in the hundreds. To kill on a larger scale, terrorists would have to possess large quantities of deadly substances and solve problems of dispersal, or they would have to resort to nuclear weapons. This raises questions of technical capacity and intentions. We will come to these in a moment.

On balance, it appears that incidents involving large numbers of fatalities will probably become more common, with deaths in the hundreds remaining for the foreseeable future the outer limit of individual terrorist attacks.

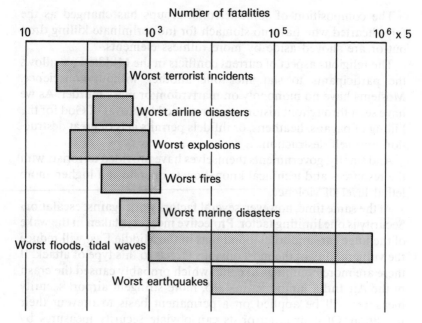

Figure 8.3 Deaths from major disasters

WILL TERRORISTS CHANGE THEIR TACTICS?

'If I were a terrorist, I would . . . ' It is the invariable preamble to the most diabolical schemes. College students, business executives, housewives, and other seemingly nice people are capable of hatching absolutely horrifying terrorist plots. Real terrorists, by comparison, are unimaginative dullards, content to follow the same script over and over.

But terrorists do not see things the way most people do. Almost everyone assumes that terrorists would want to hold cities hostage with nuclear or chemical weapons, knock out electrical grids to cause widespread blackouts, or poison the water supply. Those who study terrorists more closely are less certain that terrorists could or would even want to do these things. And from what former terrorists tell us, terrorists themselves apparently contemplate such activity rarely, if at all. Terrorists see what they do now as sufficient. They operate with a limited repertoire that has changed little and seems unlikely to change very much in the future. Six basic tactics account for 95 per cent of all terrorist incidents: bombings, assassinations, armed assaults, kidnappings, hijackings, and other kinds of hostage seizures. Terrorists blow up things, kill people, or seize hostages. Every terrorist attack is merely a variation on these three activities.

Looking at what terrorists have contemplated and discarded or tried and failed gives us some idea of the breadth of their imagination. Most of the tactics and operations they have considered are essentially 'more of the same'. They would like to have assassinated more high-ranking officials: the British Prime Minister, the President of South Korea, the entire cabinet of Chad, the gathered dignitaries at Golda Meir's funeral, the assembled senior leadership of Italy's Christian Democrat Party, the Commander of NATO.They would have given us more spectacular hostage incidents. They considered kidnapping the Pope, but dropped the idea as too risky. They planned to seize forty industrialists at a meeting in Vienna and contemplated taking a school bus filled with American schoolchildren in Europe. They would have hijacked an Italian cruise ship thirteen years before the taking of the *Achille Lauro*. They would have shot down civilian airliners in Germany, Italy, Kenya, British helicopters in Northern Ireland, taxiing airplanes in Paris and Athens. They would have destroyed oil-refineries in Rotterdam and Singapore.

What tactical innovations have terrorists produced since the late 1960s? The letter-bomb (actually an invention of the 1940s for which Jewish extremists in Palestine get credit), the car-bomb, the radio-controlled car-bomb, the radio-controlled boat-bomb, the suicide-vehicle-bomb. There have also been innovations in fusing and detonating devices: the barometric-pressure fuse invented by the Palestinians to blow up airliners in flight, the long-term-delay mechanism used by the IRA in the attempt on Prime Minister Thatcher's life. And they have added several dimensions to hostage-taking: hijacking airliners to make political demands; seizing embassies; kidnapping diplomats to gain the release of prisoners; kidnapping corporate executives to finance terrorist operations.

These innovations could all be categorised as enhancements and variations. The basic tactics have changed little over the years. Indeed, the relative percentage of the various tactics has remained stable for a long time, except for a decline in embassy take-overs. Seizing embassies was popular in the 1970s. It declined as security measures made embassy take-overs more difficult, and as governments became more resistant to the demands of terrorists holding hostages and more willing to use force to end such episodes, thus increasing the hostage-takers' risk of death or capture.

This is indicative of the kind of innovation we are likely to see. Terrorists will alter their tactics in an incremental way to solve specific problems created by security measures. If one tactic ceases to work, they abandon it in favour of another one or merely shift their sights to another target. How might terrorists respond to the new security measures that have been taken to protect embassies against car bombs? They might resort to aerial suicide attacks, which are technically and physically more demanding. Or they might resort to stand-off attacks, the traditional response to strong defences. Or they might simply attack other, still vulnerable targets. Since terrorists have virtually unlimited targets, they have little need for tactical innovation.

There are several things that appear in the scenarios of most armchair terrorists that real terrorists have not done. With the exception of a couple of minor episodes, they have not attacked nuclear reactors. Terrorists have blown up computers and set fires in data-processing centres, but they have not tried to penetrate computers in any sophisticated fashion to disrupt or destroy data.

Will we see a more sophisticated 'white-collar' terrorism, that is, attacks on telecommunications, data-processing systems, or other targets intended to produce not crude destruction but widespread disruption? Perhaps, but disruptive 'terrorism' of this type does not appear to be particularly appealing to today's terrorist groups. Such operations are technically demanding, and they produce *no immediate visible effects*. There is no drama. No lives hang in the balance. There is no bang, no blood. They do not satisfy the hostility nor the publicity hunger of the terrorists.

In sum, there is little to suggest major tactical innovations. Terrorist tactics for the foreseeable future will remain for the most part what they have been for the past fifteen years. New government countermeasures might provoke more radical departures from the traditional terrorist tactics. Or innovations might not come from those currently identified as 'terrorists', but instead from 'outsiders', entirely new types of adversaries not yet identified: computer-hackers who turn malevolent; ordinary criminal extortionists who turn political. But for the most part, the traditional tactics will predominate. Minor innovations will be devised to solve specific problems. Technical improvements may permit them to succeed where previously they have failed. Tactical innovations that appear to work will be imitated and spread rapidly, and those seen as failures the first time out will be abandoned. It is an evolutionary pattern.

WILL TERRORIST TARGETS CHANGE?

The greatest advantage that terrorists have and will continue to have is a virtually unlimited range of targets. Terrorists can attack anything, anywhere, anytime, limited only by operational considerations: Terrorists do not attack defended targets; they seek soft targets. If one target or set of targets is well protected, terrorists merely shift their sights to other targets that are not so well protected.

Over the years, the range of targets attacked by terrorists has expanded enormously. Terrorists have attacked embassies, airlines, airline terminals, ticket offices, railroad stations, subways, buses, power lines, electrical transformers, mailboxes, mosques, hotels, restaurants, schools, libraries, churches, temples, newspapers, journalists, diplomats, businessmen, military officials, missionaries, priests, nuns, the Pope, men, women, adults and children.

The future targets of terrorists will be pretty much the same as those preferred today: representatives and symbols of nations and governments – in particular, diplomats and airlines, of economic systems such as corporations and corporate executives, of policies and presence such as military officials.

Will terrorists attack high-technology targets such as refineries, offshore platforms, or nuclear reactors? They already have, although indirectly and in technically undemanding ways. Guerrillas in Latin America have frequently attacked electrical power grids as a means of waging economic warfare against governments. Less concerned with economic warfare, urban terrorists have occasionally attacked electrical energy systems to get attention, to protest government or corporate policies, or to indirectly disable nuclear power plants. Terrorist saboteurs have also attacked pipelines, oil tank farms, and refineries, again with the objective of attracting publicity or protesting specific policies.

Except for attacks on pylons and pipelines, two traditional and easy targets of sabotage, neither guerrillas nor terrorists have achieved an impressive record of success against more demanding or more easily defended targets. And seldom have they tried to attack directly, in other than a purely symbolic way, really difficult targets like nuclear reactors or offshore platforms which require technical knowledge and operational capabilities which most groups do not possess. Even their attacks on power-lines and pipelines are largely symbolic sometimes causing temporary disruptions but not sustained or directed against critical nodes so as to achieve strategic effects.

Attacks on high-tech targets will remain within the operational domain of established guerrilla groups and larger terrorist organisations. Smaller terrorist groups will continue to carry out sporadic and often symbolic attacks on energy systems and other similar targets. Sometimes they will succeed in causing widespread disruption. Often they will fail. With practice, however, even a small group can become quite good at this sort of thing and become more sophisticated in their operations as demonstrated in the growing skill of the New World Liberation Front, a tiny terrorist group in northern California that carried on a long campaign against the local power company. Groups able to recruit confederates within the labour force of a particular industry can also operate at a higher level. Insiders are always the most effective saboteurs.

Finally, the phenomenon of state-sponsorship of terrorism, if it continues, may alter terrorist targeting. States not only provide terrorists with the capabilities to take on more difficult targets but may also provide terrorists with incentives for doing so. If this happens, terrorism will truly have become strategic in its potential consequences.

WHAT WEAPONS WILL TERRORISTS USE?

What weapons will terrorists use in the future? Terrorists now use what they can buy in the gun shops or on the black market or what they can steal from arsenals. They seek powerful, rapid-fire, concealable weapons. They use commercial explosives, and military stuff when they can get it. These suffice for current operations. Since terrorists generally do not attack defended targets, they have no need for more advanced arms. Anyway, they now match the firepower of the authorities.

Terrorists will probably use more sophisticated explosives, in larger quantities, although there is no great need to increase quantity. Terrorists in the Middle East have on several occasions built bombs containing more than 1000 pounds of explosives. Car bombs with 200 or more pounds of explosives are not uncommon. 15–20 pounds of high explosives planted inside a large building will take its front off.

We will probably see increased use of stand-off weapons – mortars, rocket launchers, rocket-propelled grenades – to overcome security measures. Finally, there remains a potential for the use of portable precision-guided munitions, which terrorists have already employed on several occasions. These weapons are now manufactured in tens of thousands. They are easy to operate. They are increasingly available. According to a recent survey of law-enforcement officials and authorities on terrorism, 55 per cent thought it 'very likely' and another 29 per cent thought it 'somewhat likely' that by the year 2000, terrorists will employ shoulder-fired, precision-guided, surface-to-air missiles to shoot down civilian planes.

WILL TERRORISTS GO NUCLEAR?

Will terrorists resort to weapons of mass destruction? Will they employ chemical or biological warfare? Will terrorists go nuclear? Many people believe that nuclear terrorism of some sort is likely and may be inevitable. Reflecting the results of a poll conducted among 1346 opinion-leaders in the USA, George Gallup, Jr, in his recent book, *Forecast 2000*, wrote that 'while a war between the superpowers, the US and the Soviet Union, is a real cause for concern [a disastrous nuclear incident involving terrorists in this country], seems to be the most imminent danger'.

I happen to think that nuclear terrorism is neither imminent nor inevitable, if by nuclear terrorism we mean terrorists employing stolen nuclear weapons or a clandestinely fabricated nuclear-explosive device to kill or threaten to kill large numbers of people. Lesser terrorist acts in the nuclear domain – the seizure or attempted sabotage of a nuclear reactor, the dispersal of radioactive material, an alarming nuclear hoax that may cause panic – are possible.

The question of nuclear terrorism involves an assessment of both capabilities and motivations. It is conceivable that someone outside government who is familiar with the principles of nuclear weapons could design an atomic bomb. However, the ease with which a private citizen can build one, assuming that he or she could somehow acquire the necessary nuclear material, has been greatly exaggerated. But even if terrorists can build a nuclear weapon, would they want to? Terrorism has certainly escalated, but it is still a quantum jump from the kinds of things that terrorists do today to the realm of nuclear destruction. Why would terrorists take that jump?

Without resorting to nuclear weapons, terrorists could do more now, yet they do not. Why? Beyond the technical constraints, there may be self-imposed constraints that derive from moral considerations or political calculations. Some terrorists may view indiscriminate violence as immoral. The terrorists' enemy is the government, not the people. Terrorists pretend to be governments, and wanton murder might imperil this image.

There are political considerations as well: terrorists fear alienating their perceived constituents. They fear provoking public revulsion. They fear unleashing government crackdowns that their groups might not survive. Certainly, in the face of a nuclear threat, any rules that now limit police authorities in most democracies would change.

Terrorists must maintain group cohesion. Attitudes toward violence vary not only from group to group but also within a group. Inevitably, there would be disagreement over mass murder, which could expose the operation and the group itself to betrayal. Obviously not all groups share the same operational code, and as we have seen, certain conditions or circumstances might erode these self-imposed constraints.

What about chemical or biological weapons, which are technically less demanding than nuclear weapons? The same self-imposed constraints apply. Moreover, although there have been isolated incidents, neither chemical or biological warfare seems to fit the pattern of most terrorist attacks. Terrorist episodes have a finite quality – an assassination, a bombing, a handful of deaths, and that is the end of it. That is quite different from initiating an event that offers no explosion but instead produces indiscriminate deaths or lingering illness, an event over which the terrorists who set it in motion would have little control.

Still, we must take note of a disturbing trend. Product contamination is a crime clearly on the rise. Criminal extortionists, seeking huge pay-offs, malevolent pranksters, mentally unbalanced persons seeking revenge for real or imagined grievances or dramatic forums from which to express themselves on a variety of issues have poisoned, or have threatened to poison food, pharmaceutical products, or water supplies. Most of these threats turn out to be hoaxes, and many go unreported, but there have been moments of public alarm. The poisoning of Tylenol capsules with cyanide killed six people and nearly caused a national panic in 1982. The episode received enormous publicity and it inspired numerous copycat crimes around the world. It also demonstrated the obvious vulnerabilities of society to this type of crime and the tremendous economic losses faced by firms confronted with such threats. The Tylenol case cost the manufacturer $100m in lost product and sales. Facing financial disasters of this magnitude, corporations may decide to pay quietly rather than risk the consequences if news of a threat leaks out.

No one claimed responsibility, no perpetrator was ever arrested, no motive ever discovered in the Tylenol case. When authors of these threats are apprehended, they usually turn out to be ordinary criminals, angry former employees or genuine crackpots. Seldom have their motives anything to do with political causes or those whom we currently label terrorists.

One exception was the 1979 poisoning of Israeli oranges by Palestinian extremists. No one was harmed by the mercury-injected oranges, but fear sent sales of Israeli oranges in Europe plummeting. A Palestinian group claimed credit for this apparently effective economic warfare but then promptly abandoned the tactic. Israeli officials later hinted that quiet threats of retaliation against Arab states prompted the Palestinians to end the campaign.

More recent contamination threats have involved issues beyond personal gain or individual revenge. In one case, the money demanded by extortionists was to have been used to finance the political activities of an *émigré* group. In another case, the intent may have been to humiliate certain public officials. Another involved demands to drop criminal charges against a popular figure. Still another sought to discourage shopping at supermarkets involved in a labour dispute. Animal-rights extremists have threatened to poison the products of corporations using animals in laboratory tests. Publicity, economic warfare, ransoms to finance operations, punishment for despised policies – these are the stuff of political terrorism. While the more ambitious schemes of chemical or biological warfare are likely to remain beyond the technical reach and outside

the motives of most political terrorists, at least for the near-term
future, we must anticipate the possibility of more limited scenarios
involving political demands based upon product contamination.

Over the longer term – the next ten to fifteen years – my concern is
that chemical weaponry will be acquired by unstable, dangerous
countries like Iraq, Iran, or Syria, and will increasingly be used in
warfare. If chemical warfare becomes more commonplace, particularly in a region like the Middle East, we cannot dismiss its
potential use by terrorists. The same is true of nuclear weapons, but
probably over a longer time-period.

WILL TERRORISM BECOME ANOTHER KIND OF WAR?

Where will terrorism fit in the future of armed conflict? The current
trend toward state-sponsorship of terrorism will probably continue.
Limited conventional war, classic rural guerrilla warfare and international terrorism will coexist and may appear simultaneously. The
Iranian revolution and its spread to Lebanon, which has involved
the effective use of international terrorism as an instrument of
policy, may provide a model for other Third World revolutions and
revolutionary states, just as the Cuban model inspired a generation
of imitators in Latin America. If it does, we are in for a lot of
trouble.

We may also see international terrorism emerge as a new kind of
global guerrilla warfare in which terrorist groups sally forth from the
political jungles of the Third World to carry out highly publicised
hit-and-run attacks, militarily insignificant but of great political
consequence, avoiding confrontations where they might run into
well-equipped, well-trained, specialised anti-terrorist forces.

Terrorists now avoid seizing embassies in Western capitals. They
hijack airliners, keep them on the move to evade any rescue attempt,
and retreat with their hostages to sanctuaries like Teheran or Beirut.
In the absence of government, as in Lebanon, or the presence of a
hostile government, as in Iran, these sanctuaries lie beyond the reach
of the world regime of treaty and law. If Iran defeats Iraq and the
Gulf States fall, then the world's 'badlands' might be centred in the
Middle East, a crescent reaching from the Mediterranean to
Persia.

HOW WILL TERRORISM AFFECT SOCIETY?

Finally, what developments will we see in security? The 'privatisa-tion' of violence has been matched by the 'privatisation' of security, as illustrated by the tremendous growth of private sector security expenditures. In the USA, a total of $21bn is now spent annually for security services and hardware (as compared with $14bn spent annually on all police). The figure will reach $50–60bn a year by the end of the century.

We will see the further proliferation of inner perimeters, the rings of security that now surround airline terminals, government buildings, and, increasingly, corporate offices. From this last development, however, emerges a cynical counter-terrorist strategy. By protecting the most obvious symbols, terrorists' preferred targets, terrorists will be forced to become less discriminate in their attacks. That will create greater public outrage, which governments can exploit to obtain domestic support and international cooperation to combat terrorists.

All these security measures, however, will not buy us a feeling of security, but only remind us of our vulnerabilities. Terrorism is not an objective threat measured in body-counts. It is a subjective threat. News of the latest terrorist attack will still penetrate protected perimeters, making us vicarious victims. Behind our alarms, sensors, surveillance cameras, reinforced walls, we will live in fear.

CONCLUSION

This survey offers a depressing but conservative view of future trends in terrorism. Terrorism persists. It may double in volume, but the world does not end in terrorist anarchy. Few changes are foreseen in terrorist tactics or targets.

Terrorists will escalate their violence, their attacks will become more indiscriminate, we may see political demands based upon threats of food contamination, but terrorists will probably not enter the Armageddon world of mass destruction. Terrorism will become institutionalised as a mode of armed conflict for some, no less legitimate than other modes of conflict. The media will increase its ability to cover terrorist incidents; we will *see* even more terrorism. The extraordinary security measures taken against terrorism will have become a permanent part of the landscape, of our life-style. They will no longer attract comment.

That may be the most insidious and perhaps the most worrisome development in the coming years. Terrorism will become an accepted fact of contemporary life – commonplace, ordinary, banal, and therefore somehow 'tolerable'.

Index